The Mystery beneath the Real

The Mystery
beneath the Real

Theology in the Fiction of George Eliot

Peter C. Hodgson

FORTRESS PRESS
Minneapolis

THE MYSTERY BENEATH THE REAL:
Theology in the Fiction of George Eliot

Cover design: Joseph Bonyata

ISBN 0-8006-3436-5

Manufactured in Great Britain   AF 1-3436
05   04   03   02   01   1   2   3   4   5   6   7   8   9   10

Contents

Preface

George Eliot was born Mary Ann(e) Evans on 22 November 1819 near Nuneaton, Warwickshire, on the Arbury estate of the Newdigate family, where her father Robert Evans was agent. A precocious child, at the age of nine she was sent to boarding school where she came under the influence of a teacher, Maria Lewis, who awakened in her an intensely evangelical form of Christianity. Mary Ann also had frequent conversations with her Aunt Elizabeth Evans, a one-time Methodist lay preacher. In 1836 her mother, Christiana Pearson, died and Mary Ann began keeping house for her father, educating herself in her spare time.

In 1841 she moved with her father to Foleshill near Coventry, where she became acquainted with Charles and Caroline Hennell Bray, and through Caroline with her sister Sara Sophia Hennell and her brother Charles Hennell. The Brays and Hennells were Unitarian free-thinkers who helped to free Mary Ann from her evangelical orientation. In 1838 Charles Hennell had published a book about the origins of Christianity that came to conclusions surprisingly similar to those of David Friedrich Strauss. He was asked to arrange a translation of Strauss's *Life of Jesus,* which proved to be a more daunting task than he had anticipated. Hennell turned to Mary Ann Evans for help, and she, having taught herself German, took over the translation in 1844 at the age of twenty-four, finishing it brilliantly in a year and a half.

Following her father's death in 1849, Marian (as she now called herself) spent several months in Geneva, reading broadly. In 1851 she went to work in London for John Chapman, publisher of her translation, as assistant editor of *The Westminster Review*. The Chapman house was a gathering place for liberal and radical thinkers of various persuasions. Here she met Herbert Spencer, to whom she was briefly attracted, and George Henry Lewes, a versatile man-of-letters. In 1854 her translation of Ludwig Feuerbach's *Essence of Christianity* was published. During the same year she began living with Lewes, who was permanently separated from his wife but could not obtain a legal divorce. She and Lewes declared themselves husband and wife and were united in a stable and loving relationship for twenty-four years until his death in 1878. They lived in London and made frequent, extended trips to the European Continent where they worked on their writings and enjoyed a rich cultural life.

Marian Evans had long desired to write fiction, and with the encouragement of Lewes she composed three novellas that were published under the title *Scenes of Clerical Life* in 1857–8, using the pseudonym 'George Eliot' to disguise her identity as a woman. 'George' was Lewes's Christian name, and 'Eliot,' she said, was 'a good mouth-filling, easily pronounced word.' *Adam Bede* appeared in 1859 and almost immediately was a commercial and critical success. Soon the true identity of the author became known, but by then Marian Evans had in the public mind become George Eliot. Three more novels followed in rapid succession: *The Mill on the Floss* (1860), *Silas Marner* (1861), and *Romola* (1862–3). *Felix Holt, the Radical* appeared in 1866 and *The Spanish Gypsy*, a poetic drama, in 1868. The 1870s brought George Eliot's two greatest novels, *Middlemarch* (1871–2) and *Daniel Deronda* (1876). After Lewes's death she was despondent, but in the spring of 1880 she married John Walter Cross, an old friend and admirer twenty years her junior. Following her death on 22 December 1880 he became her first biographer, but it was Gordon Haight who wrote the first critical biography based on his exhaustive edition of her letters, which he began in the 1950s. At the time of her death she was recognized as the greatest English writer of her time, and since then has been acknowledged as one of the greatest of all time – the author, in Rosemary Ashton's words, of 'some of the most wonderful works of fiction ever written.'

George Eliot possessed a diversity of interests and skills, including history, philosophy, aesthetics, ethics, politics, psychology, natural science, and the place of women in society. In addition she was a deeply religious thinker, despite having abandoned orthodox forms of Christian belief, and religious themes and figures appear in all her novels. The recent critical literature on George Eliot, while illuminating in particular her brilliant feminist and psychological insights, has for the most part ignored the religious aspect of her life and writings. It is the latter on which the present study proposes to focus, with the conviction not only that this aspect of her work has been accorded scant justice, but also that her ideas are of considerable interest to theological efforts at rethinking the meaning and substance of religious faith in our own time. The chapters that follow make no attempt at considering all the complex themes at work in her novels but concentrate just on the religious and theological elements. I offer my own reading of the texts. The body of critical literature is extensive, and I have worked with it on a selective basis, incorporating references where it seemed helpful. This literature demonstrates the wide diversity of approaches to the texts.

My own interest in George Eliot goes back to 1971–2 when I edited a new edition of Strauss's *Life of Jesus*. I read Mary Ann Evans's correspondence about her work on the translation and was attracted by her engaging personality, extraordinary mind, and keen sense of humor. Many years later, when I began assigning *Adam Bede* for a course in nineteenth-century theology, I came across a sentence George Eliot wrote to Barbara Bodichon: 'The highest "calling and election" is to *do without opium* and live through all our pain with conscious, clear-eyed endurance.' I pondered that statement many times and came to appreciate its profound truth. I have a sense of gratitude to George Eliot, as have countless others. Subsequently I read through all her novels and determined that one day I would attempt a theological reading of her fiction. It should be clear that I am not a specialist in literary criticism but a theologian who has found in George Eliot a surprising resource for reflecting on one of the most difficult questions: whether and how it is possible to speak meaningfully of the presence and action of God (or of the Divine Mystery) in the world today. Since I am writing principally for nonspecialists, for persons whom I would like to entice into reading (or re-reading) George Eliot, I thought it appropriate to provide summaries of each of the stories. Of course the summaries are already part of the interpretative process, but in addition I believe that the religious and theological meanings are deeply embedded in the structures of the plots.

George Eliot's novels are published in different editions. For the sake of consistency I have used the Penguin Classics editions, which are the most widely available and include all the novels. To facilitate reference to other editions, I cite chapter as well as page numbers. Biblical passages are normally quoted from the New Revised Standard Version, but in some instances (as noted) from the Authorized or King James Version.

The core of this book was presented as the Samuel Ferguson Lectures at the University of Manchester in March 2001. I appreciate the opportunity the lectureship provided to bring the project to completion, and I am indebted to David Pailin for his hospitality and support. David Jasper of the University of Glasgow has provided helpful criticism and advice, as have several friends who graciously read the manuscript: Joann Wolski Conn, Neumann College; Wendy Farley, Emory University; Leonard and Elizabeth Hummel, Vanderbilt University; and James Laney, Emory University. I am thankful to John Bowden and Alex Wright of SCM Press and Michael West of Fortress Press for their willingness to undertake the publication of what I have written. During the spring semester 2000, I taught a seminar on the religion of George Eliot in the Divinity School of Vanderbilt University. I was impressed at the diversity of insights that emerged from our discussions, and at the way in which students identified different passages that were especially illuminating. I was reminded of the inexhaustible wealth of these texts and of the modesty of my own effort to elucidate them. A book three or four times as long could not do them justice. I invite you to read and enjoy these wonderful works of fiction on your own.

Peter C. Hodgson

I

George Eliot's Religious Pilgrimage

1. Experiments in Life

The conventional wisdom about George Eliot[1] is that, after her exposure to higher criticism and German theology, she abandoned the fervent evangelical faith of her youth and became a disciple of the 'religion of humanity.' Thereafter, it is thought, she lost interest in religion and turned to the exploration of other subjects in her novels.

On a simple factual level the latter statement, at least, is demonstrably false. Religion is a topic of central interest in her first novels (*Scenes of Clerical Life* and *Adam Bede*) and in the last (*Daniel Deronda*), and it plays a significant role in the others as well (*The Mill on the Floss, Silas Marner, Romola, Felix Holt*, and *Middlemarch*). Moreover, religious figures, roles, beliefs, and practices are treated with both an understanding and a sympathy rare in modern literature. Yet the recent critical studies of George Eliot virtually ignore her engagement with religious issues or find various deconstructive devices to explain it away. The critics simply assume that she was a nonbeliever who used religion to achieve certain aesthetic, psychological, political, or moral effects.[2]

Basil Willey, noting Lord David Cecil's remark that George Eliot was 'not religious,' responds as follows:

'Religious' seems to me to be just what she was . . . the whole predicament she represents was that of the religious temperament cut off by the *Zeitgeist* from the traditional objects of veneration, and the traditional intellectual formulations. She was not, of course, a 'practising Christian', but in her estrangement from the 'religion *about* Jesus' she was none the further from the 'religion *of* Jesus.' She knew the hunger and thirst after righteousness, and the need for renunciation – the need to lose one's life in order to gain it. And, though her religious consciousness was pre-eminently moral, it was not exclusively so; she also had the faculty of reverence, the capacity to acknowledge the reality of the unseen.[3]

I believe that Willey is correct, and I want to expand his interpretation by proposing that George Eliot's life and literary career form a kind of religious pilgrimage. The young Mary Ann Evans used this image in one of her earliest letters: she wrote that those persons are happiest 'who are considering this life merely a pilgrimage, a scene calling for diligence and watchfulness, not for repose and amusement.'[4] This sense of religious calling and duty never abandoned the mature author, but in later years she expressed it differently. Four years before her death, in response to a query about her religious views, she said that her writing 'is simply a set of experiments in life' in order to determine 'what gains from past revelations and discipline we must strive to keep hold of as something more sure than shifting theory.' The 'supreme subject' with which she found herself engaged is 'how far the religion of the future must be one that enables us to do without consolation.'[5] Similarly, she wrote to Harriet Beecher Stowe that 'a religion more perfect than any yet prevalent, must express less care for personal consolation, and a more deeply-awing sense of responsibility to man.'[6] To a close friend she insisted that 'I have too profound a conviction of the efficacy that lies in all sincere faith, and the spiritual blight that comes with No-faith, to have any negative propagandism in me . . . I care only to know, if possible, the lasting meaning that lies in all religious doctrine from the beginning till now.'[7] It would be wrong, therefore, to suggest that George Eliot herself did not live by faith; but in her case it was an agnostic, apophatic faith, which kept the reality of God in suspense even as it affirmed the reality of duty and love.

It seems evident that George Eliot never arrived at any final or secure knowledge of religious meaning. Like the characters in her last novel, *Daniel Deronda*, she was on a journey, seeking an appropriate 'pathway' through life, perhaps in the hope that her pathway and those of others might, in the words of the Jewish savant she named Mordecai, be 'bound together in that Omnipresence which is the place and habitation of the world.'[8] There are many pathways, many pilgrimages, and she was convinced of the importance of a diversity of religious views and traditions to avoid cultural imperialism and to preserve what she was to call 'separateness with communication.'[9] She did not study religion as a form that was about to become extinct. Rather she was fascinated with its varieties of expression and its ability to adapt to a changing environment and evolve new patterns of survival. Over the course of her literary production she provided keen descriptions of evangelical and high church Anglicanism, of Methodism and Calvinism, of Nonconforming or Dissenting churches, of religious humanism or the religion of humanity, of Roman Catholicism, and finally of Judaism. She herself gave no unqualified allegiance to any of these forms, but she participated empathetically in all of them.[10]

George Eliot's own religious views evolved through several phases, which might be regarded as stations along a pathway or pilgrimage: evangelical Christianity, the religion of humanity, and elements of a future religion that would avoid accusation and consolation, be practical in orientation, manifest a reverence for mystery in nature and history, and in its highest form express the idea of a sympathetic, suffering, (omni)present God. The first two stations were not left behind but lingered on – incorporated into a growing and more complex vision, which was not simply theist or humanist, Christian or post-Christian, but (to introduce a term that will have to be explained later) 'cosmotheandric.' In the last phase of her life George Eliot found herself assuming a kind of spiritual or religious role as a counselor, teacher, spiritual mother or madonna to persons near and far. In a strange way, and by no direct intention, she was fulfilling a possibility she had imagined for herself in her earliest religious enthusiasm. I shall now attempt to trace these stations on a pilgrimage that reached no final destination and was always seeking its own most appropriate path.

2. Evangelical Christianity

The story of Mary Ann Evans's intense involvement with evangelicalism at an early age is well known. Through the influence of a boarding school governess, she experienced the need for conversion, repentance, and acceptance of Christ, at about age fifteen. She studied the Bible and read religious books intensively, acquiring a formidable knowledge of biblical and ecclesiastical history. Letters written during this period articulated a profound evangelical piety, which focused not on the externals of Scripture, doctrine, and creed, but on inner spiritual truth. Mary Ann Evans was by no means a biblical literalist but read the texts through a critical and literary eye, appreciative of their poetic and metaphorical character. She espoused the idea that life is a total service of God and neighbor, that suffering both internal and external is necessary for redemption, that Christians should abstain from worldly pleasures and strive to imitate Christ – ideas that reappear in several of George Eliot's fictional characters.[11] During this time she had frequent conversations with her Aunt Elizabeth Evans, who as a young woman had been a Methodist lay preacher, and who told her the story around which *Adam Bede* was constructed.[12] But this fervent evangelicalism began to collapse at age twenty-two when Mary Ann became acquainted with the liberal Unitarianism of the Bray and Hennell families after she and her father moved to the vicinity of Coventry, in 1841. She found she could no longer accept such morally questionable doctrines as that of a substitutionary atonement (according to which an innocent man is put to death for the sins of others), and it became increasingly evident to her that the biblical stories are not literal history. In a forthright letter to her father, she explained why she stopped attending church with him,[13] but she retained her own form of religious belief, never left the Church of England, began a life-long association with the Unitarians,[14] and in fact continued to attend a variety of religious services. Her deep knowledge of Scripture, her devotion to the gospel proclaimed by Jesus, her understanding of the power of the central Christian symbols, and her appreciation for all genuine religious piety are lasting heritages of her evangelical involvement.

It was the lack of such piety that chiefly bothered her in

evangelical teachers like Dr. John Cumming. In a brilliant review of his writings published in 1855, she found in him

> no indication of religious raptures, of delight in God, of spiritual communion with the Father. He is most at home in the forensic view of justification, and dwells on salvation as a scheme rather than as an experience. He insists on good works as the sign of justifying faith . . . but he rarely represents them as the spontaneous, necessary outflow of a soul filled with Divine love.[15]

She identified three striking characteristics of his theology: unscrupulosity of statement (free play of prejudices, no regard for truth), absence of genuine charity (hatred of everyone not in the clan), and perverted moral judgment (egoistic passions, dogmatic beliefs, everything reduced to serving the 'glory of God').[16]

In evangelical Christianity as a whole she found well represented what Paul Ricoeur has described as 'the rotten points' present in every religion – accusation and consolation, taboo and shelter, the fear of punishment and the desire for protection. 'In destroying the shelter offered by religion and liberating men from the taboos imposed by religion,' writes Ricoeur, 'atheism clears the ground for a faith beyond accusation and consolation.'[17] Mary Ann Evans expressed it this way in 1842: 'I cannot rank among my principles of action a fear of vengeance eternal, gratitude for predestined salvation, or a revelation of future glories as a reward.' But she continues: 'I fully participate in the belief that the only heaven here or hereafter is to be found in conformity with the will of the Supreme; a continual aiming at the attainment of that perfect ideal, the true Logos that dwells in the bosom of the One Father.'[18] The latter view accords with the Unitarian Christianity espoused by William Ellery Channing, who had considerable influence in Britain after 1830. Unitarianism provided George Eliot with a way of distancing herself from evangelical Christianity without abandoning a theological frame of reference and a form of Christian piety.

3. The Religion of Humanity

George Eliot was searching for a religion beyond accusation and consolation. And indeed in her case it was the implicit atheism of the German and French critics of mythical and dogmatic Christianity that cleared the ground for such a faith. But it would be misleading to suggest that she became a disciple of David Friedrich Strauss and Ludwig Feuerbach, whose works she trans-lated, or of Auguste Comte, whose 'religion of humanity' was in vogue among the intellectuals with whom she associated in the early 1850s.

She was put off by the 'coldbloodedness' and single-mindedness of Strauss's *Life of Jesus,* telling Caroline Bray that she was 'Strauss-sick – it made her ill dissecting the beautiful story of the crucifixion, and only the sight of her Christ-image and picture made her endure it.'[19] While endorsing the historical-critical method with its rejection of supernaturalism, and accepting Strauss's analysis of the role of myth in the Bible as well as his critique of the orthodox doctrine of the God-man, she could not have been attracted to his conclusion that the historical Jesus was an apocalyptic enthusiast (*Schwärmer*) who confused his own identity with that of the messianic Son of Man, shortly to return in triumph on the clouds of heaven. This apocalyptic version of Jesus served Strauss's own reconstructive interests well since he believed that, faced with such an unappealing figure, thoughtful persons would be driven to the philosophical conclusion that the unity of divine and human natures is realized in humanity as a whole rather than in a single individual. It is humanity to which the christo-logical predicates are properly ascribed.[20] George Eliot must have found such a conclusion to be both abstract and unproductive: we have to do not with humanity as a whole but with concrete human beings, through whom alone ideals and values become historical realities. It is a rather odd bourgeois illusion to suppose, as Strauss did, that humanity as such is the union of two natures, divine and human – working intellectual miracles, progressing toward moral perfection, triumphing over nature, etc.

The Jesus of Strauss's *Life of Jesus* is far removed from the Jesus to whom George Eliot was attracted, namely the Man of Sorrows who proclaimed the friendship of God and exemplified a life of service and self-renunciation. She would scarcely have dismissed, as Strauss did, Jesus' 'cure of some sick people in Galilee' by contrast with the advances of modern science.[21] She recognized that Strauss's work, in both its historical and its theological aspects, is more the product of a reductive rationalism than it is of genuine religious imagination or profound speculative thought. Evidence of such a rationalism is found in Strauss's conviction that philosophical concepts represent a higher order of truth than religious images, symbols, and practices, and that in the age of modernity religion is destined to be superseded by philosophy – an idea he mistakenly attributed to Hegel.[22] Given her artistic sensibility and understanding of how people actually live, George Eliot knew that such an idea is nonsense.

Feuerbach, too, disappointed her. She disliked Feuerbach's 'crudity of expressions,' warning Sara Sophia Hennell that the translation drafts of *The Essence of Christianity* that she had shared with her were quite literal, 'so you have the *raw* Feuerbach – not any of my cooking . . . With the ideas of Feuerbach I everywhere agree, but of course I should, of myself, alter the phraseology considerably.'[23] The reference to 'cooking' and the tongue-in-cheek nature of the remark about 'everywhere agreeing' – for it is quite clear that there was no single thinker with whom George Eliot could everywhere agree – should warn us that the 'cooked' version of Feuerbach that appears in George Eliot's fiction will differ in significant respects from the 'raw' version.[24] Nor is 'altering the phraseology' as innocent as it sounds, for *how* things are said shapes the substance of what is said. Later George Eliot remarked that she had 'long ceased to feel any sympathy with mere antagonism and destruction, and all crudity of expression marks . . . a deficiency in subtlety of thought as well as in breadth of moral and poetic feeling.'[25]

George Eliot found support in Feuerbach for her own conviction about the primacy of feeling and emotion in human experience, and she responded affirmatively to his emphasis on the essentially communal nature of human beings as expressed in love and the I-Thou relationship, which has of necessity for embodied beings a sensual and sexual aspect. The category of 'sympathy' that proved so important for her interpretation of religion derived in part from Feuerbach's *Mitgefühl* ('fellow-feeling'). She agreed with his (essentially Kantian) insight that religious images and theological concepts are constructions of the human imagination. But the question is what calls forth and justifies such constructions. I find no evidence in her writings that George Eliot ever embraced the central (and tediously reiterated) dogma of *The Essence of Christianity*, namely that human beings simply project onto a screen of transcendence all their own essential attributes and qualities, thereby objectifying and idealizing them in a supreme being. The source of the idea of God, Feuerbach believed, is human consciousness coming to know itself; it is a purely fanciful idea, having no reference in reality other than to the idea of humanity, the so-called species-essence (*Gattungswesen*), to which the divine attributes properly apply.[26] In contrast, as I shall attempt to show, for George Eliot the idea of God or divinity is not an illusion arising out of psychological needs but a response to something awesome, mysterious, and overwhelming that presents itself in experience and demands reverence. Expressed in Hegelian terms, which are not incompatible with her own deep conviction, the idea of God is not the self-projection of finite consciousness onto the infinite, but the self-manifestation of the infinite in finite consciousness's awareness of the infinite, an awareness that is characteristically accompanied for religious people by self-denial rather than self-seeking, a centering on God (or ultimate reality) rather than on self. The difference here is between a naturalistic and a critically realistic account of religious experience. Thus it is not surprising that Feuerbach's rationalism, as well as his materialism and naturalism, which became more evident in later writings, were of little interest to George Eliot, and after 1854 she did not discuss his ideas.[27]

As for Comte, while attracted to some of his utopian ideals, including the principles of altruism and sympathy, she found his system of positivism rigid and ideological, and she never gave unqualified approval to the 'religion of humanity.'[28] Comte thought it necessary to invent such a religion, in which the so-called 'Great Being' is identified with the ideal of humanity, in order to have a compelling basis for developing sympathetic instincts and moral values as a counterbalance to the exercise of material power in the realm of politics. But in fact his system remained utilitarian and deterministic. Pointing out that Comte did not believe that objective reality conforms to humanity's subjective values, T. R. Wright observes that 'the Religion of Humanity . . . offers a comforting fiction in the face of a hostile and meaningless universe.'[29] George Eliot was not interested in such comforting fictions, and she could not accept a disconnection between reality on the one hand and morality and religion on the other, which reduces the latter to the utilitarian function of promoting happiness and harmony. Gertrude Lenzer remarks that 'the triumph of the positive spirit consists in the reduction of quality to quantity in all realms of existence – in the realm of society and man as well as in the realm of nature – and the further reduction of quantity to ever larger and more abstract formulations of the relations that obtain between abstract quantities.'[30] Such a reduction and abstraction are utterly foreign to George Eliot's way of thinking. Moreover, Comte's compartmentalization of gender roles (according to which women are assigned to the realm of emotion as opposed to intellect, and to family as opposed to public life) must have given her pause.

While affirming that religion ought above all to promote human flourishing, her sense of human evil and historical tragedy was too deep to allow her to embrace a religion that might actually worship or idolize human beings either as individuals or as a species – those very humans whose tendency, out of ambition or fear, is to draw everything into themselves.[31] Her insight into the human condition was more profound and also more tragic than that of Feuerbach and Comte. Hers was a religion of humanity directed, not to veneration, but to service and sympathy. But what calls forth, motivates, and empowers such service and sympathy?[32] Her intent was to reorient human beings from self-centeredness to reality-centeredness.[33] But what is (ultimate) reality? The difference between Comte and George Eliot in this regard might be viewed as similar to the difference between the Sophists, who claimed that the human being is the measure of all things, and Socrates and Plato, for whom 'soul' or God or the Good is the measure of all things. In the final analysis, George Eliot's skepticism prevented her from embracing such a pretentious and totalizing system as

Comte's, which bears all the marks of modern-day sophistry. To be sure, Comtean ideas are present in her fiction, as are Feuerbachian ideas, Spinozistic ideas, Hegelian ideas, and Spencerian ideas, but she was a disciple of none of these thinkers.

George Eliot's own version of a religion of humanity can be deduced from a prospectus she wrote in 1851 describing the kind of article the editors of the *Westminster Review* would desire on the subject of Christian ethics and modern civilization. In addition to an honest, critical account of what the New Testament writers really believed and taught in their own context, the desired article

> would place in strong light the vein of asceticism in the Christian system, leading to such monstrous results in the early centuries of the Church and causing perpetual offences against conscience in simple minds of our own day, its subordination of domestic and social duties to an impractical enthusiasm and the egotistic seeking for 'salvation,' its depreciation of the present life especially as regards the culture of the intellect and taste, and its passivity towards political and social abuses – all of which had their foundation first in the dualistic theory – the antithesis of God and the world, and next in the expectation of Christ's immediate return. The writer's strictures would extend over many other particulars of Christian theory and practice, for example the creation of doctrinal belief into the condition of fellowship, but the main point would be to shew that the faith and life of the early Christians were entirely based on the idea of the special and exceptional, whereas the essence of modern advancement is the recognition of the general and invariable, and this must henceforth be the standpoint of an effective religious and moral theory.[34]

George Eliot's passion for human flourishing and justice, her suspicion of religious self-interest, her dislike of doctrinal disputes, her critique of a dualistic separation of God and world, and her belief that the 'special and exceptional,' that is the miraculous, must be replaced by the 'general and invariable' as a precondition for understanding ethical action and divine presence, are relevant to our discussion below of the elements of a future religion as she conceived it. Her own enduring religious humanism is perhaps best summed up in the following remark about Richard Congreve's efforts to establish a Church of Humanity: 'The most solid comfort one can fall upon is the thought that the business of one's life – the work at home after the holiday is done – is to help in some small nibbling way to reduce the sum of ignorance, degradation, and misery on the face of this beautiful earth.'[35]

George Eliot read widely, deeply, and continuously, and was subject to no controlling influence. Referring to Rousseau and George Sand, she commented: 'The writers who have most profoundly influenced me . . . are not in the least oracles to me. It is just possible that I may not embrace one of their opinions, that I may wish my life to be shaped quite differently from theirs.'[36] This statement should warn us against over-emphasizing the influence of Feuerbach and Comte on her thinking. Her mind was engaged by deeper thinkers and greater poets than they – not only Rousseau but also Spinoza, Hegel, Shakespeare, Goethe, Wordsworth, Coleridge, Mill, Carlyle. I cannot consider all of these influences, which are discussed in detail by Valerie Dodd in her intellectual life of George Eliot,[37] but I wish to offer a few remarks about Spinoza and Hegel.

George Eliot first read Spinoza in 1843 and began, at the request of a friend, to translate the *Tractatus Theologico-Politicus*, but neither it nor her mid-1850s translation of his *Ethics*, undertaken through an arrangement made by George Henry Lewes, was published. Spinozistic motifs are evident in her essays and novels, notably the interplay of necessity and freedom in human affairs, the antipathy toward religious dogmas and controversies, the conviction that divine providence works through entirely natural and historical processes, and the orientation to an ethical monotheism. In a universe of cause and effect, human freedom is possible insofar as rational control is exercised over physical desires and emotions, and insofar as rational insight is obtained into the ultimate connection of things (an insight that Spinoza called 'the intellectual love of God') and the ultimate goal of things (a goal that he named the 'just commonwealth'). Spinoza did not identify God with everything that is – a philosophically absurd position – but with the 'nature' or 'substance' that constitutes the most general

principles of order exemplified by things. All things have their
essential being 'in' God but are not God. When reference is made
to Spinoza's 'pantheism,' it should be taken in this sense – a sense
more precisely designated as 'panentheism.'[38]

G. H. Lewes commented that 'Spinoza's Pantheism is in truth
the grandest and most religious of all philosophies, and as such it
is recognized by Goethe and the German philosophers who all
embrace his creed.'[39] Later George Eliot claimed to have freed
herself of the influence of pantheism, writing to Harriet Beecher
Stowe: 'I do not find my temple in Pantheism, which, whatever
might be its value speculatively, could not yield a practical religion,
since it is an attempt to look at the universe from the outside of our
relations to it (that universe) as human beings.'[40] While there is
evidence that as a young woman she was attracted to a religious
mysticism or pantheism, she seems to have come to the view,
perhaps under the influence of Coleridge and Feuerbach, that
pantheism envisions a nonhuman, philosophical, rational God in
contrast to the human, personal, revealed God of Christianity and
other concrete religions.[41] But in her last work, *Daniel Deronda*, she
embraced elements of a Jewish mystical vision.

While George Eliot was attracted to speculative systems and
holistic visions, her skeptical eclecticism and her orientation to
living communities of faith prevented her from falling under the
sway of any of them. Her philosophical-theological sensibility was
similar in some respects to that of Hegel, but she clearly was not an
Hegelian and most likely was acquainted only with his philosophy
of history and his aesthetics, not his philosophy of religion or his
phenomenology of spirit, logic, and ethics.[42] While she may have
been closer to Spinoza than to Hegel in philosophical orientation –
and certainly she was more directly acquainted with the thought
of Spinoza – she did not subscribe uncritically to the Spinozistic
doctrine of substance. Reality had for her as well the qualities of
subjectivity, historicality, relationality, and difference, which are
the central Hegelian categories; and these qualities must be present
in God. Hegel's claim that in God substance is subject, and subject
substance, seems to be implicit in her thinking: thus her view
that divinity has the aspect of both moral order and infinite loving
presence. Moreover, she was closer to both Spinoza and Hegel

than to Feuerbach since from her point of view it is fundamentally wrong to confuse one's finite mode of existence or even the human species with the Whole that is God. In her views on religious feeling, divine redemption, and the inability to grasp God cognitively, she had some affinities with the theology of Friedrich Schleiermacher, although she possessed no direct knowledge of his thought.[43]

Above all George Eliot was impressed by life's complexity and the ultimate mystery of things. She resisted simplistic solutions, whether on the side of supernaturalistic theism, materialistic atheism, scientific reductionism, or political utopianism. She experimented with a form of panentheism: the belief not that all things are God, or that God and nature are one and the same, but that all things have their being *in* God, and that God encompasses the difference between God and the world. But she would have regarded that label as too abstractly philosophical, preferring instead to emphasize the way redemptive transformation is concretely experienced in people's lives. She offered an original reconstruction of religion that is not solely traceable to any of the influences that contributed to it.

4. Elements of a Future Religion

My argument is that George Eliot was seeking to move through and beyond evangelicalism and the religion of humanity toward something new. She accomplished a sublation of both evangelical and humanistic elements by means of which, purged of destructive features, they were surpassed yet continued to reverberate in her own version of a religion of the future. This would be a truthful religion without accusation and consolation, a practical religion oriented to human feelings, needs and deeds, a spiritual religion attuned to the mystery beneath the real, and a religion open to the idea of a sympathetic, suffering, (omni)present God. She lacked the categories to articulate the theological aspects of this religion very clearly. What she needed was an understanding of a God-in-process, a God who does not control the course of world events but interacts with them, becoming God through a process of self-divestment and self-reunion, a fellow-sufferer who empowers humans through a kind of sympathetic presence, a God who both preserves and transforms all things within the divine life. She did not know Hegel well enough to acquire such a vision from him, and she preceded Whitehead by some fifty years. But this is the idea of God implicit in her novels. It is expressed directly for the most part only by fictional characters such as Dinah Morris because George Eliot was reluctant to engage in God-talk, knowing how readily such talk comes to the lips of humans, and how often it serves vain and petty interests. It might be possible from her point of view to have a future religion without God-talk. At the same time she seems to have been seeking an adequate language for bringing God to speech, a language that might replace the old evangelical, mythical, metaphysical language. The language of the philosophers and theologians with whom she was acquainted was not adequate, but perhaps at the end, in Judaism, she was beginning to discover such a language (a Jewish way of speaking that, paradoxically, affirms God as Thou while denying that God can be named). In any event, the specifically theistic elements of a future religion remain at the margins, or on the horizon, of her vision. Yet it is my deep conviction that God does come to speech, indirectly, through processes of redemptive transformation, in the stories written by George Eliot.

It is clear from George Eliot's letters, some of which have already been cited, that after the initial shock of the loss of naive belief had worn off (over a period of about ten years) she no longer had any antagonism toward genuine religious piety, any destructive impulse toward religion regarded as an illusion or social pathology. Rather she had the profoundest sympathy for the human quest, under conditions of suffering and sorrow, of joyous life and authentic meaning: this is what religion is all about, and her purposes in regard to it were constructive, not destructive. Note the following statement in a letter written in 1847 at the height of her own religious struggle:

> I imagine the sorrowful amaze of a child who had been dwelling with delight on the idea that the stars were the pavement of heaven's court and that there above them sat the kind but holy God, looking like a venerable Father who would smile on his

good little ones – when it was cruelly told, before its mind had substance enough to bear such tensions, that the sky was not real, that the stars were worlds, and that even the sun could not be God's dwelling because there were many, many suns. These ideas would introduce atheism into a child's mind, instead of assisting it to form a nobler conception of God . . . – whereas the idea it previously had of God was perfectly adapted to its intellectual condition and formed to the child as perfect an embodiment of the all-good, all-wise, and all-powerful as the most enlightened philosopher ever formed to himself.[44]

Compare this with a letter written in 1873 between the composition of *Middlemarch* and *Daniel Deronda*:

All the great religions of the world historically considered, are rightly the objects of deep reverence and sympathy – they are the record of spiritual struggles which are the types of our own. This is to me pre-eminently true of Hebrewism and Christianity, on which my own youth was nourished. And in this sense I have no antagonism towards any religious belief, but a strong outflow of sympathy. Every community met to worship the highest Good (which is understood to be expressed by God) carries me along in its main current . . .[45]

In what follows I shall trace the elements of a future religion that seem important to George Eliot. These elements are not simply humanistic (oriented to human feelings, needs, practices), or cosmological (oriented to the regularities of the natural/moral order and to the mystery that underlies the processes), or theistic (the idea of the highest Good, or of God as infinitely sympathetic, suffering, omnipresent Love). Rather true religion involves all of these, coming together to form what Raimon Panikkar has called a 'cosmotheandric experience,'[46] the interaction of cosmos, theos, and anthropos in such a way as to constitute a whole in which no single element is foundational but each is essential to the others. Perhaps some such term as this (more so than 'panentheism') approximates to the complexity of George Eliot's religious vision.

a. A Truthful Religion: Beyond Accusation and Consolation

Above all, as we have seen, religion for George Eliot must be truthful: it must not be allowed to offer false shelter from present-day realities by promising future (individual) salvation, nor must it be allowed to threaten eternal punishment for designated transgressions. Such religion operates according to the logic of reward and punishment and is readily corrupted into becoming an instrument of social control. It is fundamentally misleading about how God acts in history.

Responding to Barbara Bodichon's query as to whether it was acceptable to turn to the 'forms and ceremonies' of religion for comfort, George Eliot wrote:

> I have faith in the working-out of higher possibilities than the Catholic or any other church has presented, and those who have strength to wait and endure, are bound to accept no formula which their whole souls – their intellects as well as their emotions – do not embrace with entire reverence. The highest 'calling and election' is to *do without opium* and live through all our pain with conscious, clear-eyed endurance.[47]

No statement is closer to George Eliot's own religious struggle. She was deeply aware of the human need to make sense of life, to find meaning and direction in history, to face the future with courage in the absence of certainty about one's own destiny. She knew how tempting it is to dull the pain of life through such escapes as gambling and alcohol,[48] or to provide consolation through superficial assurances of divine rescue and salvation.[49] She did not believe that God intervenes episodically in history to save people from disasters, to reward piety, to punish wrong-doing, or to bring about desired outcomes. Rather the natural and moral worlds are governed by laws that assure an invariability of sequence and the inexorability of consequences. To suggest that God contravenes these laws is immoral and irrational; rather the laws constitute God's system of government. In such a world human beings are free and responsible agents, and they must accept the consequences of their actions. Thus the effects of sin cannot be expunged, but the course of wrong-doing need not be continued. Repentance can change the future but not obliterate the past.[50] By living through our pain with conscious, clear-eyed endurance, new and higher possibilities may open up – but *we* must make them happen.[51] In all of this, truthfulness, honesty, clarity, and avoidance of illusion are absolutely essential. 'Falsehood is so easy, truth so difficult.'[52]

Is it possible for religion 'to do without opium'? Perhaps George Eliot was thinking of Karl Marx's famous comment that religion is 'the opium of the people,' offering illusory happiness in place of real happiness. But that is a sweeping dogma, true in some instances but not in others. Certainly the religion of Dinah Morris in *Adam Bede* was no opium of the people; she never tried to make things seem better or different than they were, and she avoided illusions. She provided comfort without consolation; by her sympathetic deeds and truthful speech she manifested God's presence in the world.

One of the recurrent themes in George Eliot's letters is that the only kind of redemption possible in this imperfect world is partial, fragmentary, and ambiguous. But this acknowledgment should not prevent us from accomplishing what is possible or from believing that God is somehow at work in it. Religion's temptation is to pretend that things are better than they are or worse than they are. Surely it is a strange perversion, she writes,

> to think that unless life can be made perfect, unless the prospects of humanity can be made to appear the very best, strong moral motives are gone! As if the very absence of that highest security were not a more urgent reason for at least diminishing the pressure of evil, for worshipping the goodness and the great endeavours that are at least a *partial* salvation, a *partial* redemption of the world.[53]

This idea of partial redemption as opposed to Christian perfectionism may have later attracted her to Judaism.

One of the 'old, old truths' George Eliot rediscovered is this: 'Never to bear and bruise one's wings against the inevitable but to throw the whole force of one's soul towards the achievement of some possible better . . . I use that summary every day, and could

not live without repeating it to myself.'[54] Only when we resign ourselves to inevitabilities such as the passage of time (lost opportunities of the past, a future narrowing toward death) and not seek false
consolation or escape, will we be in a position to accomplish some
good in the present moment. Human well-being is not contingent
on a supernatural rescue, nor are humans subject to a hideous
fatalism. We *can* act in such a way as to make a difference, to
promote love and justice rather than suffering and oppression.
'The progress of the world . . . can certainly never come at all save
by the modified actions of the individual beings who compose the
world.'[55] This theme reverberates in the later novels, especially
Middlemarch; it is also expressed in the poem, 'A Minor Prophet'
(1865).[56]

Other instances of truthfulness in religion are a rejection of the
illusion of spiritualism (the notion that we can communicate with
departed souls)[57] and the recognition that the doctrine of personal
immortality has led to a preoccupation with future rewards and
punishments. George Eliot came to the conviction that life after
death cannot be some sort of prolonged personal existence; rather
those who have gone before live on in the effects of their work
and the memories of their successors in what the Comteans called
'subjective immortality.' Only in this sense are their lives taken
up into and preserved in the divine life: they live not as subjects
but as objects (whose subjective immediacy has perished) in the
eternal life of God. (Whitehead called this doctrine 'objective
immortality,' a more accurate designation, I think.) Her views are
best summed up in the remark to François d'Albert-Durade that,
while reserving final judgment on 'the question of our future
existence,' she believes 'the immediate object and the proper
sphere of all our highest emotions are our struggling fellow-men
and this earthly existence.'[58]

b. A Practical Religion: Feeling and Deed Rather than Doctrine

In *Adam Bede* the narrator observes: 'Faith, hope, and charity have
not always been found in a direct ratio with sensibility to the three
concords; and it is possible, thank Heaven! to have very erroneous
theories and very sublime feelings.'[59] And Adam Bede himself says

that 'it isn't notions sets people doing the right thing – its feelings.' 'Doctrines,' he adds, simply are 'finding names for your feelings.' Rather than arguing about doctrines, 'I found it better for my soul to be humble before the mysteries o' God's dealings.'[60]

By these statements George Eliot is telling us to trust our emotions, our feelings, to regard them as putting us in touch with what is real and true, and to view doctrines as interpretations of feelings rather than vice versa. While she seemed to have no objection to doctrines in principle, she saw them often being used to impose inhumane, rationally indefensible beliefs and practices, or to push a sectarian agenda. And she regarded the role of the artist to be the evocation of feelings in relation to concrete figures and experiences rather than the advancement of the writer's religious, philosophical, or moral theories.[61] There is, to be sure, a powerful didactic element in George Eliot's novels, but it is a teaching that proceeds inductively from experienced realities rather than deductively from abstract principles. It arises out of her genius for acute observation and penetrating description.

Religious feelings have both a mystical and a practical dimension. Mystically, they entail the fruits of the Spirit, the peace of God, the 'bathing of the soul in emotions which overpass the outlines of thought';[62] practically they lead to a life of service and sympathy, a sharing in the suffering love of Christ.[63] Already as a young woman George Eliot was motivated by a deep sense of social injustice and by the urgency of effective action. In one of her more apocalyptic letters she lashed out at 'the loathsome fawning, the transparent hypocrisy, the systematic giving as little as possible for as much as possible that one meets with here at every turn. I feel that society is training men and women for hell.'[64] She believed that people could be persuaded to act through 'the truth of feeling as the only universal bond of union,'[65] rather than by abstract arguments and doctrines. 'The reason why societies change slowly is, because individual men and women cannot have their natures changed by doctrine and can only be wrought on by little and little.'[66] Here the artist has a peculiar role to play, for the artist is capable of evoking feeling and creating emotional bonds, of 'wroughting on' people. 'I have had heart-cutting experience that opinions are a poor cement between human souls; and the only effect I ardently long to produce by my writings, is that those who read them should be better able to *imagine* and to *feel* the pains and the joys of those who differ from themselves in everything but the broad fact of being struggling erring human creatures.'[67] Art and religion share the domain of feeling, and as such they are both oriented to humanizing practices rather than to metaphysical theories.

c. A Spiritual Religion: Reverence for the Mystery beneath the Real

Commenting on Darwin's *Origin of Species,* George Eliot made another revealing observation to Barbara Bodichon: 'To me the Development theory and other explanations of processes by which things came to be, produce a feeble impression compared with the mystery that lies under the processes.'[68] This letter was written shortly after the publication of *Adam Bede,* in which she was concerned with both the divine mystery and realism in art. The mystery that lies under the processes is 'the mystery beneath the real'[69] – a phrase that can serve as a motto for her work as a whole. The narrator of *Adam Bede* associates the mystery with the kind of deep love, religious feeling, and musical harmony[70] that 'bring with them the consciousness that they are mere waves and ripples in an unfathomable ocean of love and beauty: our emotion in its keenest moment passes from expression into silence; our love at its highest flood rushes beyond its object, and loses itself in the sense of divine mystery.'[71] This mystery is to be found not above and beyond the real but beneath and within it. What is required to find the mystery is not a denial of the real and commonplace but an imaginative penetration and intensification of it, a discovery of the good, true, and beautiful in the midst of the common, ugly, and everyday – a discovery that is possible only for those who have eyes to see. This is the 'rare, precious quality of truthfulness' in many Dutch paint-ings, which find beauty not simply in the 'secret of proportion, but in the secret of deep human sympathy.' We may paint angels and madonnas if we like, but 'do not . . . banish from the region of Art those old women scraping carrots with their work-worn hands, those heavy clowns taking holiday in a dingy pot-house, those rounded backs and stupid weather-beaten faces that have bent over the spade and done the rough work of the world.'[72] In these common human faces may be seen the face of God; in ordinary human sympathy, the divine sympathy. The presence of the ideal in the realism of Dutch painting is a theme articulated in similar terms in Hegel's *Aesthetics*.[73]

George Eliot's emphasis on realism in art was influenced by John Ruskin, while her sense of mystery was nurtured by Rousseau, Wordsworth, Coleridge, and Carlyle. With the English Romantic poets she shared the intuition of a nonmaterial dimension of the natural world. Immaterial beauty, the beauty of soul or spirit, shines through material beauty, but it can also shine in the midst of the commonplace and ugly. Thus hers was not a positivist, empirical realism, but an imaginative, spiritual realism, which sought a dimension in reality beyond the visible truth of material objects, a mystery that pervades space and time and reveals itself in the manifestation of goodness, love, and beauty within the real world.[74] The category of revelation is not inappropriate here. George Eliot embraced R. W. Mackay's idea that divine revelation is not contained in the facts and scriptures of one particular age but is co-extensive with the history of human development, perpetually unfolding itself to widened experience.[75] Imagination is required to apprehend such revelation and to participate in its power, which is the power of spirit, not of natural forces.

Thus we should not confuse George Eliot's realism with a naturalistic or materialistic worldview. She did indeed have to comes to terms with the challenge of natural science to traditional religious worldviews, especially as that challenge presented itself in the form of Darwin's evolutionary theory, which called radically into question any literal reading of biblical cosmology. She was well acquainted with the science of her time and accepted the validity of its explanations.[76] But she knew that natural science is precisely an empirical discipline and cannot make judgments about nonempirical questions, such as the ultimate origin and destiny of the world (the religious question), or the determination of what is good and what is evil (the ethical question). She would have agreed with the now widely-accepted view that religious and ethical interpretations must be *consonant* with natural science but cannot be derived from natural science. She herself avoided scientific reductionism. Her attempt at working out the interface between science and religion would have been aided had she had access to the organic, relational, process-oriented models that came to fruition in the twentieth century as distinct from the mechanical, deterministic models that still prevailed in the nineteenth century.[77]

d. The Idea of a Sympathetic, Suffering, (Omni)present God

George Eliot's artistic vision clearly refers the reader to a mysterious reality that transcends the self and nature, reverberates in the rhythms of nature and the events of history, draws the self out of itself into an unnameable whole, molests and drives human beings until they collapse or are reborn.[78] Sometimes it comes under the guise of the 'hard unaccommodating Actual, which has never consulted our taste and is entirely unselect.'[79] Other times it appears as 'a pitying, loving, infinite Presence, sweet as summer to the houseless needy.'[80] But what is it in and for itself? Is it simply the fatality and necessity of history, the cosmic and moral law that exacts consequences for every action?[81] Is it an impersonal trans-individual substance, having perhaps the quality of 'maternity,' a nurturing, sacrificial love?[82] Or is it a God who, while not personal in any finite sense, nonetheless is experienced as subject, present and active in nature and history? On this question I think George Eliot did not arrive at a clear and definitive answer; she remained agnostic.[83] She seems to have oscillated between a more personal view of a compassionately engaged, suffering God, as in *Adam Bede,* and a more impersonal, Spinozistic view of a divine omni-presence at work in things, as in *Daniel Deronda*. In some ultimately inconceivable sense God is both subject and substance.

To her former landlord in Geneva George Eliot wrote:

Ten years of experience have wrought great changes in [my] inward self: I have no longer any antagonism towards any faith in which human sorrow and human longing for purity have expressed themselves; on the contrary, I have a sympathy with it that predominates over all argumentative tendencies. I have not returned to dogmatic Christianity – to the acceptance of any set of doctrines as a creed, and a superhuman revelation of the Unseen – but I see in it the highest expression of the religious sentiment that has yet found its place in the history of mankind, and I have the profoundest interest in the inward life of sincere Christians in all ages.[84]

Note the qualifiers in this statement: she has not returned to *dogmatic* Christianity, to the acceptance of doctrines *as a creed,* or to a *superhuman* revelation. This leaves open the possibility of reconstructing a nondogmatic, noncreedal form of Christianity (the highest expression thus far, she claims, of human religion), and of affirming an innerhuman revelation of the Unseen.

In her critique of Dr. Cumming's evangelical teaching, George Eliot sketched an intriguing alternative to his vengeful, compensatory God.

The idea of God is really moral in its influence . . . only when God is contemplated as sympathizing with the pure elements of human feeling, as possessing infinitely all those attributes which we recognize to be moral in humanity. In this life, the idea of God and the sense of His presence intensify all noble feeling, and encourage all noble effort, on the same principle that human sympathy is found a source of strength: the brave man feels braver when he knows that another stout heart is beating time with his; the devoted woman who is wearing out her years in patient effort to alleviate suffering or save vice from the last stages of degradation, finds aid in the pressure of a friendly hand which tells her that there is one who understands her deeds, and in her place would do the like. The idea of a God who not only sympathizes with all we feel and endure for our fellow-men, but who will pour new life into our too languid love, and give firmness to our vacillating purpose, is an extension and multiplication of the effects produced by human sympathy; and it has been intensified for the better spirits who have been under the influence of orthodox Christianity, by the contemplation of Jesus as 'God manifest in the flesh.'[85]

There are, to be sure, Feuerbachian elements in this statement, but there are also important differences from Feuerbach. Some 'cooking' has occurred: the role of human imagination is affirmed, but also the reality of what is imagined. The idea of God may be a fiction, but a true and necessary fiction. After all, theology as a whole is a kind of fiction that creates imaginative variations on what history offers as 'fact.' The theologian and the artist alike are engaged in a creative act, a *poiēsis*, an envisionment of a possible world in which human beings might dwell humanly. In this case, George Eliot is telling us that we need the sympathetic presence of a friend in order to have the courage and strength to act under difficult circumstances. But human friends alone often are not enough, given the fragility and transience of the human condition: we need the idea of a God who not only sympathizes with our feeling but also will *pour new life* into our languid love and *strengthen* our vacillating resolve. 'Pouring' and 'strengthening' are metaphors associated with the Holy Spirit. God does not act directly, miraculously, superhumanly, but through the indwelling of the Spirit and the mediation of human friends: just this is the meaning (for Christians) of God becoming manifest in the flesh of Jesus.

The idea of God, if it is a 'true' idea, necessarily affirms the reality of God, for an unreal or purely imaginary God is a contradiction in the very concept of God (Anselm's ontological argument, reformulated by Hegel). The question for George Eliot (as well as for us) is whether the thought-project 'God' is a truthful or an illusory construction of the human imagination. The test of the truth of the idea, and hence of the reality, of God is in the experiencing of new life as a gratuitous empowerment, as a gift that is not reducible to any given thing and is not at our disposal. Such testing occurs in the stories written by George Eliot, and it leads me to suggest that for her the idea of God does not satisfy a psychological need or serve a social function, as claimed by Feuerbach and Comte; rather it has to do with the fundamental condition of being human and existing morally in a tragically conflicted world. God comes forth as real in redemptive transformations wrought by the power of sympathy and love.

George Eliot experimented with the concept of the Good as an ethical name for God. There are scattered references to it in the earlier letters,[86] but it seems to have become more predominant later. The 'highest Good' is what is expressed by the word 'God,' she told John Walter Cross, and she added that religious worship is important because it is a way of recognizing a 'spiritual law which is to lift us into willing obedience and save us from the slavery of unregulated passion or impulse.'[87] To a despairing friend who had come to the view that modern natural science allows no room for morality, she wrote that human fellowship is not dependent upon something miraculous and supernatural. Rather 'the idea of God, so far as it has been a high spiritual influence, is the ideal of a goodness entirely human (i.e., an exaltation of the human).'[88] I think it is important to note the nuances here: the idea of God is the *ideal* of a goodness, an *exaltation* of the human. It has the status of ideality, but it permeates reality and gives to humanity its distinctive ethos and telos. It is the ideal-real. It appears in history in both impersonal lawlike forms and personal incarnations. The naming of God as the Good is found also in the Jewish parts of *Daniel Deronda*,[89] which suggests that this idea has for the author its roots in Hebraic piety as well as in Platonic theology.

5. The Vocation of Spiritual Motherhood

Part of George Eliot's religious pilgrimage was a quest for vocation.[90] In early letters she struggled with the question as to what she was to do with her life.[91] The options were severely limited for a precocious young woman – certainly nothing by way of a religious or academic profession was open to her – and she sometimes despaired, even after a significant accomplishment such as the translation of Feuerbach.[92] She found her vocation as a novelist, which carried with it for her an almost religious sense of duty. At the end of 1857, having completed her first book, *Scenes of Clerical Life*, she wrote in her journal: 'My life has deepened unspeakably during the last year: I feel a greater capacity for moral and intellectual enjoyment, a more acute sense of my deficiencies in the past, a more solemn desire to be faithful to coming duties, than I remember at any former period of my life.'[93] But the completion of each new novel brought a fresh spiritual crisis, a sense that 'much work . . . remains to be done in life.'[94] She observed in 1864 that she had been reading Newman's *Apologia pro Vita Sua* and found, despite a life so different in form from her own, a close fellowship in 'spiritual needs and burthens.' In the same letter she noted that 'inspiration is a rare and incalculable thing': sometimes it will 'flash out' in unexpected ways (as in a mere fragment of a painting), but normally it leaves one 'to wonder at its absence.'[95] As an acutely sensitive artist George Eliot suffered the vagaries of inspiration and experienced both manic and depressive states. In a journal entry written about the same time as this letter in 1864 (following an extraordinary six-year period in which she had published five novels), she acknowledged experiencing 'horrible scepticism about all things – paralyzing my mind. Shall I ever be good for anything again? – ever do anything again?'[96]

One thing she proved 'good for' came surprisingly and unintentionally. From the beginning of her literary career, but especially after the publication of *Middlemarch* in 1872, she received letters of appreciation and pleas for help or counsel from people all over the world. One young man from California wrote, 'You, who are a great lady, yet know so well how all the little fishes struggle.'[97] Another, a poor working man, asked for a cheap edition of her 'inimitable books,' adding, 'I can get plenty of trash for a few pence, but I am sick of it. I felt so different when I shut up your books . . . Many of my working brethren feel as I do, and I express their wish as well as my own.'[98] Some persons, women in particular, became devotionally (even pathologically) attached to her, but for George Eliot friendship with men was just as important. Gordon Haight says that people felt in her a 'charismatic force' attributable to 'deep sincerity . . . and genuine human interest.' He adds that since their Italian travels George Henry Lewes sometimes called her 'Madonna,' while others referred to her as the 'Great Teacher,' a 'spiritual mother,' 'die Mutter.' Persons great and small came, in Charles Dickens's words, 'to attend service at the Priory' (the house she and Lewes owned in London).[99]

Thus George Eliot took on something like a religious or pastoral vocation – a possibility hinted at in her earliest letters.[100] She became, figuratively speaking, the Madonna with whom some of her greatest heroines (Dinah, Romola, Dorothea) were associated. She herself was fascinated and overwhelmed by Raphael's *Sistine Madonna*, which she saw in Dresden in 1858 while writing *Adam*

Bede. She seems to have had some kind of religious experience while viewing (repeatedly) the sublimely beautiful, tender yet prescient, sensuous yet spiritual young woman – the divinely human mother – depicted in this great painting.[101] She who bore no children of her own, and lacked physical beauty, became a spiritual mother to her own and successive generations – to all readers who have found in her writing extraordinary wisdom, sympathy, courage, hope, and moral beauty.

She who ministered also needed to be ministered unto: thus she continued to attend religious services with some regularity throughout her life, not only Unitarian services (as noted above) but also Anglican, Calvinist, and dissenting services, and occasionally Roman Catholic and Jewish services.[102] She explained to John Cross that, 'if there were not reasons against my following such an inclination, I should go to church or chapel constantly for the sake of the delightful emotions of fellowship which come over me in religious assemblies.'[103] She made it clear that she was brought up in the Church of England and never joined any other religious society: she gloried in its liturgical grandeur while deploring its moral failures; and in the end she was married and buried in it (though the funeral service was conducted by a Unitarian).[104] To be sure her religious devotion had an eclectic, experimental quality. She was attracted to Lessing's advocacy of religious tolerance, but repelled by sectarian squabbles and the fruitlessness of religious and doctrinal controversies.[105] To Harriet Beecher Stowe she wrote: 'Will you not agree with me that there is one comprehensive Church whose fellowship consists in the desire to purify and ennoble human life, and where the best members of all narrower churches may call themselves brother and sister in spite of differences?'[106] The spiritual mother and religious skeptic needed and belonged to the spiritual church.

6. A Theological Reading of the Texts

George Eliot was reluctant to discuss religious ideas directly.

I must tell you that I am always a little uneasy about my share in the talk when it has turned on religion . . . My books are a form of utterance that dissatisfies me less, because they are deliberately, carefully constructed on a basis which even in my doubting mind is never shaken by a doubt . . . The basis I mean is my conviction as to the relative goodness and nobleness of human dispositions and motives. And the inspiring principle which alone gives me courage to write is, that of so presenting our human life as to help my readers in getting a clearer conception and a more active admiration of those vital elements which bind men together and give a higher worthiness to their existence; and also to help them in gradually dissociating these elements from the more transient forms on which an outworn teaching tends to make them dependent.[107]

Art in the form of fiction was the chosen medium for expressing this 'inspiring principle,' for depicting the unifying and elevating elements of the human condition. In another letter she explained that she hesitated 'to adopt any formula which does not get itself clothed for me in some human figure and individual experience, and perhaps that is a sign that if I help others to see at all it must be through the medium of art.'[108]

If art is the medium by which George Eliot's deepest religious convictions and searchings were expressed, we must recognize that this is an indirect medium that does not permit a direct reading of the author's mind from the stories, characters, speeches, and actions that make up her fiction. Thus far we have obtained glimpses of this mind from letters that were never intended to be public and from the few essays that bear on the subject. What is principally available to us from George Eliot is a series of fictional texts that reverberate with religious images, motifs, and characters. We *can*, I believe, offer a *theological reading* of these texts, attempting to identify not only compelling ideas but perhaps even an encompassing vision whose relevance for present-day theology is noteworthy. The extent to which these ideas and vision coincide with George Eliot's own point of view is ultimately unanswerable. More important is what is written in the texts themselves. Surely a theological reading of George Eliot's fiction is as plausible as a feminist reading, a humanist reading, or a psychological reading. Ideas and insights may be presented in her work that prove illuminating to theological reflection in ways not intended or foreseen by the author. Theology itself, I have suggested, is a kind of fiction, which, very much like the work of the novelist, creates imaginative variations on what history offers as real in a quest for the mystery beneath the real. The theologian is an artist, and the artist (at the highest reaches of imagination) a theologian.

In the final analysis, the reader provides the hermeneutical lenses that bring the texts into focus in particular ways. As a theological reader I may find descriptions of 'redemptive transformation' taking place in which 'God comes forth as real,' without having to claim that this is how the author herself would interpret the fictional construct. It is quite possible that she arrived at theological (or psychological, or feminist) insights that she herself did not fully recognize. I suspect that the great painters and poets see and express more than they themselves ever fully comprehend. They serve as a medium of something that manifests itself through them,[109] and there is an element of inexhaustibility and mystery in their work.

In this book I will offer theological readings of each of George Eliot's novels.[110] The chapters that follow are concise and focused. They make no attempt to do justice to the rich complexity of these writings, each of which could be the subject of a book of its own. I will tell enough of the stories to enable readers who are unfamiliar with them to follow what is being said. My purpose is to identify the distinctive religious and theological themes of these novels, with a view toward assessing in the final chapter George Eliot's significance for theological reconstruction today. The themes considered – the experience of divine presence in the lives of ordinary people (clerical and otherwise), the discovery of the clue of life through suffering and self-renunciation, the quest for a kingdom of justice, the role of unhistoric acts in widening the skirts of light, and the insight of Judaism into the mysterious pathways that converge upon the divine Unity – reflect not so much an evolution in George Eliot's own views as they do an increasingly multifaceted appreciation of religious life.

Unspoken Sorrows, Sacred Joys:
Scenes of Clerical Life

In her journal George Eliot described how she came to write fiction. She had always had a 'vague dream' that she might write a novel but doubted her capacity for the dramatic as opposed to descriptive aspects. It was George Henry Lewes who encouraged her to try, during their first trip to Germany in 1854–5, and the idea eventually occurred to her of 'writing a series of stories containing sketches drawn from my own observation of the Clergy.'[1] She and Lewes agreed that, if her authorship was to have any chance of success, it must not be known that the author was a woman. So Lewes submitted a draft of the first story, 'The Sad Fortunes of the Rev. Amos Barton,' to the Edinburgh publisher John Blackwood on behalf of an anonymous 'friend' who was trying his hand at fiction. He added that the proposed series of stories 'will consist of tales and sketches illustrative of the actual life of our country clergy about a quarter of a century ago; but solely in its *human* and *not at all* in its *theological* aspect; the object being . . . [to] represent the clergy like any other class with the humours, sorrows, and troubles of other men . . . The tone throughout will be sympathetic and not at all antagonistic.'[2]

The distinction drawn by Lewes is ironic since, as I shall attempt to show, *Scenes of Clerical Life* is profoundly theological – and it is theological precisely in its human aspect, its insistence on treating the clergy as ordinary human beings.[3] What constitutes theology is not a supernatural, idealized view of things, but insight into how redemptive transformations occur in real, concrete, human life with all its pathos and tragedy, but also its joy and comedy. George Eliot herself knew better than to say that her work was not theological (nor did she describe it as theological). Rather she put it this way in a letter to Blackwood: 'Art must be either real and concrete, or ideal and eclectic. Both are good and true in their way, but my stories are of the former kind. I undertake to exhibit nothing as it should be; I only try to exhibit some things as they have been or are . . . The moral effect of the stories of course depends on my power of seeing truly and feeling justly.'[4] 'Moral' here includes 'religious,' and it is clear that George Eliot intended to have a religious as well as a moral effect on her readers. Reflecting at the end of 1857 on the accomplishment of having written her first book, she noted in her journal: 'I feel a deep satisfaction in having done a bit of faithful work that will perhaps remain, like a primrose root in the hedgerow, and gladden and chasten human hearts in years to come.'[5] A few days later she added that she was heartened by 'indications that I can touch the hearts of my fellow-men, and so sprinkle some precious grain as the result of the long years in which I have been inert and suffering.'[6] The author is using the images of a religious mission – speaking to the heart, doing faithful work, gladdening and chastening, offering precious grain that ripened through her own spiritual struggles – but these are certainly not ordinary religious stories.

Scenes of Clerical Life first appeared as three novellas by 'George Eliot'[7] in successive issues of *Blackwood's Magazine* during 1857, then was issued in a single volume in 1858. The stories are loosely connected and together constitute an extraordinary first piece of fiction.

'The Sad Fortunes of the Rev. Amos Barton'

The Reverend Amos Barton[8] was curate of the Shepperton church some 'five-and-twenty years ago' (about 1830). As curate he was paid a starvation wage of £80 per year, insufficient to support his wife and six children.[9] There was nothing unusual about him. He was just 'palpably and unmistakably commonplace.' 'His very faults were middling – he was not *very* ungrammatical. It was not in his nature to be superlative in anything; unless, indeed, he was superlatively middling, the quintessential extract of mediocrity'

('Amos Barton,' 5.43, 57). We are told that he could not preach ex-tempore, that he rambled and did not stick to his text, that he had the oratory of a 'Belgian railway horn' and a 'knack of hitting on the wrong thing in garb as well as in grammar' (1.13; 2.20, 25). He also had a knack of hitting on the wrong thing in church doctrine and politics. Thinking he was wise as a serpent, and intending to launch a two-pronged attack on religious dissent, 'he preached Low-Church doctrine,' as evangelical as anything the Dissenters could mount, but 'made a High-Church assertion of ecclesiastical powers and functions' (2.18). He was a 'Low-Church onion' who was beginning to take on a High-Church odor (2.31). Despite these doctrinal and ecclesiastical vanities, which absorbed theological energy and had nothing to do with the real needs of the people, he was a hard-working pastor who went regularly to the workhouse (although he had not a clue how to communicate with the paupers there) and served his parishioners moderately well (although they grumbled and gossiped about him and mocked his foibles) (2.18, 24–7).

In setting forth this picture, the narrator notes that many readers will undoubtedly prefer 'the ideal in fiction.' But in point of fact the vast majority of our fellow citizens are of this same insignificant stamp.

> Yet these commonplace people – many of them – bear a con-science, and have felt the sublime prompting to do the painful right; they have their unspoken sorrows, and their sacred joys; their hearts have perhaps gone out towards their first-born, and they have mourned over the irreclaimable dead. Nay, is there not a pathos in their very insignificance – in our comparison of their dim and narrow existence with the glorious possibilities of that human nature which they share? (5.44)

This passage sets the framework for *Scenes of Clerical Life*. The stories are all about ordinary people who know both unspoken sorrows and sacred joys, who discover God's sacred, transforming presence precisely in and through their sorrows and sufferings – people who sometimes realize their human potential in ways they (and we) could not have imagined possible. In these stories George

Eliot was attempting to show how religion works in ordinary life, including clerical life, providing men and women with the strength to endure rather than illusory promises for the future. Her view of religion thus contrasts sharply with one of Feuerbach's principal criticisms of religion, namely, that by placing its hope for salvation in heaven and the world to come, it disregards the misery, suffering, and injustice of this world, and diminishes the value and importance of earthly life.[10] Of course it is *possible* for religion to take on the character of other-worldly compensation, which is a distortion of its true nature, but it *need* not and in these stories it *does* not.

One of those ordinary persons was Amos's wife Milly, who is described as 'a large, fair, gentle Madonna,' a woman whose devotion to her husband and family seemed boundless, although we are warned that her body was weary and that she seemed paler than normal (2.19, 23). Milly was sustained by faith in a resource greater than herself: 'her heart so overflowed with love, she felt sure she was near a fountain of love that would care for husband and babes better than she could foresee' (2.23). The family's economic and her physical condition gradually worsened: 'the howl of the wolf was audibly approaching,' and the parishioners of Shepperton 'were more likely to have a strong sense that the clergyman needed their material aid, than that they needed his spiritual aid' (5.45–6). Under these circumstances Amos did not need the additional burden of the Countess Caroline Czerlaski, a strange self-preoccupied widow in her mid-thirties who was looking for a second husband and took an unusual interest in Amos and his ministry. Following a falling-out with her brother with whom she lived, she asked to visit the Bartons briefly but remained for months. With 'inky swiftness did gossip now blacken the reputation of the Rev. Amos Barton' (5.50). Rumor had it that Amos had become the Countess's maid and lover, while his poor wife waited on them hand and foot even as she was expecting a seventh child. Gossip is one of the destructive forces in this story, practiced by clergy as well as housewives (1.11–16; 6.53–8). Only the Rev. Martin Cleves warned his brethren that the reality might be quite different than they suspected.

The denouement came suddenly. Milly was on her death-bed

after giving birth to a premature baby that died within a day. The children were brought to say goodbye. Only the eldest, nine-year old Patty, fully understood what was happening, and to her she said, 'Patty, I'm going away from you. Love your papa. Comfort him; and take care of your little brothers and sisters. God will help you.' Milly's last words to Amos came in a slow whisper: 'My dear – dear – husband – you have been – very – good to me. You – have – made – me – very – happy' (8.66–9). Too late Amos realized that 'he could never show her his love any more, never make up for omissions in the past by filling future days with tenderness.' The narrator reminds us of this painful human failing: 'O the anguish of that thought that we can never atone to our dead for the stinted affection we gave them . . . ' Amos became emotionally alive just as his wife was dying. Milly was buried with her baby in her arms 'while the Christmas snow lay thick upon the graves' (9.70–1).

Then a strange thing happened: Milly's death, which came in the season of the Redeemer's birth, brought a rebirth to her husband and the village. The many villagers who stood in the churchyard that day and who had made vulgar jests about their pastor now saw him stricken with grief, and they took pity on him. 'No outward solace could counteract the bitterness of this inward woe' – and we should note that Amos did not seek inward solace through an appeal to afterlife. 'But,' continues the narrator, 'outward solace came. Cold faces looked kind again, and parishioners turned over in their minds what they could best do to help their pastor' (9.70–1). Food and money were given, the children were cared for, the refurbished church was opened, and Amos went back to work.

'Outward solace came.' That is the sober, realistic way that redemptive transformation comes about in human affairs. There is nothing magical about it, but it has an amazing, mysterious quality nonetheless. Milly's memory 'hallowed her husband,' and he was 'consecrated anew by his great sorrow' (9.70, 72). Out of suffering and death new life is born. God is at work in this story – an old, old story – but in this case the suffering and death are those of a woman who poured out her life for the sake of motherhood and family. Milly's faith in a fountain of love proved not to be an illusion. The metaphor suggests that the divine fount is not a fixed and static thing but something fluid and flowing, a passionate vitality that pours new life into languid love. It is not exhausted by any single human being. We are told that 'Milly did not take all her love from the earth when she died. She had left some of it in Patty's heart' (9.75). Likewise, through the kindness and support of his neighbors, Amos began to feel 'that Milly's love was not quite gone out of his life' (9.72). But just when a real bond was forming between Amos and his flock, he learned that his duties as curate were being terminated because the vicar intended to install his brother-in-law. 'It was another blow inflicted on the bruised man' (9.72–3). 'Amos' means 'burden,' but like Job the Reverend Amos Barton endured and found peace in later years. Patty cared for him, and together they once again, 'in the calm and softened light of an autumnal afternoon,' visited Milly's grave (Conclusion, 75–6). The ending reminds us that in this life there are no final victories, only faith, hope, and love. If redemption is occurring, it is in a not-yet-redeemed world.

'Mr Gilfil's Love Story'

The second 'Clerical Scene' is not as stringently realistic as the first and not as theologically profound as the third. There are surely impressive features of it, such as a devastating portrayal of how women are treated as pets, animals, playthings ('Mr Gilfil's Love Story,' 2.100; 4.114, 117), and a depiction of the condescending attitude of the English aristocracy (3.108–10). Here a first glimpse is provided of the feminist and social criticism of future novels, but George Eliot did not again employ the story's rather exaggerated gothic style. Yet the title of the story anticipates that all of George Eliot's stories will prove to be 'love stories' in one form or another.

Maynard Gilfil[11] was Amos Barton's predecessor in Shepperton some forty years earlier, having become vicar in 1790. We are told already at the beginning of the first *Scene* that he 'smoked very long pipes and preached very short sermons' ('Amos Barton,' 1.9), and perhaps for that reason was a well-respected clergyman. But few of his parishioners knew about his personal history and the deep, anguished love he had experienced as a young man. That love had been for a young girl, Caterina Sarti, the orphaned daughter of an impoverished Italian singer, who had been brought to Cheveral Manor by Sir Christopher Cheveral and his wife following a journey abroad, and raised, not as their daughter, but as a servant and provider of musical entertainment. Caterina was dark, foreign, sickly, delicately beautiful, and very flirtatious. She and Maynard played together as children; but, failing to appreciate his qualities, she set her heart on Sir Christopher's nephew, Captain Anthony Wybrow. The captain understood that marriage between Caterina and himself was out of the question, but he encouraged the flirtation. When arrangements were finalized for Anthony's wedding to Miss Beatrice Assher, Caterina knew that she had been dealt with duplicitously. In a fit of rage she stole a dagger with the intent of killing Anthony at a rendezvous in the rookery, but when she arrived she found him already dead of heart failure. Frightened and racked by guilt, she fled from Cheveral Manor, and when she disappeared it was assumed that she had committed suicide.

Who should care about someone as insignificant as poor little Tina? How trivial her problems seemed as compared with the 'unmoved and terrible beauty' of nature and the 'mighty torrent' of human affairs, 'rushing from one awful unknown to another' ('Mr Gilfil's Love Story,' 5.132). Well, the coachman Knott cared. He and his wife took her into their humble home, and it was there that Maynard Gilfil found her. Putting aside his own feelings, he did his best to persuade Caterina that she was not wicked and that God would not punish her. In a remarkable reversal of the doctrine of just retribution ('those who do wrong will find it the worse for them, and those who do well will find it the better for them'), which was the customary logic of his sermons and indeed of Christian preaching in general (1.85–6), Mr. Gilfil told the distraught young woman:

> No, my Tina, we mean to do wicked things we never could do, just as we mean to do good or clever things that we never could do. Our thoughts are often worse than we are, just as they are often better than we are. And God sees us as we are altogether, not in separate feelings or actions, as our fellow-men see us . . . We don't see each other's whole nature. But God sees that you could not have committed that crime. (19.185)

God, and God alone, sees us whole and judges us whole, knowing the underlying goodness that is in most of us. For human beings to be seen and measured as a whole, a divine conspectus is needed, from which arises the divine mercy. This message, wrung from Mr. Gilfil in a moment of anguished insight, was heard by Caterina, on whom it had a transforming effect. She was slowly nursed back to psychological and physical health by Mr. Gilfil. More than this, the bond of love between them grew and two years later they were married. They enjoyed a few happy months together and Tina became pregnant. 'But the delicate plant had been too deeply bruised, and in the struggle to put forth a blossom it died. Tina died, and Maynard Gilfil's love went with her into deep silence for evermore' (chap. 21).

The effect on Mr. Gilfil is described by an analogy: 'It is with men as with trees: if you lop off their finest branches, into which they were pouring their young life-juice, the wounds will be healed over with some rough boss, some odd excrescence; and what might have been a grand tree expanding into liberal shade, is but a whimsical misshapen trunk' (Epilogue, 193). Yet the old vicar

> had been sketched out by nature as a noble tree. The heart of him was sound, the grain was of the finest; and in the grey-haired man who filled his pocket with sugarplums for the little children, whose most biting words were directed against the evil doing of the rich man, and who, with all his social pipes and slip-shod talk, never sank below the highest level of his parishioners' respect, there was the main trunk of the same brave, faithful, tender nature that had poured out the finest, freshest forces of its life-current in a first and only love . . . (Epilogue, 194)

We human beings for the most part are knotted, misshapen, but noble trees. The wounds of life damage and disfigure us but need not destroy us; instead we become stronger at the broken places. We may experience serene happiness and true love, but these are brief moments in the relentless flow of time. We must learn to cherish and remember them, thankful for the gift of life and the all-provident eye of God that redeems us from our worst moments and saves us for the best. But by what *strength* are we able to endure in this beautiful but tragic world? This is the question addressed in the final 'Clerical Scene.'

'Janet's Repentance'

Milby was a neighboring town to Shepperton in the dreary industrial Midlands. Like most towns, it was riven by sectarian prejudice and conflicts. Hatred and suspicion of others seemed to be in direct proportion to ignorance about them. The story opens with an argument about church matters in a local pub, with the lawyer Robert Dempster asserting that he will not allow the introduction of any 'demoralizing, methodistical doctrine into this parish.' The new curate at Paddiford, he claimed, was worse than a Dissenter: 'He preaches against good works; says good works are not necessary to salvation – a sectarian, antinomian, anabaptist doctrine. Tell a man he is not to be saved by his works, and you open the floodgates of all immorality. You see it in all these canting innovators; they're all bad ones by the sly; smooth-faced, drawling, hypocritical fellows' ('Janet's Repentance,' 1.197, 200).

This little speech came from the lips of a man who was himself an archetypal hypocrite and tyrant, arrogant, domineering, and ruthless. Frequently intoxicated, Dempster systematically abused and beat his wife Janet. 'An unloving, tyrannous, brutal man needs no motive to prompt his cruelty; he needs only the perpetual presence of a woman he can call his own. A whole park full of tame or timid-eyed animals to torment at his will would not serve him so well to glut his lust of torture; they could not *feel* as one woman does; they could not throw out the keen retort which whets the edge of hatred.'[12]

Janet Dempster did not suffer her abuse passively; she fought back as best she could, but she did not seek help and was herself driven to alcohol as an opium to make her suffering more bearable. Despite her strength of will, this once most beautiful and promising young woman of Milby was gradually being destroyed. In moments of despair, she cried out, 'God is cruel to have sent me into this world to bear all this misery.' Her mother's attempt at comfort with the words that we must submit and be thankful for the gift of life were to Janet words of mockery: 'God has made me a heart to feel, and He has sent me nothing but misery' (14.281–2). One evening, when the drunken Dempster flung down all the clothes she had laid out for him, she refused to pick them up or come at his bidding. He threatened to kill her but instead expelled her from the house into the cold March night, clad only in a thin night-dress. Roused by the fortuitous ringing of a church bell out of a stupor in which she might have frozen to death, Janet sought refuge with good Mrs. Pettifer, and there she thought to ask Mr. Tryan for help (chaps. 14–16). 'Perhaps he had some message of comfort, different from . . . that barren exhortation – Do right, and keep a clear conscience, and God will reward you, and your troubles will be easier to bear. She wanted *strength* to do right – she wanted something to rely on besides her own resolutions' (16.293).

Edgar Tryan was the new officiating curate at the chapel-of-ease on Paddiford Common, an adjunct to the main parish church in Milby. He was at the very bottom of the ecclesiastical totem pole. He was also something out of the ordinary for Milby: an evangelical who preached extempore, founded a lending library, expounded Scripture in the workers' cottages, lived among the poor to whom he ministered, attracted Dissenters, and filled the parish church to overflowing with evening lectures. He was just the sort of man to attract the wrath of a defender of the establishment like Mr. Dempster, who organized an unsuccessful attempt to ridicule and drive him away.

Janet shared her husband's prejudice until she saw Mr. Tryan's personal and social ministry at work. Earlier she had revealed her ignorance of religion with the following remark aimed at the new curate: 'Preaching the Gospel indeed! That is the best Gospel that makes everybody happy and comfortable, isn't it, mother' (5.236). Her mother, Mrs. Raynor, doubted that any Gospel 'will do that here below.' We are told that it was hard for Mrs. Raynor to believe that 'the future would be anything else than the harvest of the seed that was being sown before her eyes.' 'But,' the narrator adds, 'always there is seed being sown silently and unseen, and everywhere there come sweet flowers without our foresight or labour. We reap what we sow, but Nature has love over and above that justice, and gives us shadow and blossom and fruit that spring from no planting of ours' (5:237). Here Nature mirrors the superabundance[13] of God's love, which is not bound by the logic of reaping and sowing that normally governs human affairs. Mr. Tryan was proof of this superabundance, and Janet would become such too. He learned of it from a deep personal encounter with wrongdoing, guilt, and forgiveness. He also knew, and Janet would learn, that the redemption given by the Gospel is not a matter of making everybody happy and comfortable.

George Eliot remarked to her publisher John Blackwood that 'the collision in the drama is not at all between "bigotted churchmanship" and evangelicalism, but between *ir*religion and religion. Religion in this case happens to be represented by evangelicalism.' Irreligion, or immorality, is represented by Dempster, whose 'vices have their natural evolution in deeper and deeper moral deterioration . . . and death from intemperance.'[14] The story itself points out that evangelicalism had mixed effects, like all religious revivals. Some of Mr. Tryan's hearers may have gained 'a religious vocabulary rather than religious experience.' 'The old Adam . . . continued to tell fibs behind the counter, notwithstanding the new Adam's addiction to Bible-reading and family prayer.' Yet evangelicalism brought to Milby 'that idea of duty, that recognition of something to be lived for beyond the mere satisfaction of self, which is to the moral life what the addition of a great central ganglion is to animal life. No man can begin to mould himself on a faith or an idea without rising to a higher order of experience: a principle of subordination, of self-mastery, has been introduced into his nature.' People learned 'that there was a divine work to be done in life, a rule of goodness higher than the opinion of their neighbours; and if the notion of a heaven in reserve for themselves was a little too prominent, yet the theory of fitness for that heaven consisted in purity of heart, in Christ-like compassion, in the subduing of selfish desires.' Above all: 'The first condition of human goodness is something to love; the second, something to reverence. And this latter precious gift was brought to Milby by Mr. Tryan and Evangelicalism' (10.264–5). These statements come close to expressing George Eliot's own religious creed.

As for Mr. Tryan, the narrator continues:

A critic might perhaps say that he made the mistake of identifying Christianity with a too narrow doctrinal system; that he saw God's work too exclusively in antagonism to the world, the flesh, and the devil; that his intellectual culture was too limited – and so on; making Mr Tryan the text for a wise discourse on the characteristics of the Evangelical school in his day. But I am not poised at that lofty height. I am on the level and in the press with him, as he struggles his way along the stony road, through the crowd of unloving fellow-men . . . He pushes manfully on, with fluctuating faith and courage, with a sensitive failing body; at last he falls, the struggle is ended, and the crowd closes over the space he has left. (10.266)

Indeed, he 'seemed bent on wearing himself out,' consumed by an exhausting educational ministry, seeking nothing for himself, putting himself on the same level as his parishioners, knowing how to lift up those who are cast down (chap. 11). Despite his inconspicuousness, he was a Christ-like figure, prepared to lay down his own life for the sake of others. At the same time, there was a bit too much of submission and resignation in Mr. Tryan's view of religion (e.g. 18.304), an unwillingness to attend to his own needs along with those of others, to allow his own life to flourish. George Eliot affirmed the necessity of self-renunciation, but not at the cost of voluntary martyrdom or self-destruction. Later figures such as Dinah Morris would adjudicate this difficult balance between the losing and finding of self more successfully.

Edgar Tryan's last great act of ministry was to bring about the 'repentance' – or better the redemption and restoration – of Janet Dempster.[15] He did so by presenting to her a God who loves, suffers, and pities rather than rewards and punishes, a God who gives *strength* to do right rather than judging from afar. The motif of 'strength' reverberates through this story. Mr. Tryan shared with Janet his own grief at having once injured a young woman irreparably in body and soul. He had loved her and took her from her father's house, but, knowing that she was below his station in life, did not offer to marry her. Later she came under the power of a wicked woman and he found her dead on the streets of London. Overwhelmed by guilt, he was on the brink of madness when a friend showed him 'it was just such as I – the helpless who feel themselves helpless – that God specially invites to come to Him, and offers all the riches of His salvation: not forgiveness only; forgiveness would be worth little if it left us under the powers of our evil passions; but strength – that strength which enables us to conquer sin.' We need only be brought to the point of acknowledging our own helplessness, of renouncing all other hopes and trusting in God's love alone. Christ, Mr. Tryan continued,

> does not tell you, as your fellow-men do, that you must first merit his love; he neither condemns nor reproaches you for the past, he only bids you come to him that you may have life . . . You have only to rest on him as a child rests on its mother's arms, and you will be upborne by his divine strength. That is what is meant by faith . . . It is just so with God's spirit: as soon as we submit ourselves to his will . . . we are fed with his spirit, which gives us new strength.[16]

The narrator remarks that those 'unseen elements' that bring about redemption and new life despite our own best calculations Mr. Tryan called the 'Divine Will.' Thus he 'filled up the margin of ignorance which surrounds our knowledge with the feelings of trust and resignation. Perhaps the profoundest philosophy could hardly fill it up better' (22.315). This is a capsule expression of George Eliot's own agnostic faith. The authorial voice continues:

> Blessed influence of one true loving human soul on another! Not calculable by algebra, not deducible by logic, but mysterious, effectual, mighty as the hidden process by which the tiny seed is quickened . . . Ideas are often poor ghosts . . . But sometimes they are made flesh; they breathe upon us with warm breath, they touch us with soft responsive hands . . . they are clothed in a living human soul . . . Then their presence is a power, then they shake us like a passion, and we are drawn after them with gentle compulsion, as flame is drawn to flame. (19.305–6)

Abstract ideas are poor ghosts, but the idea of divine sympathy and reconciliation becomes incarnate in words and deeds of human sympathy. The *idea incarnate* takes on the character of *spirit* – not a ghostly spirit but a flaming empowering presence that draws us to itself. Here George Eliot is giving poetic expression to a strikingly Hegelian theology of incarnation and spirit.

Thus Janet was redeemed. The idea of divine sympathy became incarnate for her in the human sympathy that Edgar Tryan shared with her. She found the strength to overcome the feelings of guilt associated with her having left her husband and his ensuing death; despite powerful temptations, she fought off depression and the craving for alcohol by visiting the sick; she gained an increasing sense of divine presence, of infinite love caring for her (chaps. 24–5). As Mr. Tryan's health declined, the roles reversed and she became the care giver, bringing him to the home she inherited, and serving as a kind of minister-at-large to his parish. She filled his final days with true human affection, and when he died they shared a parting kiss, promising to meet again in paradise (chaps. 26–7). We are told that Mr. Tryan's burial service was not a 'hollow form.' 'Every heart there was filled with the memory of a man who, through a self-sacrificing life and a painful death, had been sustained by the faith which fills that [burial] form with breath and substance' (28.349). As for Janet, she 'had lived through the great tragedy of woman's life' – the loss of a true love (27.347). Her life would stretch before her as an 'autumn afternoon, filled with resigned memory.' But 'she walked in the presence of unseen witnesses – of the Divine love that had rescued her, of the human love that waited for its eternal repose until it had seen her endure to the end' (28.349).

A modern interpreter of *Scenes of Clerical Life,* Thomas Noble, believes that the 'doctrine of sympathy' is the central concept of George Eliot's moral philosophy. He is puzzled about the seemingly religious dimension of the doctrine because he is convinced that it must have a purely humanistic basis. Thus he writes:

The doctrine of sympathy embodied in the work is obviously Christian in its essential points, but it is the practical side of Christian ethics that is expressed. It is the love of man, not the love of God, that is taught here. God is mentioned in these stories, of course, because they are stories about people who believe in God in a perfectly conventional sense. But if every reference to God were taken out, the essential message of the book would be unchanged.[17]

I find this to be a confused statement. If the references to God, and thus belief in the reality of God, were removed, what would be the object of *reverence* as one of the essential conditions of human goodness? Whence would come the *strength* that enabled Janet to endure and to do right, a strength that she could not find in any human resource? Edgar Tryan's idea of a loving God who gives strength through shared suffering, rather than of an accusing/consoling God who rewards, punishes, and judges from afar, was precisely not a conventional view. Of course God does not appear directly in these or any other stories because God is not an empirical object or a supernatural agent who exercises an immediate causality. What appears is human talk about God and transformations in human relationships. God is mediated through such relationships. Faith in the reality of God does make a difference in how persons live their lives, and these differences are of central concern to the author.

Rosemary Ashton regards it as surprising that George Eliot provides a 'full and sympathetic description of Mr. Tryan's religious beliefs,' but she adds that Janet is helped as much by his 'personal kindness as by his expressions of faith' – as though personal kindness is not an often most eloquent expression of faith. She wants us to believe that good clergymen 'enact the Feuerbachian idea of the sanctity of human rather than divine relations' – as though divine relations (the love of God) could be extracted from human ones (the love of neighbor), or vice versa. In *Scenes of Clerical Life* the two kinds of relations are most intimately bound together. Ashton notes that no one was better fitted than George Eliot 'to render the inward experience of religious piety and at the same time to offer a detached, socio-philosophical view of it as a phenomenon of English life.'[18] For her description of conventional religious behavior, the latter part of this statement is true. But with figures like Mr. Tryan, and Dinah Morris in *Adam Bede*, I believe George Eliot moved beyond a detached view to an empathetic sharing of the inner piety.

Kathryn Hughes echoes Ashton's critique when she writes:

It is not Mr. Tryan's particular beliefs that save Janet, so much as the empathy he is able to extend to her as a result of his own tragic experiences. Feuerbach seeps into the narrator's voice when 'he' declares: 'Our subtlest analysis of schools and sects must miss the essential truth, unless it be lit up by the love that sees in all forms of human thought and work, the life and death struggles of separate human beings.'[19]

Both interpretations overlook the fact that it was precisely Mr. Tryan's idea of a loving, non-accusatory, empathic *God* that Janet found most helpful. And Hughes's remark misinterprets the meaning of the quoted passage in context. The point is not that religious beliefs are unimportant or that it is only *human* struggles which are at the core of what schools and sects teach, but rather that, in order to understand schools and sects such as evangelicalism, one must get beyond a bird's-eye view of a social phenomenon to feel the life and death struggles of *individual* human beings (10.266–7). There is no Feuerbachian seepage in such an observation.

Scenes of Clerical Life was a surprising success among the public, and 'George Eliot' received many complimentary letters. Among the most striking was one from Mrs. Thomas Carlyle, who commented that this was the rarest of books, 'a *human* book – written out of the heart of a live man, not merely out of the brain of an author – full of tenderness and pathos without a scrap of sentimentality, of sense without dogmatism, of earnestness without twaddle – a book that makes one *feel friends*, at once and for always, with the man or woman who wrote it!'[20] But the author, whose identity as a woman was already being suspected, had little time to savor these kind words; she was busily at work on her next novel.

3

Feeling the Divine Presence:
Adam Bede

Much of the recent critical literature on *Adam Bede* has focused on the relationship between Adam and Hetty Sorrel, and has not known what to make of the 'preacher-woman' Dinah Morris.[1] George Eliot herself saw it differently. She originally conceived of this story as another 'Clerical Scene,' with Dinah as one of the two principal characters.[2] The irony with which the novel was named *Adam Bede* reflects the irony with which Marian Evans named herself 'George Eliot.'

Adam Bede, we are told, 'was a Saxon, and justified his name' (*Adam Bede*, 1.8) – a name apparently suggested by the Venerable Bede, whose *Ecclesiastical History* (731 CE) recounted the growth of Anglo-Saxon culture in England. There was also a mixture, as evidenced by his dark eyes, of Celtic blood in this tall, handsome, good-natured man. Adam embodied the solid values and strong physique of a good rural Englishman, but he was a somewhat one-dimensional, even passive figure.[3] He certainly had good qualities, such as a depth of reverence and common sense that made him disinclined toward doctrinal religion but appreciative of mystery; he was 'at once penetrating and credulous' (4.51). Dinah remarked to the Reverend Irwine that Adam was 'like the patriarch Joseph, for his great skill and knowledge, and the kindness he shows to his brother and his parents' (8.93). But he fell for the foolish Hetty, and at the end he had to be told by his mother that he and Dinah were in love with each other (51.497–502). Adam's lack of perceptiveness reminds us also of the biblical Adam, who was formed from the dust of the ground, *'adhamah* (Gen. 2.7), and who had to be fed the fruit of the tree of knowledge by his wife Eve (Gen. 3.6). Thus Adam is not just the archetypal Englishman but the archetypal human being, an everyman who was something of a plodder but capable of growth and goodness. Perhaps 'everyman' is too strong a term, for the story-teller assures us that, while Adam was 'by no means a marvellous man,' he was 'not an average man:' he was skilful, hard-working, courageous, honest (19.213). Without such men as Adam this world would not be as good a place as it is. Yet the novel is really more a story about an extraordinary woman than a good man; and it is Dinah Morris, not Adam Bede, who becomes the second Adam, the Christ in the figure of a madonna.

In letters and in a journal entry on the 'history of Adam Bede' George Eliot described how her Aunt Elizabeth Evans told her the story around which the novel was constructed, and also suggested the figure of Dinah Morris, but who was entirely different from the Dinah of George Eliot's imagination. 'How curious it seems to me,' she wrote to Sara Sophia Hennell, 'that people should think Dinah's sermons, prayers, and speeches were *copied* – when they were written with hot tears, as they surged up in my own mind!'[4] To Barbara Bodichon, who recognized her to be the author merely from excerpts in reviews, she wrote that this book 'has come from my heart of hearts.'[5] At the end of her journal entry she said: 'I love [this book] very much and am deeply thankful to have written it, whatever the public may say of it.'[6]

George Eliot began to write *Adam Bede* in the autumn of 1857, soon after the last proofs of 'Janet' had been corrected. During the spring and summer of 1858 she and George Henry Lewes made an extended trip to Germany. In Nürnberg, by contrast with the cold formality of Protestant services, she was attracted to the Mass in the Frauenkirche, where 'the delicious sound of the organ and voices drew us farther and farther in among the standing people . . . How the music that stirs all one's devout emotions blends everything into harmony – makes one feel part of one whole, which one loves all alike, losing the sense of a separate self . . . The thought of the Man of Sorrows seemed a very close thing.'[7] This passage anticipates the narrator's comment in *Adam Bede* that music, along with tender love, autumn sunsets, and pillared vistas 'all bring with them the consciousness that they are mere waves and ripples in an unfathomable ocean of love and beauty: our emotion in its keenest moment passes from expression into silence; our love at its highest flood rushes beyond its object, and loses itself in the sense of divine mystery' (3.39).

A portion of *Adam Bede* was written during an extended stay in Dresden, where, as we have seen, George Eliot came under the spell of Raphael's *Sistine Madonna*.[8] Her description of Dinah Morris – slimness of figure, delicate beauty, total absence of self-consciousness, 'a small oval face, of a uniform transparent white-ness, with an egg-like line of cheek and chin, a full but firm mouth, a delicate nostril, and a low perpendicular brow, surmounted by a rising arch of parting, between smooth locks of pale reddish hair' (2.24) – surely mirrors the beautiful young woman depicted in that painting. We are reminded that lilies are the flower of the Virgin Mary as we are told that Dinah's 'was one of those faces that make one think of white flowers with light touches of colour on their pure petals' (2.25). The Methodist preacher-woman and her spirituality are rendered with an almost Catholic sensibility.[9]

The story may be told briefly: Adam Bede, a fine carpenter of manly virtues but limited vision, had fallen in love with Hetty Sorrel, a beautiful seventeen-year old girl with remarkable capacities for self-deception and vanity. Unbeknownst to Adam, Hetty had her eyes on Arthur Donnithorne, the landed gentleman who was to inherit the estate on which the common people of Hayslope labored, and who, like Hetty, was egocentric and self-deceiving, but also affectionate and generous. Arthur knew that the laws of social class would not permit a marriage between himself and Hetty, but nonetheless he seduced her on a fine summer's night of 1799. When Hetty discovered she was pregnant, she could not bear to tell her uncle and aunt, the Poysers, with whom she lived, and least of all Adam, to whom she had become betrothed. Instead she ran away and began a fruitless search for Arthur, who left Hayslope for a period of military service immediately after the seduction. In desperation she traveled all the way to Windsor only to discover that Arthur's militia had departed for Ireland. She retraced her journey with conflicting thoughts of drowning herself or 'going to Dinah.' The latter intention won out, but Hetty made it only as far as Stoniton, where she gave birth to a child in a stranger's house. The next day she abandoned the child in the woods, and it died of exposure after piteous crying. She was found out, placed on trial for child murder, and condemned to death, although she denied everything.

Dinah Morris was a young Methodist lay preacher whose physical delicacy and gentleness contrasted with her spiritual strength and insight. She first appears in the second chapter as she preached on the village green of Hayslope, at sunset in an idyllic setting of Loamshire countryside.[10] She worked among the poor of a cotton-mill village, Snowfield, some thirty miles away in barren hills, but frequently visited her Aunt Rachel Poyser, a wise and strongly-opinioned woman, the wife of Hetty's uncle, in Hayslope. As the story progresses, Dinah becomes the central figure.[11] She was the antitype to Hetty, utterly honest and self-giving, oriented to others rather than to herself. Whereas Hetty was preoccupied with mirrors in which to see her reflected face, Dinah delighted in her bedroom window from which she could look out upon the fields (chap. 15). For Hetty water was an image of death by drowning (35.364–5), while for Dinah it was an image of life: she experienced the inspiration of the divine Spirit as a rushing stream and a deep flood (8.90–1).

Dinah and Hetty represent contrasting types of beauty. The narrator, when the story 'pauses a little,' reflects on 'the divine beauty of form,' which deserves all honor and reverence. 'But let us love that other beauty too, which lies in no secret of proportion, but in the secret of deep human sympathy' (17.180). This is George Eliot's aesthetic theory in a nutshell: beauty is a matter not simply of harmony and proportion, as in classical views, but of ethical self-transcendence, the capacity to share in the pathos of another. A connection does not necessarily exist between physical and ethical beauty. Our expectation at finding 'some depth of soul behind a deep grey eye with a long dark eyelash' will sooner or later be disappointed. Referring to Hetty, the narrator observes: 'One begins to suspect at length that there is no direct correlation between eyelashes and morals' (15.153). George Eliot's beautiful young women must learn to acquire beauty of soul if they are to fulfill their human potential and become something other than decorative objects or tragic failures. But Dinah's problem at the outset was just the opposite: she was virtually all soul and no body. It was as though she had died to this world and was living in a post-resurrection state: clad in black by day and in a long white gown at night, she was 'almost like a lovely corpse into which the soul has returned charged with sublimer secrets and a sublimer love' (15.158). Dinah had to learn to connect with her body, to recognize the physical and sexual aspect of herself, and this she did at the end. When beauty of form and of soul truly come together in a single figure such as Dinah Morris, and in other such figures to appear in later novels, we behold something very special.[12]

When Hetty was imprisoned and condemned, Dinah went to her in the prison cell to stay with her to the last – to take her shame and suffering upon herself and to bring about Hetty's confession and repentance, knowing that there could be no healing of her soul without it.[13] Dinah called upon Jesus, who knew the depth of sorrow and had uttered the cry of the forsaken, to melt Hetty's hard heart and let her see that God encompasses her. When Hetty's heart finally melted and the story of the flight and the abandoned baby poured out, Hetty asked, 'Dinah, do you think God will take away that crying and the place in the wood, now I've told every-thing?' (45.455). Dinah did not promise that God would do that, or that God would deliver her from her fate. She rode with Hetty to the scaffold in an open cart, but Hetty was saved from the hang-man's rope by a reprieve from the magistrate brought at the last minute by Arthur (chap. 47). She was 'transported' to Australia, the colony for exiled criminals, and died before she could return home. Adam was transformed by this baptism through suffering: a fuller life and a more mature love came to him from his involve-ment with Hetty's tragedy. Dinah too was changed: she began to take more notice of her own feelings and needs. Less than two years later Adam and Dinah were married; she, proscribed from further preaching by an edict of the Methodist Conference in 1803, became a wife and mother, but carried on her ministry of human caring. On their wedding day we are told: 'Nothing like Dinah and the history which had brought her and Adam Bede together had been known at Hayslope within the memory of man' (55.533).

Dinah Morris was George Eliot's first great female figure,

although anticipations of the role to be played by women in her novels appeared in the Janet of 'Janet's Repentance.' In every respect Dinah was the antithesis of the heroine George Eliot despised in her 1856 essay, 'Silly Novels by Lady Novelists.'[14] Dinah was a working woman concerned with the needs of the poor, not an idle woman preoccupied with jewels and finery. She was a deeply spiritual woman who did not engage in flowery, pedantic discussions of religion and philosophy in parlor rooms, but lived out her faith in a ministry to widows, prisoners, and the working poor. She did not pass through a frivolous love-crisis and then reemerge more irresistible than ever, or have dreamy visions about romance. She was totally connected with the visible and the real – and with the mystery *beneath* the real, not above and beyond it. 'As a general rule,' wrote George Eliot, 'the ability of a lady novelist to describe actual life and her fellow-men, is in inverse proportion to her confident eloquence about God and the other world, and the means by which she usually chooses to conduct you to true ideas of the invisible is a totally false picture of the visible.'[15]

George Eliot's own ability to describe actual life was evident in her portrayal of Mrs. Poyser, Dinah's aunt, who is one of the most fascinating characters in the novel. Her conversation was brilliantly rendered in rural dialect, and indeed the mastery of conversation and dialect is one of the compelling features of *Adam Bede*. Of Mrs. Poyser the author writes: 'There was no weakness of which she was less tolerant than feminine vanity, and the preference of ornament to utility. The family resemblance between her and her niece, Dinah Morris, with the contrast between her keenness and Dinah's seraphic gentleness of expression, might have served a painter as an excellent suggestion for a Martha and Mary' (6.75). Mrs. Poyser was put out by Dinah's preaching and told her so in no uncertain terms: 'If everybody was to do like you, the world must come to a standstill . . . everybody 'ud be running after everybody else to preach to 'em, istead o' bringing up their families and laying by against a bad harvest. It stands to sense as that can't be the right religion.' When Dinah pointed out that God does not expect everybody to preach, and that in her case she 'didn't preach without direction,' Mrs. Poyser exploded: 'Direction! I know very well what you mean by direction. When there's a bigger maggot than usual in your head you call it "direction"; and then nothing can stir you' (6.79–80). But Mrs. Poyser had the highest regard for Dinah, whereas her opinion of Hetty was summed up in one word: 'She's no better than a peacock' (15.154). Mrs. Poyser's tendency to 'have her say out' showed itself on more than one occasion, as when she told off the old Squire Donnithorne for his abusive treatment of his tenants (chap. 32), or when she bested Bartle Massey in a spirited exchange on the nature of women (chap. 53). 'There's no pleasure i' living, if you're to be corked up for iver, and only dribble your mind out by the sly, like a leaky barrel' (32.349). Her criticism of Dinah's preaching was ironic in light of the fact that Mrs. Poyser herself was quite a preacher, as Mr. Irwine once shrewdly pointed out (49.482). Dinah was not alone in giving expression to the suppressed voice of women.

George Eliot's portrayal of Dinah Morris is quite extraordinary and of undeniable theological interest. While not exactly a Christ figure, Dinah was the mediatrix of a divine redemptive presence. She was in fact, as we have seen, a madonna figure. Not only did she resemble the *Sistine Madonna*, but also other associations with madonnas occur in this story – one in a discussion of beauty in art: 'paint us yet oftener a Madonna, turning her mild face upward and opening her arms to welcome the divine glory' (17.180); another when Seth Bede saw in Dinah, by contrast with other women, 'the beauty and greatness of a pictured Madonna' (26.281); yet another, indirectly, in Lisbeth Bede's identification of Dinah with the angel seated on the tomb of the risen Lord (10.110; 51.499). God is not seen or known directly in this world but is reflected, made manifest, in the speech and actions of madonna figures like Dinah.

Dinah's speech had a clarity, simplicity, and insight that were luminous and transformative. The preaching on the Hayslope green (chap. 2) was the most remarkable instance of this. George Eliot created an eighteenth-century Methodist evangelical sermon, using as a historical model the preaching of Mary Bosanquet Fletcher. But the sermon and other speeches were her own artistic creation, composed, as she said, 'with hot tears, as they surged up in my own mind.' We are told that Dinah preached for about an hour, no book in her hand, speaking directly to the people gathered before her, using words and ideas they could readily grasp, but with no condescension and no avoidance of difficult questions. Her text drew upon the words of Jesus from Luke 4.18: 'The spirit of the Lord is upon me, because he hath anointed me to preach the gospel to the poor' (KJV). This was the theme of the sermon, that Jesus came to 'tell good news about God to the poor.' 'The simple things she said seemed like novelties, as a melody strikes us with a new feeling when we hear it sung by the pure voice of a boyish chorister; the quiet depth of conviction with which she spoke seemed in itself an evidence for the truth of her message' (2.29). The narrator continues: 'Nothing could be less like the ordinary type of the Ranter than Dinah. She was not preaching as she heard others preach, but speaking directly from her own emotions, and under the inspiration of her own simple faith' (2.29). Yes, but the 'simplicity' of her faith evoked the radical kind of relationship to God that characterized Jesus' own faith. It was a relationship of direct trust, without resentment, conditions, calculation, cultic and moral paraphernalia – an instance of the feeling of utter or simple dependence[16] that is at the heart of true religion. Dinah was capable of evoking powerful emotions when she believed repentance was called for, but she ended by conveying a sense of divine peace and love. This, she concluded, 'is the good news that Jesus came to preach to the poor. It is not like the riches of this world, so that the more one gets the less the rest can have. God is without end; his love is without end' (2.33). Dinah's simplicity was the simplicity of purity and truth, and her theology was in fact quite profound, as I hope to demonstrate.

Dinah often spoke in biblical phrases, such as her first words to Adam Bede: 'I trust you feel rested and strengthened again to bear the burthen and heat of the day' (11.116). These words, which are reprised at the very end of the story (Epilogue, 539), reflect Jesus' parable of the vineyard in Matthew 20.1–16. Stephen Gill points out that many Victorian novels made a satire of such speech and represented it as hypocritical, whereas for Dinah it was entirely natural and appropriate 'because she is steeped in the Bible and feels no distinction between the world of her religion and everyday life.'[17] This seems to me the crucial point: Dinah's life was a whole, without a split between the sacred and the secular. It was just this split, the product of modernity, that George Eliot recognized as problematic, for it signaled the marginalization of religion and the emptying of ultimate meaning from culture.

Dinah's actions were as effective as her speech. She soothed, touched, calmed, fed, and healed by her physical presence. She did not deny suffering when it was real, did not offer false assurances, did not engage in abstract exhortations. She knew intuitively when quiet sympathy was best, and when it was appropriate to speak. As she comforted Adam's mother Lisbeth after the death by drowning of her drunken husband Thias, we are told that 'there was faith, love, and hope pouring itself forth that evening in the little kitchen' (10.109–14). Indeed, the scene in the little kitchen took on a sacramental quality as Dinah shared food and drink with the distraught woman,[18] and as Dinah herself, through her face and voice, became an embodiment of the divine nurture. She reminded Lisbeth of what David did when God took away his child (2 Sam. 12.15–23). While the child was yet alive, David fasted and wept in hopes that God would be gracious and allow the child to live. But when he died, David said: 'Why should I fast? can I bring him back again? I shall go to him, but he shall not return to me' (*Adam Bede*, 10.113–14). This brief homily (which might have been an Easter text) had a revivifying effect on Lisbeth, who resolved to take up her life again, knowing that Thias would not come back to her but that someday she might go to him. The words Dinah spoke to Lisbeth, intimating that in death there is yet life, were the opposite of the words Mr. Irwine chose for Thias Bede's funeral, 'In the midst of life we are in death' (18.202). Both are true words: but one is theological speech, the other philosophical.[19]

Who was Dinah's God? The central theme was announced in her sermon: God is one who is present and available to those who have need of God, especially the poor, the broken-hearted, those who are lost and who suffer. God is not remote and lofty but has come near and is our friend – above all in the words and deeds of Jesus, who was not just a good man: 'He was the Son of God – "in the image of the Father," the Bible says; that means, just like God, who is the beginning and end of all things – the God we want to know about. So then, all the love that Jesus showed to the poor is the same love that God has for us.'[20] Dinah seemed to address and answer George Eliot's central religious question: 'Will God take care of us when we die? and has he any comfort for us when we are lame and sick and helpless? Perhaps, too, he is angry with us; else why does the blight come, and the bad harvests, and the fever, and all sorts of pain and trouble? For our life is full of trouble, and if God sends us good, he seems to send bad too. How is it? how is it?' The answer is that God does not directly cause these things, is not angry with us, does not reward or punish us. Rather God simply 'lasts when everything else is gone.' God is our everlasting, ever-present friend, who sustains us when we are sad and rejoices with us when we are happy. 'What shall we do if he is not our friend?' (2.27).

Dinah herself embodied the message of her sermon when she befriended the forsaken Hetty in prison. She told Hetty that her suffering would be less hard if she knew somebody was with her, to feel for her, to care for her. 'But Hetty, there is some one else in this cell besides me,' said Dinah. 'Some one who has been with you through all your hours of sin and trouble . . . If you had a friend to take care of you after death . . . some one whose love is greater than mine . . . if God our Father was your friend . . . if you could believe he loved you and would help you, as you believe I love you and will help you, it wouldn't be so hard to die on Monday, would it?' There is no false consolation here, no promise of divine rescue or of personal immortality, only the assurance that 'whether we live or die, we are in the presence of God' (45.449–50).

While Dinah herself, in accord with her evangelical faith, believed in the 'showing' and 'leading' of God's providence, and in scriptural 'direction' received upon the random opening of the Bible (3.37–8), this is not the way that providence actually works in this story if something supernatural or miraculous is implied. Rather providence works through very ordinary events, feelings, insights, and contingencies. It does not grant special favors or guarantee happy outcomes. It does not prevent bad things or the inevitable consequences of deeds from happening, but provides resources for living in the face of what happens. The quiet ministry of Dinah Morris *is* God's providence at work, and her deep conviction was simply that God is our ever-constant friend who gives us strength by sharing in the joys and sorrows of this mortal life. What is called 'providence' is often Dinah's acute sensitivity to situations, her intuition as to when and how to act, her practical wisdom or 'prudence,' and this could be regarded as evidence of her spiritual attunement to God. Today providence is appropriately thought of in terms of divine 'influence,' 'persuasion,' or 'lure' rather than of direct causality, overt signs, or predestined goals; and this accords well with Dinah's sense of divine presence and provision.

The theme that ran through Dinah's discourses was that of the presence of a suffering, infinite love, which is God's very being.[21] Those to whom she spoke had their souls 'suffused . . . with the sense of a pitying, loving, infinite Presence, sweet as summer to the houseless needy' (3.39). The divine presence is 'the presence of a Love and Sympathy deeper and more tender than was breathed from the earth and sky' (15.156). The infinite love is a suffering love. As she meditated on 'the Redeemer's cross,' Dinah wrote to Seth:

> I feel it, I feel it – Infinite Love is suffering too – yea, in the fulness of knowledge it suffers, it yearns, it mourns; and that is a blind self-seeking which wants to be freed from the sorrow wherewith the whole creation groaneth and travaileth. Surely it is not true blessedness to be free from sorrow, while there is sorrow and sin in the world: sorrow is then a part of love, and love does not seek to throw it off . . . Is there not pleading in heaven? Is not the Man of Sorrow there in that crucified body wherewith he ascended? And is He not one with the Infinite Love itself – as our love is one with our sorrow?'[22]

Mary Wilson Carpenter offers a different interpretation of this passage than the one I am proposing. She believes that Dinah's words express 'the thematic heart of the novel, defining the cross of Christianity as a narrow doctrine and "enlarging" it to the doctrine of sympathy, or George Eliot's "religion of humanity."'[23] But for Dinah the cross and sympathy are deeply connected: as this passage demonstrates, the cross is precisely the manifestation of the divine *sym-pathos*. Dinah did indeed reject the 'narrow thought' that 'taking up the cross' refers to the troubles and persecutions that Christians bring on themselves by following Jesus.

While this is a commonly espoused attitude, it is not an authentic Christian theology of the cross. Rather, as Dinah herself said, 'The true cross of the Redeemer was the sin and sorrow of this world – *that* was what lay heavy on his heart – and that is the cross we shall share with him, that is the cup we must drink with him, if we would have any part in that Divine Love which is one with his own sorrow' (30.330). I find no basis for the view that George Eliot sought to replace the religion of the cross by the religion of humanity; rather as she saw it the religion of the cross offers the profoundest resource for human flourishing – just because it links love and suffering.

Sorrow must be part of love because sorrow is everywhere present in the world. The narrator remarks that, sometimes when traveling in foreign (mostly Catholic) lands, one comes across something that seems strangely out of place in the midst of a pleasant landscape – 'an image of great agony – the agony of the Cross' (35.363). A stranger to this world might wonder about these roadside crucifixes. Why are they there? He would not know that just out of sight 'there might be a human heart beating heavily with anguish' – Hetty's, for example, as she prepared to run away because of her advancing pregnancy. 'Such things are sometimes hidden among the sunny fields and behind the blossoming orchards; and the sound of the gurgling brook, if you come close to one spot behind a small bush, would be mingled for your ear with a despairing human sob. No wonder man's religion has much sorrow in it; no wonder he needs a Suffering God' (35.364).

We need a suffering God. This is often thought to be a Feuerbachian statement, but in fact it expresses a deep theological insight. The classical theological tradition for the most part maintained that God is impassible, incapable of suffering, although such a view stood in tension with the concrete imagery of the Bible and a subversive patripassianist counter-tradition. Medieval mystical writings and Luther's theology of the cross broke with the doctrine of impassibility, as did Hegel's speculative theology of divine self-divestment, and, more recently, process, feminist, and post-Holocaust theologies with their insistence that God is affected and changed by the suffering of the world. This is the kind of God George Eliot envisioned through her own religious sensibility and artistic imagination. Her God is 'fictional,' of course, but not for that reason an illusion or wish-fulfillment, the product simply of human need. Rather it is the product of deep poetic insight into the human condition and what presents itself through and transpires in that condition. We not only need a suffering God; we also find such a God, as Dinah testifies. Implicit in George Eliot's idea of God is the Hegelian conviction that love, sympathy, and suffering even unto death are not illusory projections of human qualities into God but qualities that inhere within the divine life itself.[24] That the suffering God (the divine pathos) is apprehended in the modality of feeling (itself a pathos, an affective as opposed to a cognitive form of knowing) does not diminish but rather enhances the reality of such a God.

Dinah 'felt the Divine Presence more and more' as she sat in the prison cell with Hetty. She felt 'as if she herself were a part of it, and it was the Divine pity that was beating in her heart.' God, she thought, 'manifest[s] himself by our silent feeling, and make[s] his love felt through ours' (45.449). A bit later we are told that 'the pitying love that shone out from Dinah's face looked like a visible pledge of the Invisible Mercy' (46.460). Dinah, in other words, was a mediatrix of the redemptive divine presence; she was an instrument by which this presence can become a transformative reality in people's lives. Without such human mediation there would be no divine presence.

But how do we know that it is really the *divine* presence that is mediated, as opposed, let us say, to merely the innate human capacity for love and sympathy? There is no way that we can know this with logical certainty, no way to disprove irrefutably the Feuerbachian inversion of theology into anthropology. But we can listen to the testimony of those like Dinah who are filled in a special way with the divine presence. What they testify to is a sense of being *channeled, called, laid upon* and *led on* by a gratuitous power not at their disposal. Those who so testify include women. Dinah had such a calling at the age of twenty-one. While discussing 'women's preaching' with Mr. Irwine, the tolerant and somewhat disengaged rector of Broxton and Hayslope,[25] she remarked wryly: 'It isn't for men to make channels for God's Spirit, as they make channels for the water-courses and say, "Flow here, but flow not

there."' 'Sometimes,' she continued, 'it seemed as if speech came
to me without any will of my own, and words were given to me that
came out as the tears come . . . Sir, we are led on, like the little
children, by a way that we know not. I was called to preach quite
suddenly, and since then I have never been left in doubt about the
work that was laid upon me' (8.90–1). In another context, the
authorial voice intercedes: 'As Dinah expressed it, "She was never
left to herself; but it was always given her when to keep silence and
when to speak." And do we not all agree to call rapid thought
and noble impulse by the name of inspiration? After our subtlest
analysis of the mental process, we must still say, as Dinah did, that
our highest thoughts and our best deeds are all given to us'
(10.114). Is this the gospel according to Feuerbach or another,
truer Gospel – the Gospel not of achievement but of gift?

Mr. Irwine asked Dinah if she ever felt embarrassed by the fact
that she was 'a lovely young woman on whom men's eyes are fixed.'
She responded this way:

> When God makes his presence felt through us, we are like the
> burning bush: Moses never took any heed what sort of bush it
> was – he only saw the brightness of the Lord. I've preached to as
> rough ignorant people as can be in the villages about Snowfield
> – men that look very hard and wild; but they never said an
> uncivil word to me, and often thanked me kindly as they made
> way for me to pass through the midst of them. (8.92)

Dinah, then, was a holy, inspired figure, and we are told that as
she passed through the crowds with Hetty on the way to the
scaffold the people became silent and gazed upon her with awe
(47.462). But at the same time George Eliot is careful to depict
her as a real, flesh-and-blood, warm and sensuous human being,
capable of falling in love with a handsome man. She wept at the
thought of her repressed affection for Adam (49.481; 50.487).
Dinah was attracted to the sensible, sensuous, down-to-earth
Adam rather than to his more ascetic, religious brother Seth,
whose proposal of marriage she declined. It was Adam who warned
against the danger of being 'over-speritial; we must have something beside Gospel i' this world' (1.11); it was Adam whose hard

common sense along with reverence for mystery made him disinclined toward doctrinal religion (4.51). Something about this common sense appealed to Dinah, and it is fair to say that she needed Adam to save her from her own excessive tendencies just as he needed her for a true soul-mate. Thus she, whose calling was to minister to others and not to have joys and sorrows or even a life of her own, as she told Seth (3.37) and later Adam (52.509), allowed herself to be drawn into the human community and to be ministered unto. In doing so she feared the temptation of becoming a 'lover of self' instead of one who 'bears willingly the Redeemer's cross' (52.510). She faced the dilemma common to many of George Eliot's heroines and heroes: whether love of self can be reconciled with love of neighbor and of God. Adam tried to persuade her that love is not a fixed quantity that can be measured in such precise ways.

Dinah attained a better balance in her life than Edgar Tryan did, but what she found was not a perfect harmony. In gaining Adam, she benefited from the loss of another woman, Hetty Sorrel, and had to live with the knowledge of that fact. She consented to marriage, recognizing that her love of Adam might compete with her love of God, but she was convinced that their union was God's will since without Adam hers would be but a divided life.[26] And after her marriage she acquiesced in the prohibition against women preaching – even though she was not completely silenced, for, as Adam observed, Dinah went on 'talking to the people a bit in their houses' and was 'not held from other sorts o' teaching' (Epilogue, 538) – a hint that in a subversive way her ministry continued. But for the most part she had to give up one aspect of the madonna role, proclamation and spiritual guidance, to assume another aspect, that of motherhood and domesticity. It is after all only fragile human beings, caught in life's ambiguities and the reality of hard choices, who mediate God's presence.

Dinah took Hetty's victimization, shame, condemnation, and judgment upon herself, and in this sense she earned the meaning of her name in Hebrew, 'judged.' As a victim of the history of patriarchy and its silencing of women, she was linked to the story of her biblical namesake in Genesis 34, who was seduced by a Canaanite and then betrayed by her brothers.[27] But she who was judged overcame judgment, and she who suffered victimization converted it into a mission of proclamation and caring. In this her model was Christ, condemned, humiliated, crucified, yet still alive and at work in the world. It is not inappropriate that one with the name of Dinah should become a figure of the Christ.

In *Adam Bede,* redemption prevails over loss, but not un-ambiguously. Hetty repented and was saved from execution, but she died before she could return home. Arthur obtained her reprieve, was genuinely remorseful, and after a self-imposed exile of nearly eight years was accepted back into the community, but he agreed with Adam that 'there's a sort of wrong that can never be made up for' (48.468; Epilogue, 539). Earlier, on more than one occasion, Adam had emphasized that the evil of Hetty's ruin 'can never be undone' (41.424). The narrator summarized his view as follows: 'Evil's evil, and sorrow's sorrow, and you can't alter its nature by wrapping it up in other words' (54.529). *Adam Bede* teaches this hard truth: deeds cannot be revoked, and the agents of deeds must live with the consequences of their actions. 'Our deeds determine us, as much as we determine our deeds' (29.315). It is a false consolation to suggest, as Bartle Massey did to Adam (46.459), or as Arthur deluded himself into thinking after the seduction of Hetty (29.314), that good may come out of evil in some simple, painless, miraculous fashion. If good does come out of evil, it requires a sustained and difficult process of confession, repentance, forgiveness, sacrifice, mutual suffering, painful re-building. The apparently happy ending of the novel bears the scars of the events that led up to it. Far from being an artistic failure, the ending brilliantly succeeds in showing the ambiguities and com-promises that are the ingredients in any 'comic' resolution of human affairs. Even the happy marriage of Adam and Dinah was darkened by their difference on the subject of women preaching (Epilogue, 538). Dinah chose to avoid the subject and to direct her energies elsewhere.[28]

The realism of the ending contrasts with the millennial expecta-tions that form part of the backdrop to the story. The beginning of a new century and of a new day for the people of Hayslope was celebrated at Arthur Donnithorne's coming-of-age party on 30 July 1799 (chaps. 22–6). The tenants were quite sure that things would be different when he became Squire of the estates: 'there was to be a millennial abundance of new gates, allowances of lime, and returns of ten per cent' (7.87). In deflating such expectations, George Eliot offers a 'counter-apocalyptic' intuition: not a cynical dismissal of hopes for a new tomorrow, but a transmutation of them into the struggle to make things a little better day by day.[29]

The brief history of Dinah Morris's ministry – a 'clearing' in the history of patriarchy – came to an end. Yet life goes on. Tragedy is clearly present, but it does not prevail; the vision is comic, or better tragicomic. In George Eliot's later fiction, the tragic elements of the vision deepened. She never again created a hero or heroine as purely good as Dinah Morris. Daniel Deronda was the closest approximation, and we shall have occasion to compare these two figures. In the later novels, while there were no more scenes of clerical life at the fictional centerpiece, George Eliot continued to explore religious traditions and practices; and the fundamental themes of sin and guilt, suffering and loss, grace and redemption were present in all of them.

Within a few months of its publication in 1859, *Adam Bede* had become a sensational success. Only *Middlemarch* surpassed it in initial sales, and with it George Eliot's reputation as a novelist was firmly established. For the author it proved to be a hard act to follow. In a journal entry for 28 August 1860 she noted that she was feeling 'much depressed just now with self-dissatisfaction and fear that I may not be able to do anything more that is well worth doing.'[30]

4

The Clue of Life: *The Mill on the Floss*, *Silas Marner*

The Mill on the Floss

Published only a year after *Adam Bede*, in 1860, and likewise set in rural England, *The Mill on the Floss* nonetheless offers a very different kind of story. It is much more darkly and deeply tragic, ending with the deaths of the heroine and hero, and concerning itself throughout with the inscrutability of nature and the mystery of the human lot. It differs from other George Eliot novels by beginning the story of the central characters in childhood and tracing their development through youth into young adulthood. It is a *Bildungsroman*, showing how human beings grow *out of* nature while remaining embedded *in* nature. There occurs a sublimation of nature in spirit, an elevation to the moral life, while at the same time persons remain subject to natural drives and hungers. In the first instance it may be the 'superior power of misery' that distinguishes the human being from even the most melancholy chimpanzee.[1] Maggie Tulliver, the heroine, was, as a girl, a nature-creature: dark-skinned, rebellious, half-wild like the gypsies (to whom she once ran away), worshipper of a fetish in the form of a defaced wooden doll (*The Mill on the Floss*, 1.4.11). Throughout her short life she experienced the contradictory pulls of nature and spirit, but in the end she found 'the clue of life' in a renunciation modeled on the cross of Christ.[2]

The role of nature in this story is signaled by the River Floss. The fictitious name 'Floss' suggests that it is the representative river, *der Fluss*, that which flows and floods, bringing both life and death – the River Jordan of the New Testament, the river of time and history that is crossed to the heavenly city in Bunyan's *The Pilgrim's Progress,* the river over which there is no bridge, a river dry for some, flooded for others.[3] George Eliot did historical research on floods and found her model for the Floss in the River Trent in Lincolnshire, a portion of which she rowed with G. H. Lewes from Gainsborough down to the Idle – presumably the fictitious Ripple, where Dorlcote Mill was located, near the village of St. Ogg's on the Floss.[4]

The Floss and the Mill provide the backdrop to the story, and we are warned early on that a disaster may be brewing. Tom and Maggie Tulliver liked to play along the river, and their mother feared that they would tumble into it and drown (1.2.60–1; 1.10.166). No floods had occurred in recent years and people had become complacent, forgetting the giant forces of nature (1.12.184). The author created a legend of St. Ogg, complete with Roman and Norse roots. Ogg the son of Beorl was a boatman who ferried passengers on the River Floss. On one windy evening, only he would take a woman in rags with a child in her arms. When she reached the other side, her rags changed into flowing robes and her face became bright and beautiful. She told Ogg that henceforth he would be saved from peril in storm and flood. Upon the visitation of floods after his death, Ogg was always seen with his boat, 'and the Blessed Virgin sat in the prow shedding a light around . . . so that rowers in the gathering darkness took heart and pulled anew' (1.12.182–3). Another legend, about Dorlcote Mill, told that whenever the Mill changed hands the river would be angry (3.9.352).

And the Mill did change hands. Its owner, Mr. Jeremy Tulliver, was a proud and righteous man, determined to defend his rights against persons attempting to draw water from the Ripple for irrigation purposes. Although he already had financial problems, he insisted on 'going to law' over water-rights. When their father lost his lawsuit and all his property, and was forced into bankruptcy, 'the golden gates of childhood' closed on Tom and Maggie Tulliver (2.7.270). The Mill passed into the ownership of lawyer Wakem, who allowed Mr. Tulliver to manage the business for thirty shillings per week. The old man's spirit was utterly broken ('this world's too many for me . . . I'm nought but a bankrupt'). He put his neck into harness and resolved never to forgive Wakem until his dying day (3.8.350; 3.9.355–7).

Mr. Wakem had a son, Philip, deformed and crippled from a childhood accident. Philip happened to be Tom's schoolmate: he was an excellent student, bright, industrious, well-informed, sensitive, whereas Tom struggled constantly to understand the relevance of Cicero and Euclid to real life. The boys became natural rivals, but between Philip and Maggie, who occasionally visited Tom at school, there was an instant attraction. Maggie was a precocious, self-taught girl of eleven, with lovely, tender eyes – eyes that 'were full of unsatisfied intelligence and unsatisfied, beseeching affection' (2.5.253). Philip thought that her eyes were trying to speak kindly to him, whereas the stares of most people were hurtful. Maggie, Philip later observed, had 'such wealth of love in her, and there was no one to claim it all' (5.1.404).

Several years later, when Maggie had grown into a beautiful young woman of seventeen, she began meeting clandestinely with Philip in the Red Deeps, an exhausted stone quarry near the Ripple (5.1, 3, 4). She tried at first to stop the meetings for the sake of their alienated families and especially her embittered father, but the attraction between them was too strong. It was for Maggie principally an intellectual and spiritual attraction, not a physical one. She found in Philip a sensitive conversation partner, who knew about books, art, music, culture. They talked about these things eagerly, and Philip pleaded with Maggie not to destroy her brilliance and vitality for the sake of a senseless renunciation, a sacrifice to other people's feelings. Through their words and glances they were making love to each other. This is the only kind of love-making that ever explicitly occurs in George Eliot's stories, but it can be very powerful. When Tom found out about the secret meetings, in a shockingly cruel fashion he forced Maggie to give up Philip (5.5). She lashed out at him:

> You have always enjoyed punishing me – you have always been hard and cruel to me – even when I was a little girl, and always loved you better than any one in the world . . . You have no pity – you have no sense of your own imperfection and your own

sins. It is a sin to be hard – it is not fitting for a mortal – for a
Christian. You are nothing but a Pharisee . . . You have not even
a vision of feelings by the side of which your shining virtues are
mere darkness! (5.5.450)

Thus began an alienation between brother and sister that was overcome only in their last embrace.

Two years later Maggie met handsome, supercilious Stephen
Guest, who was engaged to her best friend and cousin, Lucy Deane
(whom Maggie had pushed into the mud when they were little
girls). Stephen was the son of the owner of the business for whom
Tom had gone to work, earning enough to pay off his father's
debts. Once his eyes locked onto Lucy's beautiful cousin, he could
not take them off her, and Maggie felt herself blushing deeply. She
was in fact beginning to experience a sexual attraction that she had
never felt with Philip. Maggie knew that it was utterly absurd for
her to fall in love with Stephen, and she struggled mightily
between feelings of vanity and sensual pleasure on the one side,
and love, pity, and discipline on the other (6.2–3, 6–7, 9–10). She
concluded that she must leave St. Ogg's and take a situation in
another town. But she thought a final parting with Stephen would
do no harm. Through a sequence of improbable events, Stephen
and Maggie ended up alone together in a boat, borne along by the
tide down the River Floss, 'enveloped in an enchanted haze' (6.13).
Maggie experienced a kind of intoxication in which everything but
the present pleasurable moment was blotted out. They drifted so
far that it would be impossible to return home before nightfall. She
found herself yielding to Stephen's proposal that they elope, and
they climbed aboard a Dutch sailing vessel headed to the seacoast.
Maggie fell asleep with sweet dreams of a future life no longer filled
with sacrifice.

She awoke, however, to a nightmare in which she was in a boat
with Stephen and saw the Virgin seated in St. Ogg's boat (6.14).
The Virgin was Lucy and the boatman Philip, or rather Tom, who
rowed past them without a glance. Their own boat overturned and
began to sink. The whole terrible truth now flooded in upon her.
She had committed an irrevocable wrong that would bring sorrow
into the lives of those whom she most loved: by an act of cruel

selfishness she had betrayed Lucy and breached the trust of Philip. 'She had let go the clue of life' (6.14.597) – a clue that she had learned years before from an old monk. What this clue was we shall examine below.

Maggie knew that she must now inflict pain on Stephen by insisting on an irrevocable parting. Stephen argued that the natural law of attraction was more powerful than earlier promises and obligations. Maggie said that 'if we judged in that way, there would be a warrant for all treachery and cruelty – we should justify breaking the most sacred ties that can ever be formed on earth . . . We should have no law but the inclination of the moment.' To his appeal that constancy without love is hollow, she rejoined that 'faithfulness and constancy mean something else besides doing what is easiest and pleasantest to ourselves. They mean renouncing whatever is opposed to the reliance others have in us.' She told Stephen that it was not her intention to sacrifice him, but she could not believe in a good for him that would be a wrong toward others. She was moving toward her definitive ethical and religious judgment: We humans 'can only choose whether we will indulge ourselves in the present moment or whether we will renounce that for the sake of obeying the divine will within us – for the sake of being true to all the motives that sanctify our lives. I know that belief is hard – it has slipped away from me again and again; but I have felt that if I let it go for ever, I should have no light through the darkness of this life' (6.14.599–605).

In the critical moment Maggie held on to that hard faith, and she returned to St. Ogg's without Stephen. She was not welcomed with open arms. Public opinion – 'not the world, but the world's wife' – would have judged Maggie more kindly if she had actually married Stephen and come back a rich wife. That would have been easy to rationalize, but her degraded and outcast condition proved that she had been the temptress and schemer, and it was to Stephen's credit that he had shaken her off as quickly as he did. No matter that Stephen had written a letter placing all the blame on himself, public opinion knew better and could not, thankfully (for the benefit of social order), be deceived (7.2). Dr. Kenn, the local clergyman, told Maggie that no evidence would save her from false imputations from persons who would not believe her conscientious struggle because they were incapable of it themselves. He regretted that churches for the most part had utterly failed to realize the original Christian vision of a true fellowship in which members exercised mutual responsibility and forgiveness toward each other (7.2.624–7). The ladies of St. Ogg's felt a greater obligation to 'society' than to a 'higher authority' that gave a very explicit answer to where social duties begin, an answer that turned not 'on the ultimate good of society, but on "a certain man" who was found in trouble by the wayside' (7.4.637).

But Maggie found forgiveness and understanding from the two persons in whom it mattered most (7.3–4). A letter arrived from Philip: he believed that the strong attraction which drew her and Stephen together 'proceeded only from one side of your characters, and belonged to that partial, divided action of our nature which makes half the tragedy of the human lot.' He rejoiced that there was something stronger in Maggie than her love for Stephen. He reaffirmed his own undying affection: 'I think nothing but such complete and intense love could have initiated me into that enlarged life which grows and grows by appropriating the life of others . . . This gift of transferred life which has come to me in loving you, may be a new power to me.' 'And remember,' he concluded, 'that I am unchangeably yours: yours – not with selfish wishes – but with a devotion that excludes such wishes. God comfort you, – my loving, large-souled Maggie' (7.3.633–5). As for Lucy, she came secretly to Maggie to say that she understood that she had not meant to deceive her, and that Maggie had in fact given Stephen up through a hard struggle. Maggie reported that Stephen had struggled too, that he had wanted to be true to Lucy. 'He will come back to you. Forgive him – he will be happy then' – words were that wrung, we are told, from the depths of Maggie's soul (7.4.641–2). A healing and redemption were beginning to happen in the lives of Maggie, Philip, and Lucy. But what of Tom and Stephen?

Maggie faced one final trial. Heavy rains came. As they beat against her window one midnight, she was reading a letter from Stephen in which he begged her to let him return to her. Moved by his palpable pain and misery, she was tempted to write, 'Come!' But then she remembered the words in a little book she had read long ago: 'I have received the Cross, I have received it from thy hand; I will bear it, and bear it till death, as thou has laid it upon me.' As she burned his letter, she sobbed, 'Forgive me, Stephen! It will pass away. You will come back to her'.[5] Confronting her own weakness – 'How shall I have patience and strength? O God, am I to struggle and fall and repent again?' – Maggie's soul went out 'to the Unseen Pity that would be with her to the end.' Then she felt the flood waters rising under her feet. She managed to get into a boat with the one resolve to find the Mill and rescue Tom and her mother. Tom, stranded in the attic, was amazed to see her. This was 'an entirely new revelation to his spirit, of the depths in life, that had laid beyond his vision.' Together Maggie and Tom went out into the current to rescue Lucy and others, but huge floating masses were bearing down on them, their boat capsized, and they drowned 'in an embrace never to be parted' (7.5.649–55). The rescue effort was a selfless act, which through an accident, a contingent natural occurrence, brought Maggie's life to an end. I do not support the view that it was a death wish or an incestuous drive – these seem to be ideological overinterpretations. Rather, the rebellious, divided Maggie became in the end, through her courage and resolve, something like the young woman, the Virgin, who was seen on the waters during storm and flood, shedding light that others might be safe.

Two forms of religion confront each other in this novel. One is described, in the title to Chapter 1 of Book 4, as 'a variation of Protestantism unknown to Bossuet.'[6] This is the religion of the Tullivers and Dodsons, and of most other citizens of the modern world. The days are gone, we are told, when people can be greatly wrought upon by their faith (1.12.184–5). What remains is a tepid, prosaic religion with no sublime principles, no romantic visions, no active, self-renouncing faith, no strong passions, no rough simplicity of wants, no outlet toward something beautiful, great, and noble. Men and women seem to be living out of keeping with the earth, out of touch with the world's mighty heart. 'A vigorous superstition that lashes its gods or lashes its own back, seems to be more congruous with the mystery of the human lot, than the mental condition of these emmet-like Dodsons and Tullivers' (4.1.362–3).

Insofar as a belief in the Unseen manifests itself at all, it is rather more pagan than Christian. But moral notions are held with a strong tenacity, based on the standard not of the suffering, sympathetic God of the Bible but of hereditary custom. The negative aspect of this morality is an impulse to accuse, blame, humiliate, and punish those who do not conform to social custom or who defile family honor. It is right that children should be made to suffer for their father's faults, asserted the Dodson aunts and uncles in the aftermath of Mr. Tulliver's downfall. Young Maggie lashed out at this hypocritical, accusatory religion:

> Why do you come, then, talking, and interfering with us and scolding us, if you don't mean to do anything to help my poor mother – your own sister – if you have no feeling for her when she's in trouble, and won't part with anything, though you would never miss it, to save her from pain. Keep away from us then, and don't come to find fault with my father – he was better than any of you – he was kind – he would have helped *you*, if you had been in trouble. (3.3.287–96)

Seeing people we dislike reduced and humiliated without special efforts of our own has a soothing, flattering influence. 'Providence, or some other prince of this world, it appears, has undertaken the task of retribution for us.' Thus Mr. Wakem derived pleasure from doing the very thing that would cause Mr. Tulliver the most deadly mortification – the purchase of the mortgaged Mill and the employment of Tulliver as a hired hand. 'To see an enemy humiliated gives a certain contentment, but this is jejune compared with the highly blent satisfaction of seeing him humiliated by your benevolent action of concession on his behalf. That is a sort of revenge which falls into the scale of virtue' (3.7.340). 'Benevolent vengeance' is the name of this morality. It is driven by egoism, fear, and self-interest, and it legitimates the primitive, punitive impulse by locating it in the deity itself.

A similar egoism underlies the positive form of this semi-pagan moralism. The principle here is to revere whatever is customary and respectable: thus to insure one's eternal salvation it is necessary to be baptized, to take the sacrament before death, but also to have the proper pall-bearers and well-cured hams at one's funeral. Obedience to parents, faithfulness to kindred, industry, rigid honesty, thrift are unquestioned maxims, which if followed will yield honesty with wealth: this is a proud, honest egoism, which has a certain social utility (4.1.363–5). Such maxims are the glue of culture – but the authorial voice reminds us that 'the mysterious complexity of our life is not to be embraced by maxims.' Maxims are human, but sympathy is divine (7.2.628).

The other form of religion that appears in *The Mill on the Floss* is one that provides the clue of life. Following the humiliation and impoverishment of her family, Maggie was looking for something that would make sense of the tragic mystery of the human condition. 'She wanted some key that would enable her to understand and, in understanding, endure, the heavy weight that had fallen on her young heart' (4.3.379). One day a childhood friend, simple and kind Bob Jakin, brought Maggie a bag of books to replace her books that had been sold at auction. He did not know what books were in the bag but had just taken them off a shelf in a bookstore. They were a strange potpourri, and what an odd coincidence that they all happened to be books read by Mary Ann Evans![7] Among them was Thomas à Kempis's *De Imitatione Christi*.[8] This is a summary (not a direct quotation) of what Maggie read from the little book:

> Know that love of yourself hurts you more than anything in this world. If you seek your own will and pleasure, you will never be free from care; seek rather the Cross and follow it. Blessed are those who hear the whispers of the divine voice and listen not to the whisperings of the world. Hearken to the truth that teaches inwardly and tells the one thing necessary: go wholly out of yourself, retain nothing of self-love, resign yourself, and you shall find inward peace. (4.3.382–3)

Here was a 'secret of life' that would enable Maggie to renounce all other secrets and outward supports; 'here was insight, and strength, and conquest, to be won by means entirely within her own soul, where a supreme Teacher[9] was waiting to be heard.' Perhaps the miseries of her young life derived from orienting everything to her own pleasure, whereas she might now look 'at her own life as an insignificant part of a divinely guided whole.' She read on and on, 'devouring eagerly the dialogues with the invisible Teacher, the pattern of sorrow, the source of all strength.' She passed too quickly over the old monk's deepest insight that re-nunciation requires sorrow, for Maggie was 'panting for happiness, and was in ecstasy because she had found the key to it' (4.3.383–4). Thus it is not surprising that 'she threw some exaggeration and wilfulness, some pride and impetuosity even into her self-renunciation . . . She often lost the spirit of humility by being excessive in the outward act; she often strove after too high a flight and came down with her poor little half-fledged wings dabbled in the mud' (4.3.386). So it is with most of George Eliot's heroines and heroes – Romola, Dorothea, Gwendolen, Felix, Daniel – they are, after all, ordinary mortals, not gods and angels. In Maggie's case, bitter experience taught her the sorrow that accompanies renunciation, but also the recognition that the denial of egoism does not require a denial of selfhood, a refusal to *be* loved, to enter into relationships of love. Philip warned her against a narrow asceticism: 'every rational satisfaction of your nature that you deny now, will assault you like a savage appetite' (5.3.429). Maggie oscillated between excessive renunciation and excessive gratifica-tion, but in the end she clung to the clue of life.[10]

What makes the clue a genuinely religious insight as distin-guished from a moral or humanistic one? The answer, I think, remains implicit in this novel. It is that human renunciation, suffering, sympathy, pathos-for-the-other are empowered by the divine renunciation, suffering, sympathy – incarnate in the anguished love of the Cross. What is entailed is an imitation not of ourselves but of Christ, of God-in-Christ, of a God who appears in the face of the suffering other. Only God is able to break the cycle of self-securing and retribution. No finite source can do that because it is part of the cycle. Something utterly self-giving and gratuitous is needed to interrupt the vicious logic. Maxims are human but sympathy is divine: sympathy is not something arbi-trary and illusory but is the manifestation of a mysterious cosmo-theandric order, of the Unseen Pity that Maggie felt would be with her to the end. Without ontological orientation, without a sense of being connected with something that is awesome, holy, and right, it is difficult to imagine how a life of compassion, resignation, and active love for the other could long sustain itself against 'the tone of good society,' where, observes the narrator, moderation and irony prevail. Good society has little time or need for 'emphatic belief,' considering that the privileged can satisfy their needs with thoroughbred horses, exclusive clubs, and superior clergy – and the less privileged may find their *ekstasis* in gin. Emphatic belief, by contrast, or what good society calls 'enthusiasm,' is 'something that will present motives in an entire absence of high prizes, something that will give patience and feed human love when the limbs ache with weariness and human looks are hard upon us – something, clearly, that lies outside personal desires, that includes resignation for ourselves and active love for what is not ourselves' (4.3.385–6). Emphatic belief does not lend itself readily to a Feuerbachian interpretation of religion.

Journeying down the Rhône, writes George Eliot in a journal-like passage, you see dreary ruined villages 'telling how the swift river once rose, like an angry, destroying god sweeping down the feeble generations whose breath is in their nostrils and making their dwellings a desolation.' These Rhône villages, she continues, 'oppress me with the feeling that human life – very much of it – is a narrow, ugly, groveling existence, which even calamity does not elevate, but rather tends to exhibit in all its bare vulgarity of conception' (4.1.361–2). Is this the principal message of the novel? Is the flood on the Floss to be interpreted as the work of a divine destroyer who sweeps away human pretension and pride? Is human life simply a 'gross sum of obscure vitality, that will be swept into the same oblivion with the generations of ants and beavers' (4.1.362)?

I do not think so. The 'Conclusion' of the story (656–7) is not so unrelievedly tragic as these oppressive feelings – brought on by contemplating the 'sordid life' of the Tullivers and Dodsons – suggest. The flood is an act of nature, of natural rhythms and forces, not of an angry, vengeful God. The story reminds us of the fragility of human existence in the world, and of the fact that good and innocent people sometimes suffer indiscriminate harm. The situation is tragic in that, were it not so, the conditions of possibility for goodness, responsibility, purpose, freedom, and change would be lacking. What happens in the world is not attributable to 'a Providence who arranges results' (5.3.430). Why it is that human beings are not blessed impartially is hidden in the great mystery of time (2.2.223–4). But the presence of tragedy does not rule out the possibility of redemption. Nature repairs her ravages, and human life goes on in a perpetual process of building, wearing down, and rebuilding. To be sure, not all ravages are repaired, and marks remain of the past rending. In Dorlcote churchyard a new tomb was erected for two bodies found in close embrace – a tomb that was visited from time to time by Stephen and Lucy Guest and by Philip Wakem. Their lives were scarred but ultimately changed for the better by their companionship with Maggie Tulliver. They survived the flood. As for the two who did not survive, they found reconciliation. Tom had redeemed the Mill and honored the memory of his father. Maggie held on to the clue of life and in the end was faithful to those whom she loved the best. These were good and remembered deeds.

Silas Marner

During a visit to Italy in the spring of 1860, George Eliot became interested in creating a historical romance, set in Florence at the close of the fifteenth century. That was to become *Romola*. 'But I want first to write another English story,' she told her publisher, John Blackwood.[11] In a journal entry the following autumn she noted, 'I am engaged in writing a story . . . which has thrust itself between me and the other book I was meditating. It is "Silas Marner, the Weaver of Raveloe."'[12] Later she explained to Blackwood that the idea for the story 'came to me . . . quite suddenly, as a sort of legendary tale, suggested by my recollection of having once, in early childhood, seen a linen-weaver with a bag on his back; but as my mind dwelt on the subject, I became inclined to a more realistic treatment.' She hoped he 'will not find it at all a sad story, as a whole, since it sets . . . in a strong light the remedial influences of pure, natural human relations.'[13]

A legendary tale with a realistic treatment: this is *Silas Marner*. The legendary aspect of it illumines the perennial story of Christmas, since it shows how a little child brings about a redemptive transformation in human affairs. The realistic treatment shows that the redemption is accomplished through pure and natural human relations, not by a miraculous intervention of God – but this is not to say that God is not present and active in the story.

Silas Marner came to the village of Raveloe with a bag on his back about fifteen years before the beginning of the story. No one knew about his background, but he was reputed to possess healing powers, perhaps even to be in contact with preternatural agents. He had in fact inherited from his mother some acquaintance with medicinal herbs, and at his previous home he had belonged to a narrow religious sect in which he seemed marked for leadership. But a friend framed Silas to make it appear that he had murdered an elderly man and taken his money. Lots were drawn, which determined that Silas was guilty; and his fiancée ended their engagement to marry the treacherous friend. Silas, convinced that 'there is no just God that governs the earth righteously, but a God of lies, that bears witness against the innocent,' left his home and became a wandering linen-weaver.[14]

He settled in a stone cottage at the Stone-pits near Raveloe, and became a recluse, working unremittingly at his loom. 'He seemed to weave, like the spider, from pure impulse, without reflection.' He became 'a spinning insect.' Nothing called forth love and fellowship toward his new neighbors, 'for there was no Unseen Love that cared for him' (*Silas Marner*, 2.16–17). Having few expenses, he began to hoard the gold coins he received for his linen goods. He hid his growing treasure in a hole below the bricks of the floor beneath his loom. During the days he weaved; at night came his revelry, when he drew forth the coins, spread them out in piles, and worshiped the glistening gold in the flickering fire (2.17–21).

But about Christmas time of his fifteenth year in Raveloe, something momentous happened: one evening Silas's gold mysteriously disappeared (chaps. 3–10). He did not know whether a thief had taken the bags of coins, or whether a cruel supernatural power had 'delighted in making him a second time desolate' (5.44). *We* know that it was a thief, Dunstan Cass, the dissolute son of the wealthiest landowner in Raveloe, Squire Cass. Dunstan's elder brother, Godfrey, was secretly married to a woman of low estate, Molly Farren; and Dunstan had to be bribed to keep the secret from their father (the brothers hated each other and were among the most degenerate of George Eliot's characters). Having squandered his funds, Dunstan thought to himself, as he passed by Silas Marner's cottage, that the old fool of a weaver must have a great deal of money hidden somewhere. Finding the cottage unlocked and empty, he searched the floor, removed the loose bricks, and stole the entire treasure, some two hundred and seventy-two pounds. Dunstan was never seen again in Raveloe. Silas spent Christmas Day in loneliness, pressing his head between his hands and moaning softly.

A few days later, on New Year's Eve, a great dance was hosted by Squire Cass. This afforded a fine opportunity for Godfrey to re-kindle his on-again-off-again romance with Nancy Lammeter, the belle of Raveloe. While Godfrey 'was taking draughts of forgetfulness from the sweet presence of Nancy . . . Godfrey's wife was walking with slow uncertain steps through the snow-covered Raveloe lanes, carrying her child in her arms' (12.107). Molly was on her way to the party with the intent of disclosing herself as the Squire's daughter-in-law. Unfortunately, poor Molly was addicted to opium. Feeling cold and weary, she took her last draught and sank down into the snow in a death-like torpor. As the mother's arms loosed their grip, a golden-headed two-year old girl toddled off toward a distant light, which emanated from the open door of Silas Marner's cottage. The child walked right up to the warm hearth where there was a bright fire, lay down on an old sack and fell asleep (12.108–9). Silas did not see her enter because at just that moment he suffered a cataleptic seizure. When he regained consciousness, he glimpsed something golden on his hearth. Reaching out to grasp it, he felt not familiar hard coins but soft warm curls. 'In utter amazement, Silas fell on his knees and bent his head low to examine the marvel: it was a sleeping child.' He sensed immediately that somehow the child had come to him in place of the gold (12.110–11). The symbolism hints that the child was a kind of Christ-child: the lowly mother, the absent father, the mysterious appearance in the season of Christmas on the hearth of an outcast, the act of veneration, and Silas's intuition that this child was to be his salvation.

When she awoke, he fed the little girl porridge and by following

her tracks discovered the mother's body in the snow. Shortly thereafter Silas Marner appeared at the New Year's Eve party carrying
Godfrey Cass's child and asking for a doctor for a woman lying in
the snow at the Stone-pits. Of course only Godfrey recognized the
child as his own, and (fortunately for him) the woman was found to
be dead. Silas told Godfrey that he would keep the child until 'any-
body shows they've a right to take her away from me. The mother's
dead, and I reckon it's got no father: its a lone thing – and I'm a lone
thing. My money's gone, I don't know where – and this is come
from I don't know where' (13.114–18). He sensed that something
unknown was dawning on his life: 'He could only have said that the
child was come instead of the gold – that the gold had turned into
the child' (14.122).

Silas's determination to keep the 'tramp's child' evoked sympathy and support from the citizens of Raveloe. Dolly Winthrop
taught him how to dress, feed, and care for a baby. She had a
religious faith that she shared with Silas as he attempted to cope
with the great mystery that had come into his life. One thing goes
and the other comes, she said, we know not how nor why. All we
can do is to trust and to do the right thing as far as we know. 'For
if us as knows so little can see a bit o' good and rights, we may be
sure as there's a good and a rights bigger nor what we can know'
(14.121; 16.145). Silas began to share this view. 'There's good i'
this world – I've a feeling o' that now; and it makes a man feel as
there's a good more nor he can see, i' spite o' the trouble and the
wickedness. That drawing o' the lots is dark; but the child was sent
to me: there's dealings with us – there's dealings' (16.145). We
need not assume, as Silas and Molly did, that these 'dealings' are a
direct manifestation of divine providence, as though God had
planned and directed all of it – the false accusation against Silas,
the hoarding and loss of the gold, and the coming of the child.
Such things happen by causes entirely natural, but it is possible to
believe nonetheless that there is a prevailing goodness in the world
– a divine goodness that empowers us to make something good of
the opportunities that present themselves. For the good actually to
happen *we* must act, *we* must seize the opportunity and assume
responsibility. This is what Silas Marner did. His response to the
contingencies that affected his life was the direct opposite to that of

the Cass brothers, who worshiped 'blessed Chance' in the hope that their luck would hold and their deceitful deeds would escape detection (9.73–4). Chance is everywhere present but it need not rule our lives or become our god. What should rule our lives is a trust in the ultimate power of goodness, which includes the power to bring good out of evil, and a recognition that deeds have inescapable consequences.

Rosemary Ashton suggests that the phrase 'natural supernaturalism' may be appropriate to characterize the view being expressed here – a phrase used in Carlyle's *Sartor Resartus* (1836), which George Eliot had admired as a young woman.[15] Natural supernaturalism implies that nature has its ground in the divine life, and that the latter manifests itself in and through natural processes. George Eliot shared this sacramental view of nature (and of history as part of nature) with Carlyle, Wordsworth, and Coleridge, and their influence is especially felt in *Silas Marner*. The religion of Chance, by contrast, deprecates the principle that 'the seed brings forth a crop after its kind' and hopes for some unforeseen turn of fortune or magic rescue. 'Favourable Chance is the god of all men who follow their own devices instead of obeying a law they believe in' (9.73–4).

Dolly told Silas that the child must be christened, and for that she needed a name. His mother's name had been Hephzibah – a biblical name meaning 'the LORD's Delight Is in Her' (Isa. 62.4) – and his little sister, who died when she was very young, was named after her mother. She was called Eppie for short, and it was appropriate that the child too should have this name (*Silas Marner*, 14.124). As the weeks passed into months, Eppie drew Silas out of his narrow isolation into fresh links with life. 'Unlike the gold which needed nothing, and must be worshipped in close-locked solitude . . . Eppie was a creature of endless claims and ever-growing desires, seeking and loving sunshine, and living sounds, and living movements' (14.125). 'As her life unfolded, his soul, long stupefied in a cold narrow prison, was unfolding too, and trembling gradually into full consciousness' (14.126).

Near the end of the first part of the story, the narrator draws out its theological implications in the following way:

In old days there were angels who came and took men by the hand and led them away from the city of destruction.[16] We see no white-winged angels now. But yet men are led away from threatening destruction: a hand is put into theirs, which leads them forth gently toward a calm and bright land, so that they look no more backwards; and the hand may be a little child's.[17]

To this should be added the epigraph from Wordsworth printed on the title page:

A child, more than all other gifts
That earth can offer to declining man,
Brings hope with it, and forward-looking thoughts.[18]

Silas Marner found the clue of life not in the words of an old monk but in the hand of a little child. But what is it that a child actually accomplishes to bring about the redemption and rebirth of suffering humanity? It is certainly not that the child (or the man who grows from the child) must be sacrificed as a substitutionary atonement for the sins of the world. This punitive theology has had too many destructive consequences in the history of humanity, and it makes a mockery of the goodness of God. The answer is found in the phrase from Isaiah that echoes in George Eliot's legend: 'A little child shall lead them' (Isa. 11.6). A child leads us out of ourselves, our preoccupations and self-centeredness, into an encounter with the other – in the first instance a very needy other, who is totally dependent on us for its well-being – but then into ever-deepening relations with the human family. A child also leads us into the future, into new hopes and possibilities, into 'a calm and bright land,' which must be the land envisioned by Isaiah in which the wolf shall live with the lamb, and the leopard shall lie down with the kid. This is the messianic land, and every child is the messianic child (the anointed child in whom the Lord delights) insofar as he or she embodies anew the human promise – the promise of the fullness of life in a community of love, sympathy, peace, and justice. This 'leading' of the child is the profoundest meaning of the Christmas story. George Eliot offers a remarkable demythologization of the Christmas symbols. God is present (but

not miraculously, via a virgin birth) in the gentleness, vulnerability, and innocence of the child, leading us, as it did Silas
Marner, into a new life.[19] The beginning of the story at Christmas
anticipates its end on Good Friday, when worldly power over-
whelms divine powerlessness. The same clue of life is found at the
end (in the cross of renunciation) as at the beginning (in the child
of promise).[20]

In the second part of the novel the story jumps ahead by sixteen
years. Godfrey Cass and Nancy Lammeter were married, but their
relationship had been haunted by the secret Godfrey felt he could
not share with his wife, and Nancy's only child had died at birth.
Their childless marriage weighed on Godfrey as a privation that
Nancy could not fully understand, but she refused his desire to
adopt Eppie Marner, believing that somehow it was not right
(chap. 17). Godfrey began draining some fields near the Stone-pits,
and as a consequence the water level of the pits was lowered. One
day a skeleton was found in the dried-out pits: it was the body of
Dunstan Cass, and scattered about him lay Silas Marner's gold;
Dunstan must have fallen into the pits immediately after robbing
the weaver. Shaken by this revelation, Godfrey went to his wife
and said: 'Everything comes to light, Nancy, sooner or later. When
God Almighty wills it, our secrets are found out' (18.162). Then he
told Nancy that Eppie's mother had been his wife and that Eppie
was his child. Nancy's response was not, as Godfrey had feared,
one of condemnation: rather she said that had she known the truth
from the first they could have taken Eppie into their home and
their life together would have been happier. Now she felt that it
was Godfrey's duty to acknowledge Eppie and provide for her
properly (chap. 18).

Godfrey and Nancy went to Silas Marner and condescendingly
assumed that the humble weaver would see the rightness of their
finally taking Eppie into their home and making a lady of her (chap.
19). But Silas 'felt the spirit of resistance in him set free.' He asked
Godfrey why he had not come forward sixteen years ago to 'claim
her before I'd come to love her, i'stead o' coming to take her from
me now, when you might as well take the heart out o' my body?
God gave her to me because you turned your back upon her, and
He looks upon her as mine: you've no right to her! When a man

turns a blessing from his door, it falls to them as take it in' (19.169). These words stung Godfrey, but he acknowledged their truth. After Eppie made it clear that she had no intention of leaving her only true father, and that she preferred to live among the working poor, one of whom she had promised to marry, the Casses returned home, sadder but wiser (chap. 20). Godfrey recognized that one of the consequences of his earlier irresponsibility was that his daughter should remain permanently alienated from him. At least he had Nancy, and he resolved to work at mending their relationship. In the end we sense that Godfrey had grown up morally and emotionally: there was hope for him, whereas his brother had been lost years ago. Godfrey and Nancy resolved that it would do no good to make the parentage of Eppie known publicly. They left her to the happiness she had found, but they did provide for her wedding feast and in other ways as well. It was understood by the villagers that Godfrey Cass should take an interest in the weaver who had been wronged by one of his own family; and of the weaver himself it was widely agreed 'that he had brought a blessing on himself by acting like a father to a lone motherless child' (Conclusion, 182). People marvelled at the strange history of Silas Marner and knew that he had found the clue of life.

5

The Kingdom of Justice:
Romola, *Felix Holt*

Romola

In May of 1861 George Eliot and George Henry Lewes returned to
Florence for a second visit. She intended to immerse herself in the
history, literature, and atmosphere of the city for the purpose of
writing a story set during the time of the rise and fall of Fra
Girolamo Savonarola. It proved to be the most difficult of all her
novels to write, partly because she felt she could never acquire
sufficiently detailed knowledge of the historical context, and partly
because of frustrations experienced in getting the story under way.[1]
Many journal entries written in 1861 and 1862 gave vent to her
despair. Cross remarks: 'The writing of *Romola* ploughed into her
more than any of her other books. She told me she could put
her finger on it as marking a well-defined transition in her life. In
her own words, "I began it a young woman – I finished it an old
woman."'[2] What accounted for the aging process was not merely
the complexity of the historical material but the scale and tragedy
of the story itself. *Romola* anticipated the last and greatest of
George Eliot's novels, *Middlemarch* and *Daniel Deronda*, which
came a decade later. Henry James regarded it as her finest achievement.[3]

The action of the novel runs from 9 April 1492, the day after the
death of Lorenzo de' Medici, who had ruled Florence as head of a
patrician oligarchy for over twenty years, until 23 May 1498, the
day on which Savonarola was executed for heresy and treason. In
November 1494, republican government was reestablished in

Florence following the invasion of French troops, and for two-and-a-half years Savonarola, the Dominican friar and Prior of San Marco, was the intellectual and spiritual leader of the city. He fell out of favor with the ecclesiastical and political powers, and ultimately lost the support of the people themselves. George Eliot was fascinated by his combination of charismatic power, prophetic courage, and religious fanaticism; and she brought her fictional heroine, Romola de' Bardi, into a decisive encounter with him. In the novel historical and fictional characters are interwoven in such a way as to suggest that history itself is fiction, and fiction history.[4] History and fiction blend together with religious and theological concerns in a remarkable literary construction, whose underlying motif is the never-consummated struggle for justice in human affairs, a struggle that occurs against the backdrop of duplicity, hypocrisy, violence, egoism, and realism on the one hand, and integrity, courage, charity, self-renunciation, and idealism on the other.[5]

The details of the novel are very complicated, which helps to account for its being little read today – regrettably so, for it is a wonderful story. Tito Melema, an Italian-born Greek, arrived in Florence on the day after the death of Lorenzo, representing himself as a scholar whose only fortune consisted of a few gems that he wished to sell. The painter Piero di Cosimo observed that Tito's dark handsome face would make a fine model for a picture of Sinon deceiving Priam. 'A perfect traitor should have a face which vice can write no marks on – lips that will lie with a dimpled smile – eyes of such agate-like brightness and depth that no infamy can dull them – cheeks that will rise from a murder and not look haggard' (*Romola*, 4.42). We learn shortly that Tito had not only the face but also the heart of a traitor. His first act of betrayal was toward his own adoptive father, Baldassarre Calvo, whom, he claimed, had been lost at sea on a voyage to Delos. Shortly after his arrival in Florence, Tito learned that his father had in fact been taken captive by the Turks. He found it easy to rationalize a decision to remain in the city, where a soft and prosperous life awaited him, rather than to undertake the uncertain and hazardous mission of ransoming Baldassarre with the 500 florins gained from the sale of the gems, which had actually belonged to the old man. He followed the impulse of the moment, which was to conceal half the facts from his new friends and to convince himself that Baldassarre was by now most likely dead (9.98–100). From this one little lie there developed an ever-expanding web of falsehoods, each new one necessary to protect the previous deception.

Part of this web was Tito's attachment to a simple-minded and affectionate peasant girl, Tessa, whom he pretended to marry in a mimic ceremony at a fair (chap. 14). Unfortunately poor Tessa always believed it was a real marriage and tried to attach herself to Tito at inconvenient times. Later she bore two children by him. 'He had spun a web about himself and Tessa, which he felt incapable of breaking . . . it seemed to him that the web had gone on spinning in spite of him, like a growth over which he had no power' (34.299). Indeed the novel is a fascinating study of how a duplicitous character like Tito becomes ever more deeply entrapped in his own lies until they destroy him. Baldassarre found out that Tito was in Florence and came to the city bent on revenge. When he burst into a dinner party and accused his son of treachery, Tito boldly denied that Baldassarre was his adoptive father, claiming instead that the old man was a former, half-mad servant. At this point we are told that 'he had borrowed from the terrible usurer Falsehood, and the loan had mounted and mounted with the years, till he belonged to the usurer, body and soul' (39.352).

Long before this happened, Tito had become acquainted with Bardo de' Bardi, a now-blind scholar who collected manuscripts and antiquities, and his beautiful, golden-haired, eighteen-year-old daughter Romola, whose 'girlish simplicity and ignorance concerning the world outside her father's books' belied her native refinement and intelligence (5.50, 58). It was not long before Romola and Tito fell in love. They were a study in contrasts: 'the faces just met, and the dark curls mingled for an instant with the rippling gold' (12.121). The mingling was never destined to become a true marriage. Despite a warning from her godfather, Bernardo del Nero, and a dream[6] on the part of her brother, Dino, who had become a priest and was alienated from the family, Romola allowed herself to become betrothed to Tito. They were married at Easter 1493. A year and a half later, after the death of Bardo, troubles were brewing. Tito's 'airy brilliant faculty' was not such as could stir the larger possibilities of Romola's nature: 'they lay folded and crushed like embryonic wings' (27.246). She was startled to discover one day that he was wearing armor – to protect himself against a possible dagger attack by Baldassarre, but of course Tito did not tell Romola the true reason. In fact, in order to secure sufficient funds to flee Florence and insure his own safety, Tito arranged to sell Bardo's library without Romola's knowledge or consent (exercising a husband's legal control over his wife's inherited property). Romola, who above all else had been determined to preserve her father's heritage, flew into a rage and accused Tito of being a treacherous, faithless man.

> Her eyes were flashing, and her whole frame seemed to be possessed by impetuous force that wanted to leap out in some deed . . . She could not care in this moment that the man she was despising as he leaned there in his loathsome beauty – she could not care that he was her husband; she could only feel that she despised him. The pride and fierceness of the old Bardi blood had been thoroughly awaked in her for the first time. (32.285)

You robbed my father, she said. 'Have you robbed somebody else, who is *not* dead? Is that the reason you wear armour?' (32.286). Her words lashed him like a horsewhip; the marriage was irrevocably destroyed.

Romola decided to leave Tito and on Christmas Eve 1494 she fled Florence in the disguise of a Franciscan sister (chaps. 36–7). No sooner was she outside the gates than she encountered Fra Girolamo Savonarola, who recognized her and demanded that she turn back and assume the responsibilities that would be laid upon her in the city (chaps. 40–1). Romola 'was subdued by the sense of something unspeakably great to which she was being called by a strong being who roused a new strength within herself' (40.362). She accepted the call and thus began a new life of service and renunciation. This conversion experience and Romola's ensuing religious vocation will be discussed below. In the meantime Baldassarre had made failed attempts to stab Tito (chap. 34) and expose him before the leaders of Florence (chap. 39); instead he was jailed and Tito thought he was rid of the bothersome old man.

The story jumps ahead to the autumn of 1496. Romola, clad in the black serge of a religious fraternity, was 'in her place' ministering to Florentines who were suffering from pestilence and famine (chap. 42). Tito, by now thoroughly enmeshed in Florentine politics, worked as a triple agent on behalf of the Republicans, the Medicean party, and the Papacy, depending upon which best served his interests at the moment. Among other things he was the agent of a group plotting the assassination of Savonarola. Romola found out about the plot and succeeded in foiling it (chaps. 46–7). Tito now recognized that his wife was not only hopelessly alienated from him but also dangerous, and he determined to leave her and the city as quickly as possible (chap. 48). In the meantime Romola learned from Baldassarre the whole truth about Tito, including the second 'wife' and the two children. Toward Tessa she adopted a caring attitude, for she saw 'the child's mind in the woman's body' (chaps. 53, 56). Romola now had to face the conflict between the demands of an outward law (her marriage vows) and an inner moral fact (that her marriage had become a degrading servitude). 'The law was sacred. Yes, but rebellion might be sacred too' (56.468). She resolved to leave Tito once and for all, with or without his consent.

By the summer of 1497 the ecclesial-political situation was deteriorating. Savonarola had been excommunicated, and in August Romola's godfather, Bernardo del Nero, and four other members of the Medicean party were arrested and in grave danger. Savonarola refused Romola's plea to intercede on their behalf, insisting that his own mission to further God's kingdom on earth weighed more heavily than the lives of five men (chap. 59). Eight days after their execution, a dejected Romola fled Florence for a second time in religious disguise to the fishing village of Viareggio on the Mediterranean (chap. 61). After floating overnight on the sea in a small boat with dreams of death or oblivion, she awakened to find herself near another village where pestilence had decimated the population. Among the survivors was a Portuguese Jewish child whose parents had died during their flight from the Inquisition. Romola took the child, entered the village, organized rescue operations, and remained for several months until the villagers were back on their feet (chap. 68).

When she returned to Florence in April 1498, she learned that momentous events had transpired. During the so-called Masque of the Furies, on Palm Sunday 1498, an enraged crowd dragged Savonarola through the streets, and he was tortured until he confessed his errors (chap. 66). On the same day the leader of the popular party turned against Tito and gave orders to the Compagnacci to dispose of him. Finding himself surrounded, Tito jumped from the Ponte Vecchio and floated down the River Arno to the exact spot where Baldassarre was waiting on the shore, hoping to find scraps of food. Instead he found the semi-conscious Tito and choked him to death (chap. 67). Romola learned as much as she could about Savonarola's confession, and she was present in the Piazza della Signoria on 23 May 1498 when he was degraded, burned, and hanged (chaps. 71–2). She took Tessa and the two children into her household, along with her father's cousin Monna Brigida. In a brief Epilogue set eleven years later, on the eve of the anniversary of Savonarola's death, we find her with a placidity that she had not known in youth, counseling the boy Lillo about life's choices, warning him about a pleasure-seeking man to whom she had once been near, and explaining how she had come to love Fra Girolamo despite his faults (Epilogue, 580–3).

Romola is the only one of George Eliot's heroines to have a novel named for her. In this story there is no corresponding male hero – an Adam Bede, Felix Holt, or Daniel Deronda – who might provide public cover for the female figure. Beyond this one senses a deep affinity between the author and her fictitious heroine,[7] whose name was intended as the feminine form of Romolo, the Italian equivalent of Romulus, the mythical founder of Rome.[8] Linked thus symbolically with 'the city of visible history' (as it is described in *Middlemarch*), Romola was heir to the two great Western traditions of which Rome became the intellectual and spiritual center – the Greco-Roman and the Christian. She had been brought up by her father as a pagan, committed to reason and philosophy and opposed to prostrating herself under what appeared to be a 'dim mysticism.' In her, Renaissance humanism and religious faith clashed and fused, humanism losing its impulse toward hedonism and despair, and faith its impulse toward the miraculous and fanatic. Her brother Dino, finding that philosophy had been of little help when he was in need, turned to religion and became a Dominican friar. He sought a life of perfect love and purity of soul apart from the world, whereas for Romola religion was a force that drove her back into the world (12.127; 15.152–5).

Tito represented a pagan influence of quite a different kind in Romola's life. His amoral hedonism[9] was symbolized by a painting he commissioned from Piero di Cosimo of himself and Romola in the likeness of Bacchus and Ariadne, with Bacchus seated in a ship wreathed with flowers and (in Tito's version of the fable) fair-haired Ariadne by his side, immortalized by her golden crown (18.182–5). The painting was made on a little tabernacle or triptych that Tito presented to Romola on the day of their betrothal. He locked Dino's crucifix, which had come to Romola after her brother's death, inside the triptych in the central space between the two figures, saying that all images of sadness now were buried in a tomb of youth and joy (20.197–9). The cross entombed between the god of ecstasy and wine and his Cretan princess! – this was a symbolic conflict that soon became painfully obvious.

Felicia Bonaparte suggests that the triptych and the cross represent the central myths of George Eliot's poetic imagination.[10] I think there is validity to this insight but I interpret it rather differently than Bonaparte does. It is not that the myth of Bacchus (Dionysius) embodies the essential values and truths of the Greco-Roman world, which must somehow be balanced or harmonized with the values and truths of the Christian world. Tito with his self-gratifying hedonism and genius for lying is scarcely a fair representative of classical culture. Rather what he and his Bacchus myth represent is the tragic fall of human nature into self-centeredness, egoism, excess, or (expressed in Pauline terms) existence according to the flesh. The mythos of the cross represents the only realistic alternative, a way of life oriented to self-renunciation, suffering and service on behalf of the other, a finding of self by losing self, or existence according to the Spirit. By 'realistic' alternative, I mean one that is capable of confronting the ambiguous realities of the world and providing resources to cope with them effectively. The cross properly understood does not entail a turning away from the world in life-destroying self-mortification, as Dino thought – a kind of barren antithesis to

Bacchic revelry. Rather it provides a way of finding life anew within the world, a life that is a profound mixture of joy and sorrow, love and suffering. The religion of the cross is a life-affirming religion, for crucifixion is not an end in itself but the necessary passage to the resurrection of life, its surging forth again, in anguished love.

It is clear that Romola must choose between the triptych and the cross, and it is clear also which of these myths represents the authentic way for the author of *Romola*. In choosing the cross, however, the author and her heroine demythologize it. To demythologize it is not to embrace an atheistic humanism, as Bonaparte suggests, but rather to envision a new form of religious faith. Demythologized, the cross represents not a substitutionary sacrifice of a God-man but a suffering love at the heart of the divine mystery, a mother-like love (61.504) that individuals such as Romola learn to embody in a special way. How this came about we shall now consider.

When Romola discovered that Tito had betrayed her by selling her father's library, we are told that 'Ariadne discrown[ed] herself' (chap. 36). Having determined to leave Florence in the disguise of a religious sister, she hid her golden hair under the cowl, removed her wedding ring, and hung Dino's crucifix around her neck. Thus began her religious conversion from a life of pleasure to one of renunciation and service. She did not yet know what the future held for her. 'No radiant angel came . . . with a clear message for her. In those times, as now, there were human beings who never saw angels or heard perfectly clear messages. Such truth as came to them was brought confusedly in the voices and deeds of men . . . – men who believed falsities as well as truths, and did the wrong as well as the right' (36.324).

The voice of such a man arrested Romola once she left Florence. It was the voice of Girolamo Savonarola (chap. 40). He said he knew that she was seeking, in a false disguise, to escape the lot that God had laid upon her, and he commanded her to return to Florence where duties awaited. He told her to draw forth the crucifix. 'There, my daughter, is the image of a Supreme Offering, made by Supreme Love, because the need of man was great . . . Conform your life to that image, my daughter; make your sorrow an offering: and when the fire of divine charity burns within you, and you behold the need of your fellow-men by the light of that flame, you will not call your offering great.' As a proud daughter of the Renaissance, Romola was as yet unborn to the true life of humanity; she was without love and obligation.

> You are below the life of the believer who worships that image of the Supreme Offering, and feels the glow of a common life with the lost multitude for whom the offering was made, and beholds the history of the world as the history of a great redemption in which he is himself a fellow-worker . . . The higher life begins for us, my daughter, when we renounce our own will to bow before a divine law . . . It is the portal of wisdom, and freedom, and blessedness. And the symbol of it hangs before you. That wisdom is the religion of the cross. (40.359–61)

Surrounded and overcome by Savonarola's passionate faith, Romola asked to be guided and taught, and promised that she would go back (40.362).

And so she did. She became a fellow-worker in the history of redemption. It is too simple to say that she was merely a Comtean heroine who abandoned Savonarola's dogma but retained what seemed useful and right in his teaching.[11] Neither mythical and miraculous elements nor promises of heaven and threats of hell are at the center of Christian faith. Rather at the center is the religion of the cross. This is a religion that knows the divine love to be a suffering, self-sacrificing love, that locates the agony of humanity within the heart of God, and that derives therefrom the strength to endure against overwhelming odds. Without such a religious conviction, it is difficult for an ethic of service and renunciation to sustain itself against cynicism and despair, or against the moderation and irony that prevail in good society. This was the crucial truth that Romola learned from Savonarola, and it helped her to sort out the valid from the invalid elements in his faith, tinged as it was by fanaticism and delusions of grandeur. George Eliot was not an advocate of severing a humanitarian ethic from religious faith, but the faith itself must be reimagined if it is to engender rather than hinder human flourishing.

In her ministry to the sick and starving populace while Florence lay under siege in the autumn of 1496, Romola took on the role of a madonna – not the 'unseen Madonna' of L'Impruneta, whose mysterious hidden image occasionally passed in procession (chap. 43), but a 'visible Madonna' (chap. 44) who was daily present among the people. Piero di Cosimo, who regarded her face and eyes with a painter's admiration, was the first to greet her as 'Madonna Romola,' but he was thinking of her more as 'Madonna Antigone' since he wanted to use her likeness for a painting of Oedipus and Antigone at Colonos (28.254, 257; 18.185). She became a truly religious madonna after her encounter with Savonarola. As she gave bread and wine – a secular eucharist – to an old man lying in the street (who happened to be Baldassarre), the crowd first protested but then drew back with awe when she looked at them and spoke: 'Hunger is hard to bear, I know, and you have the power to take this bread if you will. It was saved for sick women and children. You are strong men; but if you do not choose to suffer because you are strong, you have the power to take everything from the weak. You can take the bread from this basket; but I shall watch by this old man; I shall resist your taking the bread from *him*' (42.375). It was evident that Romola herself had been fasting, and she came to be addressed as 'Madonna' or 'Madonna Romola' (43.377). During her daily ministrations, little children crawled over her, and feeble voices around her said, 'The Holy Virgin be praised!' 'The Mother of God has had pity on us!' 'Bless you, Madonna! bless you!' (44.387). Along with Dinah Morris, Romola de' Bardi was the most explicit of George Eliot's madonna figures, and as such she was a figure of the Christ, who in the author's fictional world appears in many forms: male and female, religious and secular, Christian and Jewish, Protestant and Catholic. Gender, creedal, and ethnic differences are of little significance in this regard.

Romola continued to be inspired by Savonarola, notably his passionate sympathy and moral aims, his indignation at abuses and oppression. His vision of redemption had made her aware of the great drama of human existence in which she had a role to play, a role of self-denying practice. She thought little about his dogmas and his prophecies of scourge and regeneration. She entered into communion with the Church, we are told, 'because in this way she had found an immediate satisfaction for moral needs which all the previous culture and experience of her life had left hungering.' She also found in it religious resources rooted in the symbol of the cross. She needed a reason for living that was fed 'with greater forces than she possessed within herself' (44.388–9). Initially she found the strength she needed primarily through her trust in Savonarola, which was 'like a rope suspended securely by her path' (44.389). Later she had to learn to disconnect her faith from reliance on Savonarola. She became increasingly alienated from his denunciatory exclusiveness, his fanaticism and desire for vengeance, although she continued to be attracted by the energy with which he sought to make the Christian life a reality (52.444; 55.456). In her final interview with him, after his excommunication, she was shocked to learn that he placed his own mission of bringing God's kingdom on earth above the lives of five honorable men, including her godfather. What he described as a complex political calculus seemed to her sophistry and double talk. She asked how, in seeking God's kingdom, he could dare to despise the plea of mercy, justice, and faithfulness to his own teaching. She warned that 'in your visions of what will further God's kingdom you see only what will strengthen your own party.' 'And that is true!' said Savonarola. 'The cause of my party *is* the cause of God's kingdom.' 'I do not believe it,' responded Romola. 'God's kingdom is something wider – else, let me stand outside it with the beings that I love' (59.486–92).

Romola found that wider kingdom when she awoke from a night of despair after fleeing from Florence in August 1497 – her godfather dead, her marriage destroyed, and her trust in Savonarola broken. The awakening occurs in Book 3 of the novel, and it has been pointed out that the third phase in tripartite schemes is generally utopian: the age of the Holy Spirit (Joachim di Fiore), Paradise (Dante), positivism (Comte). The structure of *Romola* resonates with this pattern, but I do not agree that parts of the last book are set outside of time and history in an ahistorical ideal realm where romance triumphs over realism.[12] Rather it is a matter of bringing the utopian into the midst of the real, of realizing the wider kingdom under specific, always difficult circumstances.

Romola was now on her own, her faith no longer dependent on Savonarola or the Church. Her 'faith in the invisible goodness' (61.501) had been shaken but not lost. She drew strength directly from the goodness – the guiding voice within her soul (59.490) – and knew intuitively what must be done. Whereas Savonarola in his sermon spoke of the Israelites in abstract, metaphorical terms, Romola found a Jewish baby alive after his parents had died of pestilence and saved him from certain death.[13] When she entered the stricken village on the Mediterranean coast, word spread that the Madonna with the Babe had appeared, fetching water for the sick. 'She was as tall as the cypresses, and had a light about her head.' To the frightened local priest who had fled to the hills, she said, 'Come down. Do not fear. Fear rather to deny food to the hungry when they ask you' (68.556). She and the priest went down together, comforting those who were still alive and saving most of them. 'The suspicion that Romola was a supernatural form was dissipated, but their minds were filled instead with the more effective sense that she was a human being whom God had sent over the sea to command them' (68.558). She remained with the villagers for several months, and when she began to suffer from fatigue and languor they cared for her in return. We can appreciate how utopian and realistic elements are here inextricably linked. Legends were later told about how the Blessed Lady had come over the sea, 'but they were legends by which all who heard might know that in times gone by a woman had done beautiful loving deeds there, rescuing those who were ready to perish' (68.559). There is indeed a history of redemption, but it is not a miraculous history of divine interventions; it depends rather upon individual human beings who see the good and do it in the specific circumstances in which they find themselves.

As Romola reflected on her experience in the village she realized it was like a 'new baptism' to her, and she said to herself: 'It was mere baseness in me to desire death. If everything else is doubtful, this suffering that I can help is certain; if the glory of the cross is an illusion, the sorrow is only the truer. While the strength is in my arm I will stretch it out to the fainting; while the light visits my eyes they shall see the forsaken' (69.560). In this way (and with abundant biblical imagery) she worked out her own understanding of the religion of the cross and committed herself to the service of suffering fellow beings. She gained a faith in the inner working of a living empowering goodness. As she thought further about Savonarola after her return to Florence, 'it was impossible,' she said to herself, 'that the negative disbelieving thoughts which had made her soul arid of all good, could be founded in the truth of things: impossible that it had not been a living spirit, and no hollow pretence, which had once breathed in the Frate's words, and kindled a new life in her' (71.572). She did not arrive at any clear, articulated conception of divinity; it remained a mystery bespoken only metaphorically or left unnamed.

In the background of this novel hovers the question as to how justice and righteousness are accomplished in human affairs. The doctrine of political realism or *Realpolitik* is represented by Niccolò Macchiavelli, who appears in the story as a young man who had 'penetrated all the small secrets of egoism,' an astute observer of the role of self-interest, ruthlessness, deception, and rhetoric in politics. 'Veracity,' he said, 'is a plant of paradise, and the seeds have never flourished beyond the walls' (16.164–7; 45.393–6). His was not, he insisted, a Satanic doctrine, only the view that the ends justify the means. 'Ask our Frate, our prophet, how his universal renovation is to be brought about: he will tell you, first, by getting a free and pure government; and since it appears that cannot be done by making all Florentines love each other, it must be done by cutting off every head that happens to be obstinately in the way.' Moreover, 'The only safe blows to be inflicted on men and parties are the blows that are too heavy to be avenged' (60.495).

But this is not good enough. It makes of the human condition a war of all against all; it allows unscrupulous means to emasculate righteous ends; it confuses my party's cause with God's cause; it constricts the wideness of the kingdom. In the Proem the novelist tells us that in present-day Florence one sees the same images as of old – 'the images of willing anguish for a great end, of beneficent love and ascending glory.' These things have not changed. 'The little children are still the symbol of the eternal marriage between love and duty; and men still yearn for the reign of peace and right-eousness . . . For the Pope Angelico is not come yet' (Proem, 7–8).

Simple folk once believed that an angelic Pope would bring in a new order of things and purify the Church from corruption (6). These human yearnings are authentic, not something to be dismissed by a cynical politics. On Palm Sunday 1498 Tito was choked to death by Baldassarre while Savonarola was being tortured until he cried out in agony, 'I will confess!' Was justice done on that day? The narrator comments: 'Who shall put his finger on the work of justice, and say, "It is there"? Justice is like the Kingdom of God – it is not without us as a fact, it is within us as a great yearning.'[14]

These words tell us that justice is not a political commodity, not an accomplished fact, not a policy or program to which one can point and say, 'There it is.' Justice has a religious, visionary, utopian aspect; it is like the kingdom of God, the *basileia tou theou*, which is a metaphor of a transfigured order in which the logic of reward, punishment, and self-interest has been broken and replaced by the logic of grace, charity, and self-renunciation. The power of transformation is the power of God, not of weak, alienated, sinful human beings. We humans share in this power by having the basileia vision within us as a great yearning, and from this yearning is generated the sort of practices that make this world a tolerable, perhaps a better, place in which to live. The utopian vision can inspire a humane yet realistic politics; without it people are simply adrift, as Tito was adrift pursuing his own pleasure-seeking interests until his luck ran out. The new order, God's rule, will come not by the miraculous achievement of a Savonarola or a Pope Angelico, or by a bonfire ('the Burning of Vanities') that will 'consume impurity from off the earth' (49.419), but by the daily work of countless human beings, who learn that it will never simply arrive, that it is always both 'now' and 'not yet.'

Savonarola himself had to learn this truth the hard way. He had proclaimed quite a different version of God's justice: it would take the form not of a kingdom of peace but of a sword of vengeance by which God will punish wrongdoing and reclaim the righteous.[15] Of course he regarded himself as the prophet of this sort of justice and as a martyr prepared to suffer for the truth. But while in prison following his forced confession and awaiting execution, he wrote a document in which there was no vindication of his innocence, no protest against the proceedings against him, but only a colloquy with the divine purity – 'no lingering echoes of the old vehement self-assertion, "Look at my work, for it is good, and those who set their faces against it are the children of the devil."' The voice of sadness told him that he who had taught others had failed to learn himself. And when hope argued that the divine love had not forsaken him, it said nothing of a great work still to be done, but only, 'Thou art not forsaken.' The idea of martyrdom had been replaced by resignation. But therefore, thought Romola as she pondered these writings, Savonarola may be more fitly called a martyr. For he sought not to deceive the world but to make it noble, and he suffered a double agony – not only the agony of torture and degradation, 'but the agony of sinking from the vision of glorious achievement into that deep shadow where he could only say, "I count as nothing: darkness encompasses me: yet the light I saw was the true light."' [16]

Romola knew these truths intuitively. They were reinforced by her tragic involvement with Tito, her discovery of the religion of the cross, her mission of caring and mercy in the stricken city and village, and her recognition of the faults as well as the virtues of Savonarola. What Romola accomplished with her life was nothing grandiose and revolutionary, but she did make this earth a better place for those whose lives she touched. In the Epilogue we find her, eleven years later, an independent woman, the head of her household, counseling Tito's son Lillo about his future vocation. She who never bore children (as Monna Brigida reminded her) had become an adoptive mother, imaging perhaps the 'Great Mother' whose milk nourishes humans even if it does not always slacken their thirst (61.504). Lillo was the last of the significant males in Romola's life. The first three had failed her in one way or another: her father had isolated her from the world and burdened her with some of his own blindness; her husband had proved to be a self-serving liar, traitor, and coward; and her priest had confused his own cause with God's cause. Romola was attempting to guide the boy through such pitfalls, to pass on to the next generation the wisdom she had gained from her life experiences. It is not easy, she said, to find true happiness; certainly it cannot be directly sought.

There are so many things wrong and difficult in the world, that no man can be great – he can hardly keep himself from wicked- ness – unless he gives up thinking much about pleasure or rewards, and gets strength to endure what is hard and painful . . . And so, my Lillo, if you mean to act nobly and seek to know the best things God has put within reach of men, you must learn to fix your mind on that end, and not on what will happen to you because of it'. (Epilogue, 582).

That end is the kingdom of justice. Its strange coming, and the strength to endure what is hard and painful until it comes, is another aspect of the mystery beneath the real.

Felix Holt: The Radical

George Eliot's concern with the political and social aspects of justice continued with her next novel, published in 1866. It was written during the debates for the Second Reform Act of 1867, although it deals with events following the First Reform Act of 1832, which extended political representation to large cities like Birmingham and Manchester, but still limited the franchise to male property holders. Whether *Felix Holt* is more a political or an antipolitical novel remains to be seen.[17] It is evident that George Eliot had become more conservative than she was during the early 1850s while working in London for John Chapman. She did not regard the ballot as a panacea for political ills, and she believed that women as well as men must be educated before the franchise is extended to them.[18] In *Felix Holt* George Eliot returned to the familiar territory of Midlands England, and the novel is less ambitious in scope and less successful in execution than *Romola, Middlemarch,* and *Daniel Deronda,* although several themes and characters of the last two works are anticipated in it. Its primary fault, from the point of view of many critics, is its entanglement in legal and political intricacies, and its failure to bring its central figure fully to life. Still, what for George Eliot may have been a relative failure remains a significant work.

The story transpires between September 1832 and May 1833, during a time when the old market town of Treby Magna in North Loamshire,[19] whose character had changed with the coming of mines and manufacturing, was preparing to hold its first election under the reforms enacted the previous June. Harold Transome had just returned to his family estate, Transome Court, near the village of Little Treby, after living abroad for fifteen years, to run for Parliament as a Radical candidate.[20] At about the same time Felix Holt returned to his home, heir to nothing other than his late father's stock of quack medicines, which he quickly disposed of. Felix was a Radical of quite a different sort than Harold, and the story draws out the contrasts between them (*Felix Holt*, 46.445). Harold's Radicalism was utilitarian, compromising, self-serving, and privileged (1.17–22); Felix's was based on integrity, honest labor, opposition to privilege, and moral and educational roots far deeper than the franchise (16.181–2; 27.264). Harold figured that the Radical Party was his best route to political power, and he hired cheap political operatives to insure success by making false promises to the working men (who themselves could not vote but who could cheer for the right candidate), while Felix was a harsh critic of all political hypocrisy and chicanery (chaps. 11, 13, 17).

The third main character in the story is Esther Lyon, the daughter of an eccentric Independent minister, Rufus Lyon. How such an attractive and refined young woman could have had a father so unlike herself is one of several mysteries that has to be unraveled. It seems that her mother was a French woman, Annette Ledru, briefly married to a young Englishman, Maurice Christian Bycliffe, who was Esther's real father. When Rufus found Annette and her baby wandering in the seaport town where he pastored a large Independent congregation, he took them into his home, cared for them, fell in love with Annette, and married her when it was determined that she was a widow. He had to sacrifice his ministry to do so, but when she died a few years later he was able to resume his vocation on a more modest scale, and he reared Esther with loving care (chap. 6). Subsequently we learn that the Bycliffe family had a legal claim to Transome Court with the right of inheriting the estate should the original Transome line fail. Harold Transome's family was not part of that original line; they were distant relations instead (chap. 29). Much of the novel is occupied with the complexities of the laws of inheritance and with the games lawyers play.

Felix became acquainted with Rufus Lyon through his mother, who attended the Independent chapel. He liked the little minister for his quaint looks and ways, and for the honesty and vigor of his views. He assumed that his daughter was probably some Miss Prim in whom he would have no interest. The opposite proved to be the case, and Felix and Esther found themselves attracted to each other despite a great deal of verbal sparring (chap. 5).

On election day riots broke out, stimulated by the liquor made available by Harold Transome's agents. Felix Holt tried to bring the mob under control by leading it out of town. In the process he caused the accidental death of a constable, endangered Treby Manor, and was shot through the shoulder. He was jailed on charges of manslaughter and riotous assault. Trampled to death in the riot was half-witted Tommy Trounsem, the bill-sticker, who in fact was Thomas Transome, the last of the original Transome line (chaps. 31–3).

Shortly thereafter Harold Transome was informed by lawyer Jermyn, who unbeknownst to him was his real father, that an heiress of the Bycliffes was alive and had a legal claim on the estate; and Esther learned from a rival lawyer, Johnson, that she was that heiress (chaps. 35–7). Harold determined, in league with his mother, a gifted woman whose life had been tragically wasted, that the wisest action would be to invite Miss Lyon to visit Transome Court and to seek an amicable resolution of the matter (chap. 38). Esther gladly acceded, and for a while she enjoyed her newly found utopia. Harold concluded that by marrying Esther he could solve his inheritance problems; besides, he found himself attracted to her despite his dismissive and exploitative attitude toward women (chap. 40). Esther began to realize the trap she was falling into. She spoke eloquently in Felix's defense at his trial, then after a climactic night of soul-searching informed Harold that she loved another man and resigned all claim to the Transome estates (chaps. 43–50).

A month or so later Felix was released from prison, his sentence having been commuted through intercession by the magistrates who were moved by Esther's appeal. He was astonished to find that Esther had returned to her father's home. She informed him that she had made a deliberate choice: she did not wish to marry Harold

Transome or be rich. 'Could you share the life of a poor man, then, Esther?' he asked. 'If I thought well enough of him,' she said saucily (51.473). They were married the very next month.

Religion is present in this story through the figure of Rufus Lyon and the spiritual growth experienced by Esther Lyon under the tutelage of Felix Holt, as well as Felix's own experiences and convictions. As for Mr. Lyon, we are told that he was a small modest man who lived in small modest quarters and cared little for worldly opinion. He often was absorbed in thoughts and texts and had to be roused out of his absent-minded meditations to deal with everyday affairs.[21] He was a formidable talker, and neither the rector of the Anglican parish nor his assistant dared to accept his challenge to a debate on the constitution of the true Church (chaps. 23–4). While his ideas were rather quaint and dogmatic – he tended to find evidences of providential arrangement everywhere – he also possessed genuine insight and an incorruptible commitment to truth and justice. When Felix once jokingly remarked that the Glasgow Presbyterians sing different tunes all at once, and that it is a domineering thing to set one tune and expect everybody else to follow it, Mr. Lyon warned him not to play with paradoxes or to be scalded by his own caustic. ''Tis difficult enough to see our way and keep our torch steady in this dim labyrinth . . . The right to rebellion is the right to seek a higher rule, and not to wander in mere lawlessness. Wherefore, I beseech you, seem not to say that liberty is licence.' The minister found himself swept along by the musical analogy into a theological speculation: 'Even as in music, where all obey and concur to one end, so that each has the joy of contributing to a whole whereby he is ravished and lifted up into the courts of heaven, so will it be in that crowning time of the millennial reign, when our daily prayer will be fulfilled, and one law shall be written on all hearts, and be the very structure of all thought, and be the principle of all action' (13.150–1).

This is not far from George Eliot's own vision of a good society in which an incredible diversity of voices contributes to a harmonious whole, and in which the law of justice is written on all hearts.[22] It is the kingdom of justice – an unattainable utopian ideal, to be sure, but one that inspires concrete actions toward relative goods. Later we are told that Mr. Lyon's so-called illusions may in truth have been 'a wider vision of past and present realities,' a vision of how little things fit together into a greater whole.

> We see human heroism broken into units and say, this unit did little – might as well not have been. But in this way we might break up a great army into units; in this way we might break the sunlight into fragments . . . Let us rather raise a monument to the soldiers whose brave hearts only kept the ranks unbroken, and met death – a monument to the faithful who were not famous, and who are precious as the continuity of sunbeams is precious, though some of them fall unseen and on barrenness.[23]

Esther Lyon had to evolve from the 'silly novel' version of a heroine into the responsible and caring human being that she was capable of becoming, and she did so under the guidance of Felix Holt. In this respect the relationship between Esther and Felix anticipates that between Gwendolen Harleth and Daniel Deronda in George Eliot's last novel, although Esther was not as brilliant and complex a creation as Gwendolen was. At the outset Esther is described as a charming, saucy, strong-willed, self-centered young woman who thought it 'quite ridiculous to have a father who was a Dissenting preacher' (6.76–8). She was 'a light-footed, sweet-voiced Queen Esther' (6.78) – an allusion to the biblical Esther, whose adoptive father was named Mordecai, and who, as the wife of a Persian king, was able to save the lives of many Jewish people. She was annoyed that Felix always criticized her and did not appreciate her beauty. He ought to have been a little in love with her, she thought, although he was not suitable as a regular lover. Yet she had to admit that, by challenging her to the high achievements of which he thought she was capable, he was paying her a compliment (10.119–26). She began to see that there was something greater and better in Felix than she had imagined, and she sensed that 'if Felix Holt were to love her, her life would be exalted into something quite new – into a sort of difficult blessedness' (22.228).

Esther began to change, ironically, when she learned the details about her own actual privileged heritage. This information, combined with the humble example of her adoptive father, now turned her against privilege: the 'offending Adam' was being whipped out of her.[24] She could now imagine herself choosing hardship in a life with Felix Holt as the better lot – if only he would ask her. 'The first religious experience of her life – the first self-questioning, the first voluntary subjection, the first longing to acquire the strength of greater motives and obey the more strenuous rule – had come through Felix Holt' (27.261–3, 265).

But Felix did not ask her. He thought he must renounce her for a life of voluntary poverty and service to those in misery. Shortly after he was jailed, the invitation came for Esther to visit Transome Court, and she accepted. 'Her little private Utopia,' we are told, hitherto had been 'filled with delightful results, independent of processes.' But now that her Utopia was actually within grasp, the means to it were painful to contemplate (38.360–1). Was it her destiny to be rich and aristocratic, while Felix's was to be poor and impoverished? How incongruous it would be for her father to live in the lap of luxury (38.362–3). She was becoming aware that the choice of Harold rather than Felix would give 'an air of moral mediocrity to all her prospects.' 'Somehow or other by this elevation of fortune it seemed that the higher ambition which had begun to spring in her was for ever nullified. All life seemed cheapened' (43.307). From her observation of Mrs. Transome's desperate unhappiness, and more generally of life at Transome Court, she had the terrible prescience that she would be 'in a silken bondage that arrested all motive, and was nothing better than well cushioned despair' (49.465). So during a long night of wrestling with her soul, Esther made her decision to renounce wealth and resign all claims to the estate.[25] She did so not knowing whether she would ever again be united with Felix Holt. She came to appreciate the high price of a supreme love. 'It is not true that love makes all things easy: it makes us choose what is difficult' (49.464).

Felix had learned much earlier the necessity of choosing what is difficult. He experienced a conversion during six weeks of debauchery in Glasgow when he sought to turn his life into easy pleasure. The conversion was not inspired by preachers, but it was a religious conversion nonetheless. 'This world is not a very fine place for a good many of the people in it. But I've made up my mind it shan't be the worse for me, if I can help it' (5.62). He determined that he would live as a poor workman, not a middle-class clerk, and contribute what he could to the advancement of education and justice. Later he explained to Esther his life commitments. 'I would never choose to withdraw myself from the labour and common burthen of the world; but I do choose to withdraw myself from the push and scramble for money and position.' Men get involved in the struggle for success 'for a ridiculously small prize.' Moreover, he could not put out of mind 'the life of the miserable – the spawning life of vice and hunger.' 'The old Catholics are right, with their higher rule and their lower. Some are called to subject themselves to a harder discipline, and renounce things voluntarily which are lawful for others. It is the old word – "necessity is laid upon me"' (27.258–60). Echoing the words of Paul in 1 Corinthians,[26] Felix revealed himself very much to be a secular priest with a secular gospel. His 'congregation,' he told Mr. Lyon earlier, was the men at the Sproxton ale-house, and his ministry was educational (5.73). He had taken a vow of poverty and, so it seemed, of chastity (27.263).

His gospel was not unrelated to the Gospel of Christ, but it represented a this-worldly application of it. It took the form of a political philosophy that served as a vehicle of George Eliot's own views. In a brief speech on nomination day, Felix argued that something more radical was needed than universal suffrage, annual Parliaments, and voting by ballot. He hinted that the something more was the wisdom, discipline, education, and conviction to exercise political power responsibly – in other words what was needed was a reform of human nature. Otherwise demagoguery would take control of the electoral process (30.290–4).

Once when he was in a perverse mood Felix remarked to Mr. Lyon that universal suffrage would be equally agreeable to the devil, who would get himself more fully represented in Parliament. The minister had to warn the young man once again not to sport with paradox. 'You will not deny that you glory in the name of Radical, or Root-and-branch man,[27] as they said in the great times when Nonconformity was in its giant youth.' 'A Radical – yes,' responded Felix, 'but I want to go to some roots a good deal lower down than the franchise.' Mr. Lyon concurred with this goal, but expressed his view that 'it is our preliminary work to free men from the stifled life of political nullity, and bring them into what Milton calls "the liberal air," wherein alone can be wrought the final triumphs of the Spirit.' In this debate Mr. Lyon seemed the more earnest political reformer, while Felix doubted whether the liberal air would help very much without spiritual transformation (27.264). The two men were engaging the perennial question: which is more fundamental, the reform of self or the reform of society?

George Eliot came back to this question when she was asked to write an 'Address to Working Men, by Felix Holt' for *Blackwood's Edinburgh Magazine* on the occasion of the passage of the Second Reform Act of 1867, by which the franchise was further extended. The address, which was published in January 1868, is now customarily printed as an appendix to the novel (pages 485–99 of our edition). Here the reform of self seems to take precedence, but society has a fundamental responsibility to nurture the self, and selves must be oriented to the social good, so the relationship between them is dialectical. Felix's basic theme was that for a society to be well off it must be made up of individuals who consider the general good as well as their own. Wisdom and virtue are essential for a healthy body politic. But as a body we are not very wise and virtuous. 'Any nation . . . possessed of much wisdom and virtue would not tolerate the bad practices, the commercial lying and swindling, the poisonous adulteration of goods, the retail cheating, and the political bribery which are carried on boldly in the midst of us' (486). If the franchise is to be an instrument of political reform, it must be exercised wisely and virtuously. The political power bestowed by the franchise requires all the knowledge, ability, and honesty that can be mustered by working men as well as other men (and women?).[28] But the franchise alone will not make us wise. How can society be reformed to make it wiser?

Felix argued that it is advisable to accept certain established social structures rather than to attempt to change them too drastically or quickly, for such change risks the breakdown of order and the rule of the mob. Among these established structures are the reality of class interests, and the role of certain classes in preserving and transmitting the cultural heritage of a society. Rather than attempting to deny or destroy classes, it is better to try to convert class interests into class functions or duties.[29] The task of practical wisdom is to say, not 'This is good, and I will have it,' but 'This is the less of two unavoidable evils, and I will bear it' (495) – a characteristic formulation of George Eliot's meliorism. In light of the selfishness and weakness of human nature, compromises are necessary. The great enemy of the common good is ignorance, which causes and is reinforced by low expectations, poverty, slavery, and superstition. Society must find a way to break this vicious cycle through a program of universal public education. Thus education is the key to true political reform and the essential foundation of democracy; without it democracy is peculiarly vulnerable to propaganda and demagoguery. But education is not a panacea; it can be subverted by self-interest and used as an instrument solely of self-advancement. Wisdom is not necessarily acquired with education.

In his peroration Felix argued that getting the chief power into the hands of the wisest persons is a problem as old as the very notion of wisdom. 'The solution comes slowly, because men collectively can only be made to embrace principles, and to act on them, by the slow stupendous teaching of the world's events . . . Wisdom stands outside of man and urges itself upon him, like the marks of the changing seasons, before it finds a home within him, directs his actions, and from the precious effects of obedience begets a corresponding love.' This outside wisdom 'lies in the supreme unalterable nature of things,' and it often 'wears strange forms, wrapped in the changing conditions of a struggling world' (498).

These words can be read as an indication of George Eliot's realism and conservatism. They are also markers of her idealism and radicalism. For the wisdom that stands outside of human beings is the wisdom of nature and of God, and the work of history is the stupendous pedagogy by which wisdom builds its house within the human heart. Surely the words of Proverbs echo here:

Wisdom has built her house . . .
She calls from the highest place in the town,
   'You that are simple, turn in here! . . .
Lay aside immaturity, and live,
   and walk in the way of insight.' (Prov. 9.1–6)

When wisdom has found a dwelling place within humanity, when it has become fully incarnate, then the kingdom of justice will have come near. Savonarola told Romola that true wisdom is given by 'the religion of the cross,' as opposed to the 'dead wisdom' that leaves one without a heart for the neighbor and without a share in the divine life (*Romola*, 40.361). Wisdom dwells among humanity in the shape of the Jew of Nazareth who proclaimed God's kingdom and was crucified – and in the lives of prophets, saints, and sages of all ages. The wisdom of God, which makes foolish the wisdom of the world (1 Cor. 1.18–25), does not force itself upon humanity by supernatural interventions and demonstrations of power; rather it works its ways by a patient suffering pedagogy whose means are the ordinary events of nature and history.[30] 'Our finest hope is finest memory,' writes George Eliot in the epigraph to the Epilogue (476). The work of wisdom in history has had its redemptive effects; memory of these effects is the basis for a realistic hope.

6

Widening the Skirts of Light:
Middlemarch

Middlemarch is generally regarded as George Eliot's greatest achievement and deservedly so, although *Adam Bede, Romola,* and *Daniel Deronda* also belong among the ranks of great novels. It appeared in 1871–2 after a hiatus of five years since the publication of *Felix Holt,* and it followed a period in which George Eliot had experimented with poetry, producing 'The Spanish Gypsy' and 'The Legend of Jubal' along with other shorter poems. She began work on the novel when she was especially concerned with questions of death and immortality.[1] Asked what she thought of *Middlemarch,* the American poet Emily Dickinson wrote to a cousin, 'What do I think of glory?', and suggested that George Eliot had already 'put on immortality.' She added this enigmatic comment: 'The mysteries of human nature surpass the "mysteries of redemption," for the infinite we only suppose, while we see the finite.'[2] Perhaps the mysteries of human nature are all the greater because they occur in something we actually see; but in any event the mysteries of human nature and the mysteries of redemption are closely linked in this novel, and the latter are of themselves very great. Despite the impression that the first parts of *Middlemarch*[3] were 'melancholy,' George Eliot assured her publisher John Blackwood 'that there is no unredeemed tragedy in the solution of the story.'[4] Earlier she wrote him that her intention was 'to show the gradual action of ordinary causes rather than exceptional, and to show this in some directions which have not been from time immemorial the beaten path.'[5] Thus the mysteries of redemption appear only in and through the mysteries of human nature.

Middlemarch is a complex web of interwoven plots. There are several suggestions within the novel itself that history or human life is an intricate 'web,' an interplay of 'minute causes,' a 'stealthy convergence of human lots'[6] – and this idea is replicated in the rich density of the story in which events interact and seem to conspire to bring about inevitable consequences. The question beneath all that is going on is simply, What does it all mean? The name 'Middlemarch' – a fictitious mid-nineteenth-century provincial town in the Midlands of England – hints that life marches on in the middle of things.[7] The human condition is one of being *in medias res*;[8] and redemption, if it occurs, does so in the midst of the web of life, through 'the gradual action of ordinary causes.'

All of this conspires to make a simple summary of the plot impossible. In fact, there are three main stories or 'three love problems' (as the title of Book 4 puts it) – the triangle of Dorothea Brooke, Edward Casaubon, and Will Ladislaw; the tragic mismatch of Tertius Lydgate and Rosamond Vincy; and the seemingly doomed romance of the childhood sweethearts Fred Vincy and Mary Garth. In addition there are several subplots, especially that of the enigmatic banker Nicholas Bulstrode who gets entangled in all three of the main stories – stories that are themselves interwoven, partly through family connections and partly through fate or destiny.

The central figure in the novel, and the one on whom I shall focus in this chapter, is Dorothea Brooke, perhaps the greatest of George Eliot's heroines and certainly one of the most autobiographical.[9] While not a preacher-woman, Dorothea is a deeply religious figure. She is pointedly compared with Saint Theresa of Avila, the sixteenth-century Spanish mystic whose 'passionate, ideal nature demanded an epic life,' and who 'found her epos in the reform of a religious order' (*Middlemarch*, Prelude, 3). The narrator notes that there have been many latter-day Theresas who have found for themselves no epic life, whose spiritual qualities have lacked a 'coherent social faith and order' in which to find expression. 'Here and there is born a Saint Theresa, foundress of nothing, whose loving heart-beats and sobs after an unattained goodness tremble off and are dispersed among hindrances, instead of centring in some long-recognizable deed' (Prelude, 3–4).

Dorothea was such a Theresa, at least through most of her story. She was a beautiful young woman, not yet twenty years of age, reared by a Swiss Puritan family after losing her parents, now living with her younger sister Celia and her uncle, Arthur Brooke, on his country estate near Middlemarch. Her intense religious feeling produced a spiritual life concerned with eternal consequences rather than the trivialities of dress and ornamentation (1.7–8, 13); she is described at one point as 'a breathing blooming girl . . . clad in Quakerish grey drapery' (19.189). While naive, innocent, and inexperienced, Dorothea was intellectually precocious, her theoretic mind yearning 'after some lofty conception of the world,' her Puritan energy enamored of intensity, greatness, and martyrdom (very much like the young Mary Ann Evans) (1.7–9). She helped the sick, prayed, fasted, read theology, and produced plans for improving the living and working conditions of the tenant farmers on the Middlemarch estates (3.31–2). She told Sir James Chettam, her would-be suitor: 'I think we deserve to be beaten out of our beautiful houses with a scourge of small cords – all of us who let tenants live in such sties as we see round us' (3.31).

Later she told her uncle, who was thinking of standing for Parliament, that 'we have no right to come forward and urge wider changes for good, until we have tried to alter the evils which lie under our own hands' (39.389). As compared with the 'secondary importance of ecclesiastical forms and articles of belief,' her goal was a spiritual religion that represented a 'submergence of self in communion with Divine perfection' (3.35). She had an indefinite desire to make her life greatly effective, and (like Mary Ann Evans) was haunted by the question as to what she could and ought to do with herself. It was clear that her 'ardent, theoretic, and intellectually consequent' nature was not to be satisfied by trivial pursuits, but she found herself hemmed in by a petty social life (3.28–9). Her one sensuous indulgence was horseback riding (at which she was her 'most bewitching'), but she intended to give it up because she thought there were better uses for land than to gallop dogs and horses over it (1.10; 2.17–18). Her sister Celia observed that Dorothea 'likes giving up,' to which Dorothea responded that *liking* giving up 'would be self-indulgence, not self-mortification' (2.18–19). This little exchange anticipates the self-mortification that Dorothea actually practiced much later (chap. 80), during a night of spiritual anguish and rebirth when she gave up what she most cherished and then received an unanticipated abundance.

Not only are Dorothea's spiritual qualities compared by the narrator with the yearning of Saint Theresa for a life 'filled with action at once rational and ardent' (10.86), and with the repose of Saint Barbara 'looking out from her tower into the clear air';[10] and not only did Tertius Lydgate think she had 'a heart large enough for the Virgin Mary' (76.768); but also the painter Adolf Naumann saw in Dorothea 'the most perfect young Madonna,' 'a sort of Christian Antigone – sensuous force controlled by spiritual passion' (19.190). We may recall that Romola too was compared with Antigone by another painter, Piero di Cosimo (*Romola*, 18.185; 28.257). And Dorothea's beauty compared favorably with that of Ariadne (19.188–9), with whom Romola was fatefully linked. Both Ariadne and Antigone played redemptive roles in Greek mythology: Ariadne guided Theseus through the labyrinth with a ball of thread; and Antigone took care of her blind father Oedipus during his self-imposed exile from Thebes; later she was condemned to death for defying the prohibition of Creon against burying her slain brother. The images of guiding, caring, leading the blind suggest that Dorothea had to find her way – and to help others find their way – through the labyrinth of Middlemarch (3.29), just as Romola found her way through the labyrinth of Florence. Thus classical as well as Christian figures contribute (not without inner tension) to the definition of the two heroines.

Given her spiritual idealism and longing for an intellectual conversation partner, it is not surprising that Dorothea was captivated by the Reverend Edward Casaubon. She thought that marrying him 'would be like marrying Pascal,' and that she would then 'see the truth by the same light as great men have seen it by' (3.29). Casaubon was an independently wealthy clergyman, more than twice Dorothea's age, who turned the daily work of his parish over to a curate, reserving for himself the preaching of erudite Sunday sermons. His entire life was consumed by a pretentious and futile search for a 'key[11] to all mythologies' – the notion that all the mythico–religious systems of the world derive from an original, primordial revelation (3.24). Casaubon had accumulated many boxes of notes and was in need of an assistant to sort and organize them.[12] For this purpose marriage to a devoted young woman would serve well. Dorothea for her part wanted nothing more than to help Casaubon bring his great project to fruition, and only much later did she discover its illusory character – 'a mosaic wrought from crushed ruins,' 'a theory which was already withered in the birth,' a fanciful search for the common seed of all traditions, based on conjecture unsupported by fact (48.478).

In an epigraph written for Chapter 51 (p. 497), George Eliot expressed in verse her own view on the unity and differentiation of things (the particular case in hand being that of political parties as compared with nature):

> Party is Nature too, and you shall see
> By force of Logic how they both agree:
> The Many in the One, the One in Many;
> All is not Some, nor Some the same as Any:
> Genus holds species, both are great or small;
> One genus highest, one not high at all;
> Each species has its differentia too,
> This is not That, and He was never You,
> Though this and that are AYES, and you and he
> Are like as one to one, or three to three.

If there is an ultimate unity, it must be such as to preserve otherness and difference within itself, and no totalizing system can capture its complexity or unpack its mystery. This is a theme explored more fully in *Daniel Deronda*. The ethical implications of the One-in-Many are clearer than its metaphysical roots: they seem to entail some sort of transition from self-centeredness to other-centeredness and communal-centeredness. Dorothea understood this intuitively, whereas Casaubon's entire ego was invested in his pretentious project. When it collapsed he died in lonely isolation, having cut himself off from all human relationships, even with Dorothea (10.84–5; 29.278–80).

Casaubon took Dorothea to Rome on their honeymoon so that he could work in the Vatican Library. Tensions began to emerge between them. One day she asked, out of innocence and frustration, 'Will you not make up your mind what part of [your notes] you will use, and begin to write the book which will make your vast knowledge useful to the world? I will write to your dictation, or I will copy and extract what you tell me. I can be of no other use' (20.200). With this question she touched on a raw nerve, his awareness that the project would never be consummated (just as, presumably, the marriage would never be consummated). He responded sharply and withdrew from her physically and emotion- ally. Left on her own, a despondent Dorothea visited the Vatican museums, and there one day she met Casaubon's young cousin Will Ladislaw. Between them there was an instant communication and attraction (chaps. 19, 21).

Dorothea and Will were in most respects opposites: she was reserved, Puritanical, disciplined, idealistic, ethical; he was effu- sive, spontaneous, undisciplined, pragmatic, aesthetic. Above all he was a talker, possessed of a 'passionate prodigality of statement' (37.361). They had fervent conversations about art and painting, duty and enjoyment, religion and life, in which her ethical and his aesthetic sensibility clashed, played, and fused (chaps. 21–2). Will provided a healthy counterbalance to Dorothea's ascetic tenden- cies. She said that she could not enjoy art when she considered that most people are shut out from it; he warned against her 'fanaticism of sympathy.' 'The best piety is to enjoy,' he insisted. 'You are doing the most then to save the earth's character as an agreeable planet. And enjoyment radiates. It is of no use to try and take care of all the world; that is being taken care of when you feel delight – in art or anything else' (22.219). This is not the whole truth, but it is a part of the truth, and a part that Dorothea needed to hear. The reader is forced to ponder: yes, sympathy can indeed become excessive or fanatic; but no, Will does not understand the true character of religious piety, and there is an aspect of Dorothea's life that he will not fully share. On other subjects (social reform, for example) they were in agreement, and in general each forced the other to see things that they were otherwise blind to. Above all there was a powerful sexual attraction between them (certainly something Dorothea never experienced in relation to Casaubon, who was more like a father than a husband). That the sexuality is evoked without any explicit mention of the forbidden subject of sex is one of the remarkable feats of George Eliot's fiction.

The occasional contacts between the two would-be lovers continued after they returned to England, Will having arranged to come to Middlemarch in order to work as an editor for Mr. Brooke's political newspaper. Naturally, Casaubon grew deeply jealous and suspicious. The situation was complicated by his relationship to Will, who was the grandson of his mother's sister. The sister was unjustly disowned by her family when she married a Polish refugee musician, and as a consequence Casaubon inherited a much larger fortune than would otherwise have been the case. Will's impoverished father secured minimal support from Casaubon for his son, but it was an arrangement Casaubon deeply resented. Dorothea, when she learned all of this, made the disastrous mistake of urging Casaubon to include Ladislaw in his will (chap. 37). Instead, failing to secure Dorothea's promise to carry out his specific wishes and to avoid what he deprecated, Casaubon added a codicil to his will the night before he died specifying that Dorothea would be disinherited if she were ever to marry Will Ladislaw (chaps. 42, 48). Dorothea and Will thought they were doomed to a life apart, and they resolved, unsuccessfully, not to see each other again. They could not directly express their feelings, each waiting for signs from the other and misinterpreting what was in the mind of the other (chaps. 54–5) – a common problem in the romantic relationships depicted in George Eliot's fiction.

In order to continue the story, something must be told of the second plot, the second 'love problem.' Tertius Lydgate was a young, idealistic physician who came to Middlemarch with reform on his mind and the intent to make great discoveries, to find the 'primitive tissue.' His plan was 'to do good small work for Middlemarch, and great work for the world' (15.148–9). He and Dorothea might have been suited for each other had she not already been married and he not had rather chauvinist ideas. What he desired in a wife was a woman who would be polished, refined, docile, properly finished in the delicacies of life, and beautiful in a feminine sort of way (15.164). These qualities he thought he had found in Rosamond Vincy, the daughter of a manufacturer, the mayor of Middlemarch. She did indeed possess these qualities, but in addition Rosamond was extraordinarily self-centered and accomplished at getting her own way (27.267–8). Her mild persistence was such as 'enables a white soft living substance to make its way in spite of opposing rock' (36.345). Her goal in marriage was to rise in rank and to attain as much comfort, indulgence, and wealth as possible. She was utterly uninterested in and unsympathetic toward Lydgate's profession as a physician; rather she had her eye on his rich relatives whom she courted. When Lydgate began falling into debt because of Rosamond's extravagant life, she did not hesitate to ask Sir Godwin Lydgate for money and to cancel the arrangements her husband had made to lease their house and move to more modest quarters (chaps. 64–5). Lydgate felt himself powerless and crushed, and their marital relationship was all but dead. Between them there was a 'total missing of each other's mental track' (58.587).

Lydgate's idealism had been destroyed not only by Rosamond but also by the necessity of entering into relationship with the unscrupulous banker Nicholas Bulstrode in order to secure funding for the new hospital he hoped to build (chap. 18). Finally he was driven to borrow money from Bulstrode, and when a poor acquaintance of Bulstrode by the name of Raffles died under suspicious circumstances in the latter's home – an acquaintance who had information about the banker's shady past such as to be able to blackmail him – it was suspected that Lydgate had been complicit. Gossip about Bulstrode 'spread through Middlemarch like the smell of fire' (71.718),[13] and Lydgate was publicly vilified with him. The scandal was felt to be so important that it 'required dinners to feed it,' and the social life of Middlemarch acquired new zest. Rosamond gave credence to the rumors and concluded that her husband was worthless and her own life not worth living (chap. 75). Only Dorothea Brooke (now Mrs. Casaubon) maintained faith in Lydgate's essential goodness. She convinced herself of this through several conversations with him, and promised to help in any way that she could (chap. 76). She contributed to his hospital project, offered to lend him money, and intended to speak with Rosamond about him.

In the meantime Will Ladislaw began visiting Rosamond. He enjoyed making music and flirting with her, and on the day Dorothea called on Rosamond with the intent of speaking on Lydgate's behalf, she found them together in what appeared to be an intimate relationship (chap. 77). Dorothea was shocked into an intense jealousy, discovering feelings that she had not known she possessed; she was not, after all, a perfect saint. She went for a day and a night without food and drink, telling Celia that she was suffering 'all the troubles of all people on the face of the earth' (77.776). At night she subjected herself to physical rigors to ease her spiritual anguish, as men and women have done for ages, and she wrestled in her soul over Will Ladislaw (80.786). At length she slept and awoke to a new condition, feeling that she had been liberated from a terrible conflict.

> In her first outleap of jealous indignation and disgust, when quitting the hateful room [where she had found Rosamond and Will], she had flung away all the mercy with which she had undertaken that visit. She had enveloped both Will and Rosamond with her burning scorn, and it seemed to her as if Rosamond were burned out of her sight for ever. But that base prompting which makes a woman more cruel to a rival than to a faithless lover, could have no strength of recurrence in Dorothea when the dominant spirit of justice within her had once overcome the tumult and had once shown her the truer measure of things . . . She said to her own irremediable grief, that it should make her more helpful, instead of driving her back from effort . . . The objects of her rescue were not to be sought out by her fancy: they were chosen for her. She yearned towards the perfect Right, that it might make a throne within her, and rule her errant will. (80.788)

Morning light began piercing into the room. Dorothea looked out and saw people going about their daily activities. She took off her clothes, bathed, and put on fresh garments. Within a few hours she was under way in her second attempt to see and rescue Rosamond (80.788–90).

What is being described here, with unmistakable religious symbolism, is Dorothea's decisive spiritual transformation, her night of self-mortification and rebirth, her awakening to a new life of generosity and sublimated grief. What she experienced was a kind of amazing grace. Divine providence works not by a calculus of reward and punishment, but by an act of pure self-giving in which no reward is imagined. This is the mystery of redemption, the mystery beneath the real. Our constant tendency is to hold tight, to draw things into ourselves, but the truth is that we must learn to let go, to relinquish, to empty ourselves. In that emptiness is fullness: those who seek to save their life will lose it, those who lose their life will find it.[14] This reversal of values, which is central not only to the message of Christianity but to that of other religions as well, does not entail a weakening but a strengthening of the self. Only persons who experience an influx of new strength, or who are already intrinsically strong, are capable of it. We should avoid the misimpression that George Eliot advocated renunciation and the service of others as the characteristic virtue of the 'weaker' sex. Rather the losing of self on the way to finding self is the fundamental and most demanding condition of human well-being. It requires courage and resolution together with an acknowledgment of true justice and willingness to be ruled by the perfect Right, which is God's Right.

So Dorothea went for a second time to Rosamund, told her that she bore no resentment or anger, and that she had come to talk about the injustice that had been done to Lydgate. She said that he could have borne his trials more easily had he been able to talk about them openly with his wife, whose happiness was uppermost in his mind. Dorothea continued:

> Marriage is so unlike everything else. There is something even awful in the nearness it brings. Even if we loved some one else better than – than those we were married to, it would be no use. I mean, marriage drinks up all our power of giving or getting any blessedness in that sort of love. I know it may be very dear – but it murders our marriage – and then the marriage stays with us like a murder – and everything else is gone.[15]

When Rosamond realized what Dorothea was driving at, she responded quickly:

> You are thinking what is not true. When you came in yesterday – it was not as you thought. He was telling me how he loved

another woman, that I might know he could never love me . . . He said yesterday that no other woman existed for him besides you . . . The blame of what happened is entirely mine. He said he could never explain to you – because of me. He said you could never think well of him again. But now I have told you, and he cannot reproach me any more. (81.798)

Stunned into silence, Dorothea could only say, 'No, he cannot reproach you any more.' Her own generosity and goodness had evoked the best that was in Rosamond, and she received in return an unexpected gift. But for Rosamond the truthfulness came too late: metaphorically she had already murdered her husband – an outcome prefigured by Lydgate's earlier relationship with a married French actress who in a play actually stabbed her husband to death (15.150–3). The unhappy physician once called Rosamond his 'basil plant,' meaning thereby a plant that 'flourished wonderfully on a murdered man's brains.' They continued to live together but left Middlemarch and Lydgate established an excellent practice 'between London and a Continental bathing-place.' He died prematurely of diphtheria, regarding himself as a failure for not having accomplished what he set out to accomplish, and having sold out to values that he abhorred (Finale, 834–5). Rosamond, who remarried a wealthy physician, remained perfectly content with her life. Dorothea and Will were married within a few weeks, she renouncing her wealth and position, he finding his vocation in politics. 'They were bound to each other by a love stronger than any impulses which could have marred it' (chaps. 83–4; Finale, 835–6).

So a resolution to the stories of Dorothea and Will, Rosamond and Lydgate, was accomplished – partial, ambiguous, and ironic, to be sure. Neither Dorothea nor Lydgate attained their vocational goals, and the reader sometimes has the impression that they might have been better suited for each other than for their respective mates. But it was not to be, and rightly so, for Dorothea and Lydgate were too much alike in their drivenness to have formed a healthy relationship. Dorothea's fate was far preferable to Lydgate's, but she chose to sacrifice the wealth with which she might have improved the conditions of workers; and we are allowed to surmise that potentially harmful impulses, due to clashing sensibilities, remained in her relationship with Will despite the strength of their mutual love. She had lost a vocation while he (at last and with her help) had found one. Yet, adds the authorial voice, those who thought it a pity that so rare a woman as Dorothea had been absorbed into the life of another did not indicate exactly what else she might have done (Finale, 836). The question of women's vocation remains unresolved.[16]

Dorothea once discussed with the Reverend Camden Farebrother whether it is possible for people to resist evil or change for the better despite the terrible nemesis at work in human affairs. 'Character is not cut in marble,' said Farebrother, 'it is not something solid and unalterable. It is something living and changing, and may become diseased as our bodies do.' 'Then it may be rescued and healed,' said Dorothea (72.734–5). Farebrother himself brought about such a rescuing and healing. Though himself secretly in love with the irrepressible Mary Garth (whose practical intelligence and wit provided a welcome contrast to the always serious and somewhat ethereal Dorothea), he agreed to serve as an intermediary between Mary and Fred Vincy, assuring their future happiness by helping Fred to mend his irresponsible ways. Mary contributed to this good result by insisting that Fred must grow up before she would consider marrying him; and she foiled the possibility of his receiving an easy inheritance from his uncle. Caleb Garth, her father, saw the good possibilities in Fred and gave him the crucial opportunity of finding a vocation suited to his talents. In so doing he also assured the happiness of his daughter. Caleb once remarked, 'The young ones have always a claim on the old to help them forward. I was young myself once and had to do without much help; but help would have been welcome to me, if it had been only for the fellow-feeling's sake' (56.563). Susan Garth said of her husband that he was 'a father whose good work remains though his name may be forgotten' (40.403). Of the 'three love problems,' Fred's and Mary's turned out the best: they achieved 'a solid mutual happiness' in marriage. Fred surprised everyone by his steadiness and he became an expert in agriculture, while Mary wrote a little book for her boys that was published and well-received (Finale, 832–4).

Of the various clergymen encountered in this story – Mr.

Casaubon, Mr. Cadwallader, Mr. Tyke, Mr. Farebrother – only one of them, Camden Farebrother, manifested genuine human sympathy and wisdom about religious matters. Yet he readily acknowledged that he was 'not a model clergyman – only a decent makeshift' (17.176). He was more interested in botany than in doctrine and was a masterful player (for money) at whist and billiards. But his preaching was 'ingenious and pithy,' and people came to hear him from outside his parish. He was a likeable man, 'without grins of suppressed bitterness . . . which make half of us an affliction to our friends' (18.178). He warned Lydgate against naive idealism: 'You have not only got the old Adam in yourself against you, but you have got all those descendants of the original Adam who form the society around you' (17.173). When Lydgate out of perceived political necessity voted against him for the position of infirmary chaplain, Farebrother maintained a friendly relationship with the physician. He escaped 'the slightest tincture of the Pharisee' (18.187). After Casaubon's death, Dorothea selected Farebrother to take over the vicarage of Lowick. She had no interest in Mr. Tyke, whose sermons about imputed righteousness and apocalyptic prophecies repelled her. She told Lydgate: 'I have always been thinking of the different ways in which Christianity is taught, and whenever I find one way that makes it a wider blessing than any other, I cling to that as the truest . . . It is surely better to pardon too much, than to condemn too much' (50.495). Farebrother found ways to widen the blessing, just as Dorothea sought to widen the skirts of light. Apart from Farebrother the truest ministers in this story are not the clerical men but two strong and sensitive women, Mary Garth and Dorothea Brooke, and one non-clerical man, Caleb Garth.

There were many little acts of kindness, renunciation, and loyalty by which fellow human beings were rescued and healed in a place like Middlemarch. The narrator sums it up this way: 'It is given to us sometimes even in our everyday life to witness the saving influence of a noble nature, the divine efficacy of rescue that may lie in a self-subduing act of fellowship' (82.803). Of course, not all were saved: Casaubon died in a state of bitterness, and Raffles (Bulstrode's nemesis) in a state of debauchery, while Bulstrode left Middlemarch in a state of humiliation. But Harriet

Bulstrode accepted her husband's humiliation without abandoning him. When he came to her with downcast eyes, she said to him, 'Look up, Nicholas.' 'They could not yet speak to each other of the shame which she was bearing with him, or of the acts which had brought it down on them. His confession was silent, and her promise of faithfulness was silent' (74.750).

On the whole, life in Middlemarch went on pretty much unchanged by what transpired with Dorothea and her friends. Such deeds of goodness do seem insignificant and ambiguous, but they have their effect in history. The authorial voice says as much at the end. The determining acts of Dorothea's life were not 'ideally beautiful' but the 'mixed result' of noble ideals struggling amidst imperfect social conditions[17] – conditions that might give 'great faith the aspect of illusion,' and that would have hindered the work of even a new Theresa or a new Antigone. And yet . . .

> Her finely-touched spirit had still its fine issues, though they were not widely visible. Her full nature . . . spent itself in channels which had no great name on the earth. But the effect of her being on those around her was incalculably diffusive: for the growing good of the world is partly dependent on unhistoric acts; and that things are not so ill with you and me as they might have been, is half-owing to the number who lived faithfully a hidden life, and rest in unvisited tombs. (Finale, 838)

The Finale sounds a somewhat different note than the Prelude, which speaks more of 'tragic failure' and of the 'dispersion among hindrances' of a striving after unattained goodness, than it does of the 'incalculably diffusive' effect of Dorothea's life and of 'the growing good of the world.' Perhaps George Eliot discovered something in the writing of the novel that she had not quite anticipated. In any event, I believe that the final words tell us more about God's real presence in the world than all the sermons of glory and triumph, all the naive belief in divine providence and protection. They also hint at a form of subjective immortality to which George Eliot was attracted – the idea that a person's good work remains though his name be forgotten or her tomb unvisited.

There is indeed 'no unredeemed tragedy' in the resolution of the story, but the tragic element remains everywhere present if we look and listen closely enough: 'If we had a keen vision and feeling of all ordinary human life, it would be like hearing the grass grow and the squirrel's heart beat, and we would die of that roar which lies on the other side of silence' (20.194). To hear the sound of redemption above the roar of tragedy is the special gift of George Eliot's artistry.

The anonymity of Dorothea's life, the fact that her deeds had a diffusive effect and secured for herself no historical fame, is characteristic of many of George Eliot's heroines and heroes. Perhaps it reflects the hiddenness and anonymity of divine presence in history, and it demands of observers a recognition of what constitutes true heroism. In a letter to Sara Sophia Hennell, Mary Ann Evans once commented on 'that most beautiful passage in Luke's Gospel – the appearance of Jesus to the disciples at Emmaus.' He appeared incognito, and the despondent disciples came to recognize him only in the breaking of the bread (Luke 24.13–35) – that is, in an action that replicated and extended his good work. 'Then comes another Jesus,' wrote the future author, 'the same highest and best, only chastened, crucified instead of triumphant – and the soul learns that this is the true way to conquest and glory – And then there is the burning of the heart which assures that "This was the Lord!" that this is the inspiration from above – the true Comforter that leads into truth.' A comparable burning of the heart often occurs in the reading of George Eliot's fiction as we discover in those who lived faithfully a hidden life figures of the Christ and witnesses to the truth.[18] Reference to 'the Comforter' suggests that what is required is a spiritual discipline and guidance by the Spirit, which is usually hidden from the everyday world and confounds worldly criteria.

Dorothea had a core religious belief, which she once shared with Will Ladislaw: 'That by desiring what is perfectly good, even when we don't quite know what it is and cannot do what we would, we are part of the divine power against evil – widening the skirts of light and making the struggle with darkness narrower.' When Will characterized this as a 'beautiful mysticism,' Dorothea responded, 'Please not to call it by any name . . . It is my life. I have found it out, and cannot part with it. I have always been finding out my religion since I was a little girl. I used to pray so much – now I hardly ever pray. I try not to have desires merely for myself, because they may not be good for others, and I have too much already.'[19] Dorothea's mission in life was to widen the skirts of light a bit, knowing that the struggle with darkness would go on indefinitely.[20] She did not say that the divine power against evil would triumph, but she knew we must make ourselves a part of it, working for the better,[21] for 'mixed results,' even when we do not quite know what the best is or how to accomplish it. This is not a beautiful, otherworldly mysticism but a concrete way of life, a spirituality oriented to reality and the mystery beneath it. It entails not so much prayer as it does a turn away from self-centeredness to the needs of others.

A modern critic has analyzed this passage at length. He concludes that Dorothea could not have really believed that we are part of the *divine* power against evil. 'No longer able to pray to an "other-worldly" Power, Dorothea, like George Eliot herself, must do the next best thing and abstract Christianity into "ethics heightened."'[22] The assumption seems to be that divine power must manifest itself as 'other-worldly' rather than as an inner-worldly power that works against evil, which is what the novel depicts. The text does not say that Dorothea was no longer able to pray, only that now she rarely prayed. Her religion had evolved to a form in which prayer was no longer central. Perhaps the problem with prayer from George Eliot's perspective was its tendency to be self-serving, to express *my* needs and desires at the expense of a larger perspective.[23] But it should not be concluded from this that Dorothea had replaced her belief in the divine power against evil with belief in human power. The key religious insight is that a power greater than human power is needed to break the idolatry of self-securing and self-aggrandizement, the source of all evil. Human power is just another idol, as is 'ethics heightened.' This is where the illusion lies, not with faith in God's power. But the latter is not something that is exercised miraculously from above in the form of a supernatural causality; rather it is mediated through that human power which knows *itself* to be powerless, to be filled by a power not its own. The Christian symbol for the breaking of all idolatry is the cross, which is rarely mentioned in this novel, with one noteworthy exception: Dorothea refused to wear a cross as a 'trinket' (1.12). Her life, not her jewelry, was cruciform.

The theological and philosophical question beneath the surface of this story concerns the meaning of history and the nature and efficacy of divine purpose in history. Popular views of divine providence are expressed and criticized at several points in the novel. The narrator observes, 'What can the fitness of things mean, if not their fitness to man's expectations? Failing this, absurdity and atheism gape behind him' (14.134). In other words, providence is something that people arrange out of their own egoism and to their own advantage, just as a lighted candle as a center of illumination produces the flattering illusion of a concentric arrangement of fine scratches in a surface of polished steel (27.264). Thus 'Rosamond had a Providence of her own who had kindly made her more charming than other girls, and who seemed to have arranged Fred's illness and Mr. Wrench's mistake in order to bring her and Lydgate within effective proximity' (27.264). Similarly, providence supplied Casaubon with the wife he needed (29.279), and Fred expected providence to take care of his financial needs (36.343).

The most egregious example of such a belief was that of Nicholas Bulstrode, who thought himself guided by providence to enhance his own glory and profit at the expense of God's enemies; but ironically in his case providence also demanded of him an act of propitiation to atone for his admitted wrong-doing (53.519–25; 61.615–22). Bulstrode is a fascinating instance of a man who lived by a tortured Calvinist code that justified a double existence: morality in private life, immorality in business practices. The banker had a strange notion of 'sacred accountableness,' which required him to give close attention to the morals of Middlemarch and to point out other people's errors while rationalizing his own behavior (13.126–8). He was convinced that no one could surpass him in exalting God's cause, which required using God's enemies (the damned) as instruments for putting profits into the hands of God's servants (the elect). The narrator notes that such reasoning is typical of those who use 'wide phrases for narrow motives.' 'There is no general doctrine which is not capable of eating out our morality if unchecked by the deep-seated habit of direct fellow-feeling with individual fellow-men' (61.619).

Bulstrode's shady past gradually came to light (chaps. 53, 61). He once worked for an unethical London pawnbroker who sold stolen goods. When the pawnbroker died, Bulstrode married his wife and inherited his wealth. His step-daughter Sarah ran away from home because of her father's unethical business, and when Bulstrode later learned her whereabouts he did not share this information with his wife, who assumed her dead. Sarah happened to be the mother of Will Ladislaw. When his wife died Bulstrode became a very wealthy man, moved to Middlemarch, remarried and started a new life; and Sarah and her son did not receive what was rightfully theirs. When all of this became known in Middlemarch through Raffles, Bulstrode was humiliated and driven from town, a classic instance of a man who had calculated the providential odds too closely. We are told that he was not a coarse hypocrite but 'simply a man whose desires had been stronger than his theoretic beliefs, and who had gradually explained the gratification of his desires into satisfactory agreement with those beliefs' (61.619).

Regarding the motives that moved Bulstrode to the attempted restitution of a portion of Ladislaw's inheritance and to help Lydgate out of financial difficulty – namely the fear of divine wrath, and the hope that God might save him from the consequences of his own wrong-doing – the narrator comments: 'Religion can only change when the emotions which fill it are changed; and the religion of personal fear remains nearly at the level of the savage' (61.620). Bulstrode was in fact a fearful man, uncertain of his standing among the elect. Another sort of savagery, bred of appetite as much as fear, manifested itself in funeral practices when relatives gathered, as Peter Featherstone's did, ostensibly to mourn the departed, but in reality to prey upon the possessions of the departed, competing with each other like vultures (35.331). These 'Christian Carnivora,' as the author satirically describes them, along with most other professed Christians in Middlemarch, made a mockery of the religion of the cross.

Such views and practices contributed to the civil religion of

Middlemarch. The novel powerfully depicts the de facto secularism of modern culture. Religion had for the most part lost its
vitality, its ability to integrate all aspects of life. Instead it had been
reduced to routinized custom, a social game, a means of achieving
one's privates ends or justifying one's actions. People were religious out of fear and calculation rather than joy and thanksgiving.
They were driven by an unreflecting egoism rather than by love of
God and neighbor. Instances of this utilitarian religion are found
throughout the novel. For example, Sir James Chettam thought
that the excess religiousness alleged against Dorothea would die
out in marriage, leaving just a delightful cleverness (2.21–2). By
contrast, Mrs. Cadwallader, wife of the rector, thought that
Dorothea's 'air of being more religious than the rector and curate
together' was attributable to a deeper disease than anyone had
suspected, and would not easily be eradicated (6.61). Mr. Brooke
encouraged the marriage of his niece to Mr. Casaubon because the
latter was certain to be a bishop. 'That was a very seasonable
pamphlet of his on the Catholic Question: – a deanery at least.
They owe him a deanery' (7.66). The males of the professional
class at Mr. Brooke's dinner party, amusing themselves with a bit
of theology, debated whether the coquetry in women is attributable to providence or the devil (10.89). The casual way religion was
talked about indicated that 'the time was gone by for guiding
visions and spiritual directors' (10.86). The churches seem to
have become largely dysfunctional and institutional religion irrelevant other than as a bellwether of prevailing mores. Most
Middlemarchers lacked even the slightest understanding of what
Dorothea's religiousness was about, and she found herself isolated,
unable to converse with anyone about her beliefs. Ladislaw,
Lydgate, and Farebrother were sympathetic but did not fully
comprehend.

Divine purpose and providence have nothing to do with personal interests or with a calculus of reward and punishment. To
think of them as connected with the enhancement of selfish ends is
an utter perversion of what is really involved, for providence works
against the interests of individuals, appearing through acts of self-
renunciation, generosity, sympathy, and charity. The divine idea
(the idea of freedom, justice, love, reconciliation) *cuts across* human

passions, requiring a realignment of the latter.[24] Events and deeds have inexorable consequences, which belong to the moral order of things. In George Eliot's view, God does not interrupt this order to achieve particular results or to express anger, revenge, or approbation. Rather God created the order in such a way that the skirts of light are widened by deeds of disinterested goodness and narrowed by deeds of self-aggrandizement. In and of themselves, the events of history are like the random scratches on the surface of polished steel (27.264). These events have to be constructed and construed into meaningful patterns by human ideals, values, and goals. The ethical and religious character of these construals makes all the difference as to the concrete quality of the world in which we live: do events flatteringly fall into a concentric arrangement around ourselves, or do they take on a trajectory toward the common good? So the primary responsibility for making something of history is a human one.

But the question remains as to how the *divine power* against evil (to which Dorothea referred) actually manifests itself. Is God efficaciously present in the midst of the struggle? Does God lend strength and resolve to those who seek the good? Does God suffer along with human beings as they are stretched and sometimes broken on the rack of history? Without divine power, presence, sympathy, guidance, is it really possible for human beings to overcome their natural tendency to battle each other in the struggle for survival and supremacy? Egoism is the most powerful of human drives and seems to require a more-than-human power to break it – seems to require something ultimate in being and value that is not just another idol, a radiance that outshines every human light. These are questions that remain largely unanswered by *Middlemarch*. Its work, brilliantly accomplished by the use of irony, is principally deconstructive.

7

Finding the Pathways: *Daniel Deronda*

Daniel Deronda approximates *Middlemarch* in breadth and depth of vision and picks up several of its unfinished themes, although it is a very different sort of story. Above all, it continues George Eliot's engagement with questions of historical meaning, ethical universals, and divine providence, bringing them to a more successful resolution. Scattered hints in *Middlemarch* of a concern over prejudice against Jews[1] rise to a central motif in *Daniel Deronda*, which moves from a study of English provincial life to that of an alternative culture. Microscopic, anatomical images in *Middlemarch* become telescopic and astronomical in *Daniel Deronda*, suggesting that the novelist is engaged in not only the dissection of human feelings and thoughts but also the tracking of cosmic-historical trajectories. Gwendolen Harleth combines elements of Maggie Tulliver, Esther Lyon, Dorothea Brooke, Mary Garth, and even Rosamond Vincy into a complex and fascinating character. Daniel Deronda recalls aspects of Dinah Morris, Felix Holt, and Dorothea Brooke, while Mirah Lapidoth is similar to Dinah in her 'simple' faith (although she is a much less well-developed character). Mordecai Cohen's passion for the divine unity, deeply rooted in Jewish history and spirituality, starkly contrasts with Casaubon's abstract key to all mythologies.[2] When *Daniel Deronda* was published in 1876, George Eliot was at the peak of her fame, although the novel's controversial subject matter made it less of a critical and commercial success than *Middlemarch*.[3]

The English portion of the novel is set amongst landed estates in Wessex[4] and fashionable parts of London, while the Jewish portion is located mostly in the Jewish quarter of London. A few scenes transpire on the European Continent. The time frame is 1864–6,[5] which corresponds to the ending of the American Civil War, and several allusions are made to the war. In one of the most pointed, the narrator contrasts Gwendolen's petty preoccupations with her social life with the drama of a great ideological and political struggle, a struggle in which 'the universal kinship was declaring itself fiercely' and men died bravely in a common cause. This was 'a time when the soul of man was waking to pulses which had for centuries been beating in him unheard, until their full sum made a new life of terror or joy.'[6] The struggle to end slavery and to combat oppression and prejudice against people of color (including those in colonies of the British Empire),[7] provides part of the historical background for this novel, which focuses on the oppression and prejudice directed against the people of Israel,[8] while at the same time it offers a brilliant satire and scathing critique of British upper-class life.

While *Daniel Deronda* is composed of two interwoven plots, one involving the English gentry, the other the culture of Judaism, the main story line is fairly easy to summarize. It opens with Daniel Deronda observing a beautiful young English woman gambling away her money at a German spa. When she was called home unexpectedly because of a family financial crisis, she pawned her necklace for return fare; upon an impulse, Deronda purchased it and returned it to her anonymously. The young woman, Gwendolen Harleth, is one of George Eliot's most brilliant creations. Witty, smart, charming, vivacious, egocentric, and driven, she was full of the youthful love of life. As she and her cousin Rex Gascoigne rode horses on a fine winter day, we are told that 'the freshness of the morning mingled with the freshness of their youth; and every sound that came from their clear throats, every glance they gave each other, was the bubbling outflow from a spring of joy. It was all morning to them, within and without' (*Daniel Deronda*, 7.68). Rex was smitten by his beautiful cousin, but she cruelly rejected his advances, and as her story moved from morning to noon it took a tragic turn. She consented to marry Henleigh Mallinger Grandcourt for money rather than love, even though she knew that he had a son and daughter by a former mistress to whom he was morally obligated. The motives that drove Gwendolen into this disastrous relationship (principally the loss of her own family's fortune), and the rationalizations by which she justified what she knew to be an unethical decision, are described in fateful detail. As she reflected, prior to her wedding day, that she was about to do what had earlier seemed repulsive, her 'disregarded religious teaching' flooded back to tell her that something awful and in-exorable was about to happen, something 'with the taint of sacri-lege upon it, which she must snatch with terror' (28.311–12).

Gwendolen thought that she could master Grandcourt but dis-covered the opposite to be true: soon she was reduced to a passive shadow of her former self, her brilliant repartee silenced into seething submission. Her youthful inexperience – she was scarcely twenty-one – proved no match for the suave brutality of a man fifteen years her senior. She realized she had been 'brought to kneel down like a horse under training for the arena.' Grandcourt 'meant to be master of a woman who would have liked to master him, and who perhaps would have been capable of mastering another man' (28.320). We are reminded of how the mastering of women is described in 'Mr Gilfil's Love Story' and 'Janet's Repentance.' When Grandcourt, knowing of his wife's secret attraction to Daniel Deronda, attempted to arouse Gwendolen's suspicions about the propriety of Deronda's relation with another woman, Mirah Lapidoth, she confronted him angrily for the first time during their marriage, but he mocked her attempt to negate the rumor by speaking directly with Mirah. He then ordered her not to visit Mirah again. "'As my wife, you must take my word about what is proper for you . . . What do *you* know about the world? You have married *me,* and must be guided by my opinion." . . . He knew the force of his own words. If this white-handed man with the perpendicular profile had been sent to govern a difficult colony, he might have won reputation among his contemporaries' (48.593–4). In this way Grandcourt's governance of Gwendolen is linked with the ruthless efficiency of British colonial policy. The near-destruction and final restitution of Gwendolen Harleth are rendered with extraordinary psychological insight and make this novel a major contribution to feminist literature – an aspect of it that I cannot discuss here.

Deronda lived on a nearby estate with his guardian, Sir Hugo

Mallinger, Grandcourt's uncle. Worthy of the biblical name he bore, that of the prophet Daniel, he became a kind of spiritual counselor to Gwendolen, helping her to bear up under her misery and to reorient herself to larger human purposes. A decisive conversation occurred on New Year's Day 1866, less than two months after Gwendolen's marriage. When she acknowledged that her life was 'like a dance set beforehand,' that 'the world is all confusion to me,' he told her that the curse of her life had been to expend itself in the narrow round of personal desires. 'What sort of earth or heaven would hold any spiritual wealth in it for souls pauperised by inaction? . . . We should stamp every possible world with the flatness of our own inanity – which is necessarily impious, without faith or fellowship. The refuge you are needing from personal trouble is the higher, the religious life, which holds an enthusiasm for something more than our own appetites and vanities'.[9] This conversation had a powerful impact on both Gwendolen and Deronda: they were silent for a moment 'as if some third presence had arrested them' – a hallowed presence, for the moment marked the beginning of Gwendolen's conversion from self-centeredness and of Deronda's role as priest, mentor – and potential lover.[10] It became clear that Daniel, dark and handsome, and Gwendolen, fair and beautiful, were passionately attracted to each other despite their marked differences, but at the same time Deronda had become involved with another young woman whom he rescued from suicide by drowning. She was Mirah Lapidoth (who used the name of her Polish ancestors instead of her English surname, Cohen), a Jewess, a talented musician, a woman of delicate beauty, pure soul, and devout faith who was fleeing from a tyrannical father and had despaired of finding her long-lost brother, Ezra Mordecai Cohen. While she appeared childlike (she was not more than eighteen or nineteen), it was not from ignorance, for she had experienced the cruelty of life at first hand. As it happened, Deronda discovered Mordecai in a London pawnbroker's shop and was able to reunite brother and sister. Mordecai was a Jewish sage and mystic, modeled on Judah Halevi, a medieval Spanish poet and philosopher with whom George Eliot was well-acquainted.[11] He initiated Deronda into the history, theology, and spirituality of Judaism, adopting the young man as his disciple and successor.

Deronda eventually discovered from his mother his own Jewish identity[12] and resolved to marry Mirah rather than Gwendolen, whose husband drowned in a boating accident off the coast of Genoa, a drowning for which Gwendolen held herself partly responsible. Even after his decision for Mirah, Deronda remained aware that his feeling for Gwendolen was unlike that for any other woman. Mirah was aware of the hold Gwendolen had on the man with whom she too had fallen in love, and this gentle woman experienced jealousy, even though the idea that Deronda might actually choose her rather than Gwendolen never entered her mind (chaps. 52, 61). In the final anguished scenes between Daniel and Gwendolen, the latter underwent a kind of death and rebirth, conquering her guilt, accepting her loss of Daniel, resolving to live and to become a better person. 'Do not think of me sorrowfully on your wedding-day,' she wrote him. 'I have remembered your words – that I may live to be one of the best of women, who make others glad that they were born . . . I only thought of myself, and I made you grieve. It hurts me now to think of your grief. You must not grieve any more for me. It is better – it shall be better with me because I have known you' (70.810). Shortly thereafter, Mordecai died and Daniel and Mirah set out for the East on the vague mission of finding a homeland for the Jews.

The repentance and regeneration of Gwendolen Harleth follow a now-familiar pattern. Like Caterina in 'Mr Gilfil's Love Story,' she once thought of murdering her hateful husband and even concealed a knife in her dressing case, but never used it (56.691). Grandcourt took Gwendolen on a yachting expedition to the Mediterranean to punish her for her indiscretions with Deronda. While the yacht was being repaired in Genoa, they went out for an evening sail in a small boat (chaps. 54–5). The inexperienced Grandcourt was knocked overboard by the sail as he came about in a gust of wind. Gwendolen's immediate thought was to wish him dead, and she hesitated for an instant before throwing a rope. She was convinced that she was responsible for his death and had repeated visions of his dead face, which surfaced next to her as she leapt into the water in a belated attempt at rescue. Much earlier we learn that Gwendolen had an instinctive terror of dead faces, a terror that revealed her liability to fits of spiritual dread, her awareness of mortality and fatality, and perhaps even her remorse at having once strangled her sister's pet canary (3.25–7; 6.60–4). Now she was racked by guilt and self-condemnation. She confessed everything about her relationship with Grandcourt to Daniel Deronda, who by an unlikely coincidence was in Genoa at the same time for an interview with his mother, thus foiling Grandcourt's attempt to remove Gwendolen from his presence. He assured her that even if she had thrown the rope instantly, Grandcourt would most likely have drowned since he was not a swimmer. Gwendolen, not knowing of Deronda's attachment to Mirah, pleaded with him never to forsake her and to remain near her. She was acutely aware that if she had not foolishly married Grandcourt she and Daniel might have been lovers. But it was too late, she thought: she had sinned herself away from a possible life with him (chaps. 56–7). The brilliant, self-confident young woman who had showed off her skill at archery a year earlier had been turned into a 'crushed penitent' (58.705).

Deronda faced a dilemma: he was in love with two women, both of whom had need of him. Had all of this happened little more than a year ago, he was certain that he would have chosen Gwendolen. 'But now, love and duty had thrown other bonds around him, and that impulse could no longer determine his life' (65.765). Still, he had a 'compassionate yearning,' an 'aching pity,' for Gwendolen, and he resolved to help her as best he could. When he next saw her after their return to England he said to her:

What makes life dreary is the want of motive; but once beginning to act with that penitential, loving purpose you have in your mind, there will be unexpected satisfactions – there will be newly-opening needs – continually coming to carry you on from day to day. You will find your life growing like a plant . . . This sorrow, which has cut you down to the root, has come to you while you are so young – try to think of it, not as a spoiling of your life, but as a preparation for it . . . You have had a vision of injurious, selfish action – a vision of possible degradation; think that a severe angel, seeing you along the road of error, grasped you by the wrist, and showed you the horror of the life you must avoid. And it has come to you in your spring-time. Think of it as a preparation. You can, you will, be among the best of women, such as make others glad that they were born. (65.769)

These words had a transformative effect on Gwendolen, but she interpreted them as having reference to the possibility of a future relationship with Deronda. 'Mighty Love had laid his hand upon her; but what had he demanded of her? Acceptance of rebuke – the hard task of self-change – confession – endurance' (65.771). She must make such changes before she would be worthy to marry him. Gwendolen's expectation was understandable since from the beginning the relationship between herself and Deronda had been suffused by a powerful sexuality. By contrast, sex seemed to be absent from his relationship with Mirah. The story does not make an entirely convincing case for Deronda's choice, which was more ethical and vocational than it was emotional: duty prevailed over feeling.

Nonetheless his last and most difficult task was to disabuse Gwendolen of her false hope, to prepare her for a life in which love and loss would be inseparably joined. In their final meeting he told her about his Jewish identity, his friendship with Mordecai, his sense of mission regarding Israel, and finally his love for Mirah (chap. 69). These words came as successive shocks to Gwendolen. 'She was for the first time feeling the pressure of a vast mysterious movement, for the first time being dislodged from her supremacy in her own world . . . Here had come a shock which went deeper than personal jealousy – something spiritual and vaguely tremendous that thrust her away, and yet quelled all anger into self-humiliation.'[13] This was Gwendolen's night of self-mortification and rebirth, her encounter with 'that judgment of the Invisible and Universal which self-flattery and the world's tolerance would easily melt and disperse' (64.763). As she and Daniel gave each other a parting kiss, she said through her sobs, 'You have been very good to me. I have deserved nothing. I will try – try to live. I shall think of you. What good have I been? Only harm. Don't let me be harm to *you*. It shall be the better for me – ' (69.806). Later, in her mother's presence, she repeated again and again, 'I shall live. I shall be better.'[14] Gwendolen's future is left open, and she must face a new and painful beginning alone, without the companionship of the man she loved. Earlier she had had a sense of 'vastness in which she seemed an exile;' she had suffered from a 'world-nausea' and saw no reason why she should wish to live (6.64; 24.272). Now she was determined to live, and the reader has reason to hope that she will succeed at being better, at finding purpose and perhaps even some new happiness. As Barbara Hardy suggests, this is 'an ending which leaves us with a true sense of life's difficulties and their full complexity and toughness.'[15] Unlike most of George Eliot's other novels, *Daniel Deronda* does not provide an epilogue or finale with a glimpse into the future life of the protagonists. Yet the epigraph to the final chapter hints that endings are also beginnings, pregnant with new possibilities. 'In each of our lives harvest and spring-time are continually one, until Death himself gathers us and sows us anew in his invisible fields.'[16]

Aesthetic and ethical images are woven together in the fabric of the story, which opens with Daniel Deronda wondering whether Gwendolen was 'beautiful or not beautiful.' 'Was the good or the evil genius dominant' in her glance? Probably the evil, he thought, since he felt a certain unrest and coercion as he gazed upon her (1.7). Gwendolen possessed undeniable beauty of form and figure, but she had to learn to acquire beauty of character or moral beauty. Through the cruelty imposed on her by Grandcourt she discovered that there was such a thing as moral repulsion and that it could make beauty more detestable than ugliness; thus she could not appreciate the beauty of the Genoese sea because of her repulsion from him (54.670–1). Beauty alone was insufficient; it must be conjoined with goodness, as it was with Mirah, for whom truth and beauty were one and the same (37.466). Mirah was an artist, a gifted singer, whereas Gwendolen lacked the discipline necessary for artistic accomplishment, which entails ethical commitment as well as aesthetic talent. The musician Klesmer reminded her that the life of the true artist is the highest and most difficult calling, with little monetary reward, only a long and difficult apprenticeship (23.253–6). Beauty and goodness together constitute moral beauty or *love*,[17] and love is the beauty of holiness, the beauty of the Lord (cf. Ps. 27.4). Such beauty appears to be the *nisus* of history for George Eliot, its convergence along a multitude of pathways and through endless sufferings upon an inexhaustible, inexpressible, harmony of differences – the divine Unity at the heart of Jewish faith, for which both aesthetic and ethical images are invoked in the Hebrew Bible and subsequent Jewish writings.

The recent publication of George Eliot's *Daniel Deronda Note-books* makes clear the extraordinary lengths to which she went to immerse herself in the history, life, literature, and thought of Judaism. She visited synagogues, learned Hebrew, and read broadly in ancient, medieval, and modern Jewish literature, with a special interest in the mystical writings of the Kabbalah, thereby supplementing her knowledge of and love for the Hebrew Bible acquired in youth.[18] Her earlier engagement with the thought of Spinoza and translation of two of his major works had a formative influence. Her interest in the idea of Jewish nationalism sprang from her friendship with Emanuel Deutsch, whom she first met in 1866; he gave her lessons in Hebrew and served as a model for Mordecai.[19]

In a letter to Harriet Beecher Stowe, George Eliot explained quite explicitly her purposes in writing *Daniel Deronda*:

> Precisely because I felt that the usual attitude of Christians towards Jews is – I hardly know whether to say more impious or more stupid when viewed in light of their professed principles, I therefore felt urged to treat Jews with such sympathy and understanding as my nature and knowledge could attain to. Moreover, not only towards the Jews, but towards all oriental peoples with whom we English come in contact, a spirit of arrogance and contemptuous dictatorialness is observable which has become a national disgrace to us . . . Towards the Hebrews we western people who have been reared in Christianity, have a peculiar debt and, whether we acknowledge it or not, a peculiar thoroughness of fellowship in religious and moral sentiment.[20]

The 'spirit of arrogance and contemptuous dictatorialness' of the English upper classes is brilliantly depicted in this novel, and the cause of a Jewish national home is embraced by it. But the last sentence of the letter may provide a clue as to why she seemed so motivated to acquire an understanding of Judaism: she found in it a fellowship of religious and moral sentiment. Daniel Deronda is partly George Eliot finding her own spiritual identity. She did not

convert to Judaism, perhaps because of her appreciation for its
'separateness,' its distinctive national, ethnic, and cultural genius.[21]
Nor did she, like Deronda, depart for the East, although she and
G. H. Lewes had considered such a trip in 1874.[22] But she was
drawn to the spirituality of Judaism, its communal ethos, its ethical universalism, its sense of divine presence and historical process.
By avoiding the triumphalism and absolutism of much Christian
theology, Judaism offers a more realistic, less dangerous assessment of history. The Messiah has not yet come, there is no single
way to God, and redemption occurs as an ongoing, unfinished
process in a diverse and pluralistic world.

   To be sure, the connection between Judaism and Christianity is
long and deep. Deronda observed that 'deeper down . . . our religion [Christianity] is chiefly a Hebrew religion; and since Jews are
men, their religious feelings must have much in common with
those of other men' (32.374). When he discovered that Mirah was
a Jewess, he remarked (as Lessing did) that Jews and Christians
should not despise each other simply because individual Jews and
Christians are bad (17.193). Mirah agreed but insisted on the
necessity of maintaining her own Jewish identity. When Mrs.
Meyrick suggested that, if Jews would just keep on changing their
religion and overlook the difference between themselves and
Christians, Judaism would eventually fade away, Mirah responded
sharply: 'I will always be a Jewess. I will love Christians when they
are good, like you. But I will always cling to my people. I will
always worship with them' (32.375–6). In this fashion George Eliot
is warning against any program to convert Jews to Christianity[23] or
assimilate them to Christian culture: despite the deep spiritual
linkage between the two religions, they represent distinctive,
equally valid, and historically enduring ways to redemption.
Deronda came to appreciate this truth as he discovered his own
Jewish identity. Earlier he had regarded Judaism 'as a sort of
eccentric fossilised form'; but now, through Mirah, it was being
presented to him as 'something still throbbing in human lives, still
making for them the only conceivable vesture of the world'
(32.363). The message seems to be that Jews and Christians can
share empathetically in the spirituality of each other's religion but
should not attempt either to become the other or to assimilate the

other. (Presumably individual conversions from one religion to another remain a possibility, but this is not a matter that needs emphasis; it is assumed in a free society.)

Daniel Deronda had some of Dinah Morris's qualities. He was not motivated and driven by worldly success (16.179–80). He combined affectionateness with independence of judgment, had deep sympathy for those who were in difficulty and suffering, and seemed attracted to persons whom he could rescue (28.322–4). He was more than a moral counselor, a provider of practical wisdom: he was a priest, a confessor, a redeemer – his first act of redemption having been that of Gwendolen's necklace from the pawn shop, but later he became the redeemer of her soul (36.449–53). It was said of him that because he thought so much of others he wanted hardly anything for himself. One of his friends compared him to the Buddha who gave himself to the famished tigress to save her and her cubs from starving. While Deronda was embarrassed by the application of this analogy to himself, he took the opportunity of saying that 'it is an extreme image of what is happening every day – the transmutation of self' (37.465–6). Mirah's visionary impression that Daniel was a divinely-sent messenger (37.465) may be compared with Lisbeth's that Dinah was the angel at the grave of Jesus (*Adam Bede,* 51.499). Deronda assumed from the dying Mordecai the mission to unify his race and ultimately humanity as a whole (63.750–1). He became in fact a messianic figure. Standing on a bridge ('the meeting-place for the spiritual messengers') over the River Thames, Mordecai envisioned Deronda as the Deliverer of Israel when he saw him approaching in a boat from the West silhouetted against the setting sun (that is, at the time of the beginning of the Jewish Sabbath) (38.473–4; 40.491–4). These images are pregnant with messianic expectation. In accord with Kabbalistic doctrine, Mordecai, who had something of a messianic self-understanding, believed that his soul would be liberated from his weary body and born again in Deronda's young and healthy body (43.540). Moreover, Deronda's maternal grandfather Daniel Charisi told his daughter that 'every Jew should rear his family as if he hoped that a Deliverer might spring from it.' His mother added, 'You are the grandson he wanted;' and Deronda accepted his grandfather's trust as a sacred duty (53.662–3). Unlike Dinah, however, he initially lacked a purpose in life. He was not self-supporting, and at times he was indecisive, exhibiting a 'reflective hesitation,' a tendency to withdraw from 'the battle of the world' (16.179–80; 17.185). He needed 'either some external event, or some inward light, that would urge him in a definite line of action, and compress his wandering energy' (32.365). These he found through his encounters with Gwendolen, Mirah, and Mordecai. Gwendolen gave him a sense of vitality and passion for life, Mirah an inward faith, and Mordecai a vision and a religious orientation.[24]

What did Daniel Deronda (and his artistic creator) discover in Judaism? Put in briefest terms, he found in it a genuine moral and religious community that thrives on inner diversity and debate, that has a distinctive mission to humanity as a whole, and that believes in a God who is mysteriously present in every human face, who gives to human beings a diversity of pathways through life, and is the ultimate, incomprehensible, unnameable ground of the unity of all things. By contrast, Christianity as depicted in this novel seems to have lost its capacity for maintaining a genuine moral and religious community in which meaningful discussions about significant matters can occur; instead it has been accommodated to prevailing cultural mores and has little impact on people's lives.[25]

The novel addresses the most difficult question faced by Jews in the nineteenth century (and arguably since then as well): should they assimilate into the prevailing cultures, or should Judaism maintain its distinctive ethnic and religious identity? The question was posed most sharply in the form of a debate between Mordecai and Gideon at a meeting of 'the Philosophers,' a club of poor working-class men who were 'given to thought' (chap. 42). Gideon was a 'rational Jew' who proposed to get rid of superstitions and exclusiveness and to encourage his people to melt gradually into the populations they were living with. Mordecai rejoined:

> I too claim to be a rational Jew. But what is it to be rational – what is it to feel the light of the divine reason growing stronger within and without? It is to see more and more of the hidden bonds that bind and consecrate change as a dependent growth, yea, consecrate it with kinship . . . Is it rational to drain away the

sap of special kindred that makes the families of man rich in interchanged wealth?' (42.528)

'Each nation,' he continued, 'has its own work, and is a member of the world, enriched by the works of each.' Israel's work is to be 'the heart of mankind' – a heart of affection and reverence, a heart in which religion, law, and moral life mingle and make one growth (42.530–1). But Israel cannot play the special role to which it is called among nations if it lacks a national homeland. 'The soul of Judaism is not dead. Revive the organic centre; let the unity of Israel which has made the growth and form of its religion be an outward reality. Looking towards a land and a polity, our dispersed people in all the ends of the earth may share the dignity of a national life which has a voice among the peoples of the East and the West' (42.532). Against assimilation, Mordecai called for 'separateness.' But this was to be a separateness put into the service of humanity as a whole. The new Jewish republic would be founded on principles of equality and freedom and would serve as a meeting ground, 'a covenant of reconciliation,' between East and West (42.534–7). Mordecai did not seem to have in mind that all Jews would move to a national homeland, which would be an impossible, foolish, and discriminatory racial policy. Rather, Jews, most of whom would still live among the nations of the world, would have in Israel a 'national hearth' of great symbolic value. Diaspora Jews might be considered extended citizens of Israel if the latter, like England, is envisioned as 'a nationality whose members may still stretch to the ends of the earth' (42.536; 69.803).

By contrast with these optimistic ideas, Daniel Deronda's mother Leonora Halm-Eberstein saw the negative side of separateness and of Judaism. She told her son, 'You are glad to have been born a Jew. You say so. That is because you have not been brought up a Jew. That separateness seems sweet to you because I saved you from it' (51.630). Leonora, a talented actress, suffered the slavery of being a woman, which was made all the more intensive by a dominant father and cultural stereotypes. 'To have a pattern cut out – "this is the Jewish woman; this is what you must be; this is what you are wanted for . . ."' – that was a bondage Leonora tried all her life to escape (51.631).

George Eliot had to acknowledge the patriarchalism of traditional Judaism. She made the pawnbroker Ezra Cohen remark that 'a Jewish man is bound to thank God, day by day,[26] that he was not made a woman; but a woman has to thank God that He has made her according to His will . . . a child-bearing, tender-hearted thing' (46.575) – just the sort of attitude against which Leonora rebelled. The other Ezra Cohen, Mordecai, also expressed a stereotyped view when he told his sister Mirah that 'women are specially framed for the love which feels possession in renouncing.' He thought this was confirmed by a story in the Midrash about a Jewish maiden who sacrificed herself in place of a condemned woman who was beloved by a Gentile king. 'This is the surpassing love, that loses self in the object of love.' Mirah insisted that the maiden rather wanted the king to know that she was better than the other. 'It was her strong self, wanting to conquer, that made her die . . . The Jewish girl must have had jealousy in her heart, and she wanted somehow to have the first place in the king's mind' (61.735). Mirah said this partly out of her own anger and jealousy at the prospect of losing Deronda to Gwendolen, but she also was telling her brother that Jewish women are not immune from such emotions, and that it is not right to ascribe the role of losing self solely to women. There must also be a finding of self, for women as well as men. Mirah's strong self took the form of inward resistance and resolute endurance, but for the most part she accommodated herself to the role prescribed for women by Jewish teaching, whereas Deronda's mother did not, nor for that matter did Gwendolen. Judaism is not free of the ambiguities and oppressions that are present in every religion in one form or another. Or, as Mordecai said to Mirah as they spoke sadly of their derelict father, 'our lot is the lot of Israel. The grief and the glory are mingled as the smoke and the flame' (62.743).

In setting forth Mordecai's Zionist vision George Eliot did not consider the fact that for centuries another people also had occupied Palestine and regarded it as their homeland. Thus the establishment of a Jewish state when it actually occurred in 1948 brought with it, not a reconciliation of East and West, but a new source of conflict that has yet to be resolved. However, George Eliot was no stranger to the ambiguities of history, the necessity of tragic choices, and the incalculable consequences of actions. The narrator of *Daniel Deronda* comments that when the great movements of the world enter like an earthquake into our own lives,

> it is as if the Invisible Power . . . became visible, according to the imagery of the Hebrew poet,[27] making the flames his chariot and riding on the wings of the wind, till the mountains smoke and the plains shudder under the rolling, fiery visitation. Often the good cause seems to lie prostrate under the thunder of unrelenting forces . . . Then it is that the submission of the soul to the Highest is tested, and even in the eyes of frivolity life looks out from the scene of human struggles with the awful face of duty, and a religion shows itself which is something else than a private consolation. (69.803–4)

This passage, in which George Eliot had the American Civil War in mind,[28] could serve also to characterize the moral impact of the Israeli-Palestinian conflict over the past forty years. Presumably a religion that is something else than a private consolation must also transcend national interests and sectarian agendas. It brings judgment to bear upon all the bitter, religiously driven rivalries of history.

The apocalyptic images set forth in the passage quoted above raise the question of the meaning and goal of history – a question that fairly haunts this novel.[29] Yet the apocalyptic imagery is demythologized by a simple remark of Daniel Deronda to the effect that the 'prospect of everything coming to an end will not guide us far in practice' (32.376). The epigraph to Chapter 1 tells us that we are always *in medias res,* that no retrospect will take us to the true beginning (nor presumably any prospect to a final ending). There is an 'all-presupposing fact with which our story starts out' (1.7), a 'hard unaccommodating Actual, which has never consulted our taste and is entirely unselect' (33.380). Human beings, like planets, have both a visible and an invisible history. The threading of the latter, 'the hidden pathways of feeling and thought which lead up to every moment of action,' is the task of the narrator of human actions (16.164). Since our vantage point is always in the middle of things, and since history always has a hidden aspect, no dogmatic claims about the totality of meaning are legitimate. 'All meanings,' the narrator reminds us, 'depend on the key of interpretation' (6.57).

Conventional views of divine providence are exposed as vacuous, leaving sensitive people with little solace in the face of destiny. When Mrs. Davilow, Gwendolen's mother, told her daughter, 'We must resign ourselves to the will of Providence,' Gwendolen responded sharply: 'But I don't resign myself. I shall do what I can against it. What is the good of calling people's wickedness Providence?' She was referring to the fact that a broker lost the family's fortune through speculative investments. 'I don't call that Providence: it was his improvidence with our money, and he ought to be punished' (21.233). When her uncle tried to assure her that 'there is benefit in all chastisement if we adjust our minds to it,' Gwendolen found that it was just this that she could not do (26.289). She was becoming disenchanted with the world, forlorn that she was not immune from the calamities that seem to befall people indifferently, and she had as yet no larger vision of purpose in life.

In the epigraph to Chapter 41 (p. 509), Aristotle is quoted: 'It is a part of probability that many improbable things will happen.'[30] The improbable things that happen in this story – the chance meetings, the coincidences of time and place – are attributed by its author to probability rather than to divine plan. God's providence manifests itself differently – by creating a moral universe in which deeds yield inexorable consequences, and by empowering individuals to make something good of the opportunities that present themselves in life.[31] As an instance of the former, Gwendolen had a 'vague conception of avenging power' as she plunged ahead in her reckless plan to marry Grandcourt (28.311–12; 31.354–5), and vengeance came in the form of a letter from Lydia Glasher informing her that she had broken her promise and married a 'withered heart' (31.358–9). Yet Deronda told Gwendolen that 'no evil dooms us hopelessly except the evil we love' (57.700). She *can* make efforts to start over, but her past deeds have left her a life without future love. She must live with the consequences of her actions, yet she can create a different future for herself and accomplish something good in life. Gwendolen was a person of conscience with a sense of justice, which had been trapped within a shell of selfishness (54.669). Grandcourt, by contrast, had no conscience; but, as sometimes happens with evil-doers, he brought about his own destruction through excess – not by divine plan but through the law of consequences (cf. 54.679–82).

The Hebrew liturgy for the Day of Reconciliation that Deronda heard in Frankfurt sought for nothing special, asked for no divine favors and interventions, but rather was 'a yearning to escape from the limitations of our own weakness and an invocation of all Good to enter and abide with us.' It was 'a self-oblivious lifting up of gladness, a *Gloria in excelsis* that such Good exists; both the yearning and the exultation gathering their utmost force from the sense of communion in a form which has expressed them both, for long generations of struggling fellow-men' (32.367). Such a religion is without private consolation and without special divine intervention. It rather simply rejoices that the Good exists and abides with us, sustains us by its steadfast presence in a communion of human beings that spans the generations. Deronda sensed that the religious feeling evoked in him by the liturgy was like 'a divine influx in the darkness, before there was any vision to interpret' (32.368). David Carroll remarks: 'This is the primal religious experience, the divine influx, the spirit breathing upon the waters, not only before interpretation gets to work but even before there is a vision to interpret.'[32] The same influx was experienced by Dinah, Maggie, Romola, Dorothea, and perhaps even by George Eliot in her more liturgical moments.

Gambling is a false response to the probabilities and improbabilities of history – a veneration of the goddess of luck in the desire to escape historical necessity or to gain something for oneself at another's expense, a way of finding passion in life, of fighting boredom through amusement (1.7–14; 2.17; 15.156; 56.692). 'What we call the dulness of things is a disease in ourselves,' Deronda told Gwendolen, who learned from bitter experience that by her marriage to Grandcourt she gambled and lost everything (31.355; 35.411). Addiction to alcohol and other drugs falls under the same category as gambling in George Eliot's moral universe. Gambling itself can become a form of addiction, as it did in the case of the elder Lapidoth (66.773).

The alternative to the roulette table as an image of history in this novel is the image of the pathway. Mordecai told Deronda that 'man finds his pathways': at first they were visible foot-tracks, now they are swift and invisible, the thoughts and feelings that lead to actions and suffering (40.502, cf. 16.164). 'Has he found all the pathways yet? What reaches him, stays with him, rules him: he must accept it, not knowing its pathway' (40.502–3). 'Who shall say where the pathways lie?' (43.543). The pathway is a recurring image in Hebrew poetry, and the use of it in *Daniel Deronda* is indebted to the *Sefer Yetzirah,* 'The Book of Creation,' which is the oldest of all Kabbalistic texts. It develops the idea of thirty-two mystical paths of wisdom, which are manifest as the ten numbers and twenty-two letters of the Hebrew alphabet. These are paths that must be found and blazed by each individual. Barbara Hardy suggests that 'Mordecai uses the image to express the hidden but secure workings of Providence.'[33] In a climactic conversation, Mordecai reminded Deronda that

> from the first, I have said to you, we know not all the pathways. Has there not been a meeting among them, as of the operations in one soul, where an idea being born and breathing draws the elements towards it, and is fed and grows? For all things are bound together in that Omnipresence which is the place and habitation of the world,[34] and events are as a glass where-through our eyes see some of the pathways. (63.749)

Daniel himself, he continued, found a chief pathway by his loving will, which led him to rescue Mirah and to become a brother to Mordecai. Had he not taken this path he would not have discovered his Jewish identity and his life's vocation.

There is, in other words, a great diversity of pathways, all of which are ultimately bound together in the divine Omnipresence, and some of which are reflected in the events of history. It is up to each individual to find the pathway that is appropriate for him- or herself, and this requires a life-long pilgrimage with many false turns and much 'wandering in the mazes' (63.745). God, presumably, does not choose the right pathway for us, but provides a multitude of opportunities and possibilities. Those that are actualized contribute to the nourishment and growth of the divine life, for it is 'God, in whom dwells the universe' (43.542).

God seems to function in relation to the world in the mode of an efficacious ideality. The novel offers interesting reflections on the transforming power of ideas. 'All actions men put a bit of thought into are ideas,' said Goodwin, one of 'the Philosophers.' Ideas such as sowing seed or baking clay 'work themselves into life and go on growing with it, but they can't go apart from the material that set them to work and makes a medium for them' (42.524). Along a somewhat different line, Mirah in an earlier conversation affirmed the identity of beauty and truth: 'If people have thought what is the most beautiful and the best thing, it must be true. It is always there.' Deronda interpreted this to mean that beauty 'is a truth in thought though it may never have been carried out in action. It lives as an idea' (37.466). So it is with divinity, which, as the identity of truth, beauty, and goodness, lives as an idea. As living, the divine idea is active, it has an effect on (and is affected by) the world, it draws and grows as an immaterial force in a material medium. In Hegelian terms, the divine idea is the 'ideal-real.' Or in the Kabbalistic terms favored by Mordecai, it is the 'world soul' (cf. 40.501).

Do the pathways of history actually converge upon an Omni-presence that is the dwelling place of the whole world? Does the divine idea draw the elements toward it, by which it is fed and grows? Such at least, claimed Mordecai, is the *Shemah* of the people of Israel, the confession of the divine Unity: 'Hear, O Israel: The LORD our God is one LORD' (Deut. 6.4 KJV). 'This made our religion the fundamental religion for the whole world; for the divine Unity embraced as its consequence the ultimate unity of mankind . . . Now, in complete unity a part possesses the whole as the whole possesses every part: and in this way human life is tending toward the image of the Supreme Unity' (61.734). Parts that do not possess the whole would be merely fragmented, scattered, continuously in conflict with each other. Parts possess the whole as 'our life becomes more spiritual by capacity of thought,' thereby transcending material particularity. At the same time, the whole possesses every part: it is not an abstract totality but an infinite richness, which draws the parts into communion with each other and itself, but without reducing them to the same. This is the idea of 'separateness with communication' (or 'the balance of separateness and communication') enunciated by Deronda's grandfather.[35] Thus the premise for a genuine ethical universalism, for the great goal of human unity-in-diversity, seems to be a religious vision of the divine whole that possesses and preserves every part *as a part* (the nonhuman as well as the human parts).[36]

The idea of separateness with communication became the guiding vision of Daniel Deronda. He resolved to call himself a Jew and his first duty would be to his own people. 'If there is anything to be done towards restoring or perfecting their common life, I shall make that my vocation.' But he would not profess or believe exactly as his fathers believed, for they too had changed over time and had learned from other races (60.725). He knew that the 'Christian sympathies' in which he had been reared would never die out (53.661). Thus his distinctive pathway would be that of a Jew who could communicate with Christians (as well as persons of other faiths) and who would seek to guide human life toward its hidden common goal despite all its diversity.

What can actually be known of the divine unity, that Omnipresence wherein all things dwell? In her notebooks on the Kabbalah, George Eliot emphasized the connection of its doctrines with the negative theology of the Neoplatonists, especially Proclus.[37] The Kabbalah, she said, called God the *En Soph*, the Incomprehensible One, to whom no name can be given and no attributes applied. This is a God beyond all being, thinking, knowing, in the strict sense non-existent, *das Nichts*. This God is *arrētos* and *agnōstos*, the inexpressible and the unknown. George Eliot's own agnosticism is to be understood in this sense: to be agnostic is not to deny God's 'existence' – a term that in any event represents a category mistake as applied to divinity – but rather to honor the divine mystery in accord with the great tradition of apophatic theology. Yet this mystery comes forth, becomes kataphatic, manifests itself in the creation of the world by the Sephiroth, the emanations that disperse the divine light into the intellectual, sensuous, and material realms of reality. Each part is a microcosm of the whole and contributes to the whole by reflecting refracted light back upon it. The eye of the novelist is focused upon the parts, tracking their patterns, connections, movements, seeking therein traces of the whole, the mystery beneath the real. This was the central religious insight to which George Eliot was drawn, through her engagement with Judaism, at the end of her fictional career.[38]

In light of this engagement and the probing ideas it produced, Rosemary Ashton's central query about *Daniel Deronda* seems strange and even unworthy of an otherwise admirable work of biography. She wonders why George Eliot thought it necessary to turn away from British society toward Judaism in order to find a positive future. 'And why does an agnostic, one who respects the need for religious belief in others but repudiates it for herself, set out, without irony, a religious ideal? Moreover, is the history of Judaism any less fraught with superstition, narrowness, exclusiveness than that of Christianity? . . . It is surprising to find George Eliot engaging so deeply with a vision she did not – could not – actively share.'[39] Regarding, first, the damaging remark about Judaism, while it is undoubtedly true that it like every religion has destructive aspects, it is also evident that Jews have not been in the historical position to inflict damage on their fellow human beings to the extraordinary degree that Christians have for many centuries. Jews for the most part have been the victims of history, not victimizers, and conditions of persecution and oppression have given their religion a distinctive ethical and communal intensity that appealed to George Eliot. Moreover, it is simply not true that she repudiated a personal need for religious belief in general, or that she could not and did not actively share the vision of Judaism – which at heart is the vision of a just commonwealth (Spinoza's ideal) grounded in the divine Unity and Mystery. It is too weak to suggest, as Ashton does, that what lay behind George Eliot's last novel was simply intellectual curiosity, dissatisfaction with British insularity, a disposition to experiment with something new and different, and a disinclination to become entangled in causes closer to home.[40] These are rationalizations that avoid the plain fact that she found herself, in her own words, coming to share with Judaism a fellowship of religious and moral conviction, discovering in it an alternative to the barren Philistinism of mainstream society.

8

George Eliot and Postmodern Theology

1. George Eliot, Postmodernity, and Theology

I have argued[1] for a close connection between art and theology and have been bold or foolish enough to offer a theological reading of George Eliot's fiction, despite George Henry Lewes's claim that her first story dealt with its subject 'not at all in its theological aspect,'[2] and despite the scholarly consensus that George Eliot abandoned or never embraced a theological way of viewing things. The question turns in part on what is meant by the words 'theological' and 'fiction.' Literary critics who have written about George Eliot in recent years have tended to assume that 'theological' entails buying into the traditional doctrinal package of Christian beliefs, including mythological and metaphysical forms that are appropriate perhaps to a premodern but not to a modern and certainly not a postmodern age. The only alternative from their perspective is to abandon everything theological and to embrace instead a secular and humanist perspective – which is what they believe George Eliot did. The 'thrice-breathed breath of criticism' (to employ the author's own clever phrase)[3] has turned her into one of the modern 'cultured despisers' of religion.[4] The critics do not consider the possibility of revisioning or reconstructing a theological worldview in response to changing perceptions of reality. Yet far from being something static and unchanging, theology as an exercise of human imagination is constantly evolving. The whole of post-Enlightenment theology, from Schleiermacher and Hegel through Troeltsch, was a sustained effort both to criticize and to reconstruct the central convictions of Christian faith about God, world, humanity, Christ, sin, and redemption in forms appropriate to modern philosophy, science, and culture. In her own way George Eliot was engaged in a similar demythologizing effort.

If I am on track in suggesting that theology itself is a kind of fiction that creates imaginative variations on what history offers as real in order to bespeak the mystery beneath the real, and that it approaches this mystery in terms of how redemptive transforma- tions come about in ordinary human life, then the difference between theology and the kind of artistic sensibility George Eliot represents may not be so profound. Theology and art are both 'fiction' – a term deriving from the Latin verb *fingere*, 'to form,' 'imagine,' or 'invent' – in the sense that they entail a shaping, construing, configuring of the real in imaginative as opposed to empirical-descriptive modalities. They 'make things up,' but they do so for purposes of illuminating reality, not escaping from it into a fantasy world. They are constrained but not constricted by empirical fact since they draw upon the full range of human experience and potentiality (emotional, psychological, ethical, aesthetic, religious); what they produce must be congruent with history but not necessarily derived from it.

Both literary and theological fiction construct or project a world, 'the world of the text,' as Paul Ricoeur calls it.[5] This world is what the text is ultimately about: it is its reference, its subject matter, its *Sache*. It stands in front of the text (as something that interacts with the reader) rather than behind it (in the mind of the author) or within it (as its linguistic structure). There are many kinds of fictional worlds, ranging from the dark, destructive, and terrifying to the naive, sentimental, and idealizing. The fictional world of George Eliot is neither of these: it projects a new way of being that is poetically distanced from everyday reality even as it makes its way through the world of ordinary experience. The latter is not negated but opened up and transformed by the power of pro- jection, which is able to make a break, a new beginning, in the midst of the old and familiar. The reality status of what is poetic- ally envisioned is that of the *possible*. The possible is not the illu- sory, a product of wishful thinking, nor is it the merely ideal in the sense of a mental fantasy; rather it is the real transfigured, fulfilled as to its possibilities. The fulfillment always remains fragmentary and ambiguous, for it is something that happens in the midst of history, not at the end of history.

Not always but from time to time in the world of George Eliot's fiction, human beings find it possible to go on or start over in the midst of suffering, defeat, and despair. The decisive transformations are recounted in terms that suggest religious conversion, a process of death and rebirth, of losing and finding oneself, of creating a new kind of communal ethos defined by love and justice, which in the language of the Bible is something like the kingdom of God. God does not appear as an empirical object or a direct agent anywhere in George Eliot's fictional world. But there are hints that it is the power of God, of infinite suffering love, that constitutes the power of new predication by which redemptive possibilities come to speech, become speech-acts, in a tragically conflicted world. In this respect George Eliot's fictional world envisions something more than she herself was ever able to affirm directly. In the praxis of writing fiction she was able to overcome personal doubt and intellectual skepticism, and to enter a world of transformative possibilities. Such is the distance between text and author, notes Ricoeur,[6] that the matter of the text may escape the finite intentional horizon of the author; indeed, the world of the text may *explode* the world of the author. At its explosive limits, George Eliot's fiction becomes theological.

Certainly it is true that almost no theologians have recognized George Eliot as contributing anything of value to their subject matter. Frederick Denison Maurice may have been an exception. In August 1863 George Eliot wrote to Sara Sophia Hennell: 'A very deep delight . . . has come to me in the (to me) unexampled beauty of Frederick Maurice's conduct towards me. I should think there are very few men living who would do just as fine a thing as he did in writing a certain letter which you shall see some time.'[7] Unfortunately this letter has been lost and we shall not see it, regrettably so because Maurice, a leader of the Christian social-ist movement, was a sensitive, courageous, and open-minded religious thinker. The more common theological judgment about George Eliot was one made by H. Richard Niebuhr: 'Like Feuerbach and many other contemporaries, in revolt against what seemed a repressive orthodoxy and against the equation of the church with established social order, she sought to retain the ethos of Christianity without its faith, its humanism without its theism, its hope for man without its hope for the sovereignty of God.'[8] While allowing for a certain validity to her revolt, Niebuhr thus located George Eliot squarely in a modernist mentality with its humanism, secularism, naturalism, and atheism. But I believe, for all the evidence and reasons adduced in the preceding chapters, that this is not true, and that she was in fact closer to a certain kind of postmodern sensibility.

The term 'postmodernity' is used very loosely and perhaps ought to be avoided altogether. One recent interpreter distinguishes between three basic types.[9] The *true* or *radical postmoderns* celebrate the breakdown of all the traditional coordinates of experience (time, space, order), believe that reality is fluid and permeable, are content to live without cultural orientation in a web of highly diverse interactions, are radically historicist, and regard knowledge to be purely a function of power, desire, and self-interest with no ontological reference. From this point of view theology is often excluded a priori as an existential and intellectual possibility, and this is the perspective from which many of the recent literary-critical studies of George Eliot have been written. At the other end of the spectrum are the *countermoderns,* for whom modernity itself is the problem (its liberalism, moral relativism, secular humanism), and who celebrate its demise as an opportunity to reaffirm traditional truths and values, not by returning to pre-critical forms but by embracing a postcritical theory of knowledge that emphasizes the function of language in forming distinctive patterns of life. The theology associated with this kind of post-modernity is oriented to confessional identity and renewal.

Finally, in the middle are the *late moderns* or *critical postmoderns,* who live critically in the postmodern world, affirming some of its insights (its recognition of the fluidity, plurality, and interrelatedness of things, its decentering of Western culture and the human subject), challenging other parts of it (its relativism, atheism, aestheticism), wanting to carry the unfinished project of modernity forward (with its focus on human rights, freedom, subjectivity, critical judgment) but in a vastly changed cultural world, drawing upon various forms of pragmatism, critical social theory, or a holistic philosophy of relationality and process. This can also be described as a *revisionist* postmodernism, which allows for a type of theology – a theology which believes that, in order to preserve the heritage and identity of the Christian tradition, its traditional forms must be allowed to pass over into new and often quite different forms, which will be shaped by resources and insights presently available to us. The stress here is on transformation rather than renewal. Our task, writes one theologian, 'is to be transformed by the best of what we are now experiencing and learning and to share in the transformation of the world.'[10] I believe this is the kind of postmodernity that George Eliot most closely approximated. She was looking for ways through and beyond the aporias of modern culture (its secularism, Philistinism, cynicism, dehumanization) but without abandoning its gains and without returning to the past with its repressive orthodoxies. She did this by attempting to envision new possibilities, a religion for the future, a more perfect religion, one that affirms those revelations and disciplines of the past that are something more than shifting theory. Her question was: what is the lasting meaning that lies in all religious doctrine? In view of her commitment, as expressed in *Daniel Deronda* and elsewhere, to maintain the integrity of determinate religious traditions, we have to assume that the 'more perfect religion' and the 'lasting meaning' will appear not in a single universal religion but in a diversity of concrete religious faiths and practices.

We have seen (Chapter 1) George Eliot's conviction of the efficacy that lies in all sincere religious faith and of the spiritual blight that comes with no-faith. We have noted her lack of sympathy with mere antagonism and destruction, her insistence that she had no hostility toward any religious belief, and her affirmation of the worship of the highest Good. What she desired was that a child should be helped to form a nobler conception of God rather than to have atheism introduced into its mind. We have noted too George Eliot's own need for religious experience and worship, and her own sense of religious vocation. In 'Janet's Repentance' she provided a thumbnail sketch of what can be accomplished by religion at its best: it brings recognition that something is to be lived for beyond mere satisfaction of self, that there is a divine work to be done in life, that there is a rule of goodness higher than the opinion of one's neighbors, that one should strive for purity of heart, Christ-like compassion, and the subduing of selfish desires. 'The first condition of human goodness is something to love; the second, something to reverence.'[11] Her novels depict the doomed nature of self-centered characters such as Hetty, Tito, Rosamond, and Gwendolen (prior to her rescue), who lacked love and reverence; while Dinah, Maggie, Romola, Felix, Dorothea, and Daniel embodied the truth of the central religious insight: 'Those who seek to save their life will lose it, those who lose their life will find it' (cf. Matt. 16.25). This is the great 'clue of life,' but it must not be taken to be an act of weakness or entail self-destruction: rather it requires resolute strength of self, a finding as well as a losing, as Dorothea demonstrated, and as Mirah insisted against Mordecai. By contrast with authentic piety, the civil religion practiced in St. Ogg's and Middlemarch, and on the estates of Wessex, reflected the de facto secularism of modern culture: religion had for the most part lost its vitality, its ability to integrate all aspects of life, and instead had been reduced to routinized custom, a social game, a means of achieving one's private ends or justifying one's self-serving actions, an emotion driven by fear, vengeance, and the calculation of benefits. Neither Maggie, nor Dorothea, nor Gwendolen were able to derive any sustenance from it.

George Eliot's religion was, to be sure, a religion of humanity, but for her the objective of religion is to reorient human beings from self-centeredness to reality-centeredness, with 'reality' understood to include other persons, the larger human and natural community, and the ultimate mystery of things. She had a tragic view of the human condition and certainly did not advocate the worship or idealization of finite, fallible, sinful, narcissistic human beings. Rather what is needed is service and sympathy, the reduction of ignorance and degradation, the purifying and ennobling of human life by connecting it with something greater than itself. One of the key insights of modern theology has been the central role played by anthropology, the so-called turn to the subject, the recognition that all religious ideas are human creations in response to something that presents itself in experience. Postmodern theology has not abandoned this insight but enlarged it to a more cosmological perspective, a cosmotheandric vision, as Raimon Panikkar names it. In this vision, God is to be understood not in isolation but in relation to the creation of the world and the redemptive transformation of human beings; and the latter are to be accepted not as they are but as reoriented to a greater whole. I believe that George Eliot was pointing in this direction.

Drawing specifically upon ideas and insights provided by the novels, I shall now attempt to identify some preliminary elements of a postmodern theology, then focus on what for me is the central problematic of such a theology – whether and how God comes forth as God in redemptive transformations – and conclude with some thoughts about Judaism and Christianity.

2. Preliminary Elements of a Postmodern Theology

These elements are the first three that I sought to identify in Chapter 1 as elements of a future religion envisioned by George Eliot.

a. Truth: Beyond Consolation and Accusation

Although the mission of religion is to witness to the truth, too often it has been used in the service of illusion. The great modern critics of religion – Feuerbach, Marx, Nietzsche, Freud – have made this aspect of it the centerpiece of their critiques. Human beings project their own desires, ideals, hopes and illusions into the godhead, claimed Feuerbach and Freud. Religion is the opium of the people, wrote Marx (with echoes to come from Nietzsche), substituting illusory happiness for real happiness, illusory strength for real strength. But as we have seen, for George Eliot our highest religious duty as human beings is 'to *do without opium* and live through all our pain with conscious, clear-eyed endurance.'[12] She created characters who did precisely this: Edgar Tryan, Dinah Morris, Maggie Tulliver, Romola de' Bardi, Felix Holt, Dorothea Brooke, Daniel Deronda, and in the end Gwendolen Harleth. She said that the supreme subject with which she was engaged is 'how far the religion of the future must be one that enables us to do without consolation.'[13] In this she anticipated Paul Ricoeur's warning about the 'rotten points'[14] present in every religion – accusation and con-solation, taboo and shelter, the fear of punishment and the desire for protection; and like him she was searching for a faith beyond accusation and consolation. She depicted the logic of reward and punishment that pervades conventional religion, such as the barren exhortation against which Janet Dempster rebelled, 'Do right, and keep a clear conscience, and God will reward you;'[15] or the 'benevolent vengeance' and pious moralism so scathingly depicted in *The Mill on the Floss*; or the readiness of Middlemarchers to have a providence that conveniently served their own interests and punished their enemies. She described Maynard Gilfil's admirable reversal of the doctrine of just retribution by insisting that God sees us whole, not according to this or that good or evil deed. She did not believe that God intervenes episodically in history to save people from disasters, to reward piety, to punish wrong-doing, or to bring about desired outcomes. God not only sees as a whole but acts as a whole through natural and moral laws. God suffers along side us as a faithful friend does, and in that way strengthens and empowers us, but God does not arrange things for our benefit.

'Falsehood is so easy, truth so difficult.'[16] We are driven to various escapes from reality through addictions such as alcohol, opium, gambling, falsehood itself. Tito Melema was the most notorious example of a man who sold his soul to the 'terrible usurer Falsehood' through his systematic lying. Religion too can be an escape, especially from the reality of death. Thus George Eliot was highly critical of the prevalent spiritualism of her time – the belief that departed spirits communicate with us – which she denounced as a 'degrading folly' and 'odious trickery.' She was also suspicious of belief in personal immortality, the idea that somehow our individual selves will go on living after death, which requires that our whole effort should be directed toward assuring that we are rewarded in heaven rather than punished in hell. Without necessarily endorsing her doctrine of impersonal or subjective immortality (the idea that those who have gone before live on in the effects of their work and in the memory of their successors), we must, I believe, honestly agree with her that we have no direct knowledge about the state of life after death, and that it is better to focus our highest emotions on our struggling fellow human beings and this earthly existence. For her this is what the symbol of the kingdom of God signifies – it is neither a future heavenly kingdom nor a present political state of affairs but a 'great yearning' within human beings for justice.[17] This is a yearning by which persons are empowered to struggle for justice rather than tempted to seek consolation. Thus truthfulness about religion provides an orientation to practice.

b. Practice: Feeling, Action, Reflection

George Eliot tells us that emotions and feelings have a primacy in human life, which is affective before it is cognitive, and that we should trust them to put us into touch with what is real and true. She did not learn this only from Feuerbach but rather found in him confirmation of an early and deep conviction, a conviction that accords well with postmodern sensibilities. She also believed that people could be persuaded to act principally through 'the truth of feeling as the only universal bond of union.' Rational arguments and doctrines are not as effective; rather people must be 'wrought on by little and little.'[18] Feelings may give rise to mystical experience, but more importantly they should issue in transformative practice, a practice driven by compassion for concrete suffering human beings with whom we feel connected. Thus the one who felt God's presence most keenly, Dinah Morris, was dedicated to a ministry of service to persons in need.

Feeling has its telos in practice, but both feeling and practice require reflective interpretation. It was not the doctrines and teachings of the clerical figures – Amos Barton, Maynard Gilfil, Edgar Tryan, Dinah Morris, Rufus Lyon, Camden Farebrother – that were of principal importance, but their actions, feelings, relationships, sympathies. Several of these figures did, however, also expound appropriate theories to interpret their actions. Mr. Tryan taught Janet a new way of thinking about God, while Dinah's sermon was a powerful interpretation of the gospel she lived by, and Rufus Lyon offered a theological vision of the good society that could serve as an orientation for political reform. If Mordecai Cohen can be considered as a clerical figure, he was of a different type, for his principal function was to expound an alternative religious vision and serve as a guru to Daniel Deronda. Without such pedagogical efforts it is very difficult to break false conceptions. George Eliot herself, through the voices of her narrators, introduced a pronounced didactic element into her novels. The appeal of this kind of teaching is not to authority and tradition but to the reader's own experience.

The problem with most doctrinal teaching is that it is utterly abstract and irrelevant to concrete issues at hand. Thus Amos Barton once preached an extremely argumentative sermon about the incarnation, 'which, as it was preached to a congregation not one of whom had any doubt of that doctrine, and to whom the Socinians therein confuted were as unknown as the Arimaspians, was exceedingly well adapted to trouble and confuse the Sheppertonian mind.'[19] The practical effect of teaching dogma is often to stir up controversies over disputed points and to promote a sectarian mentality – the insistence that my group's way of interpreting the sacraments or Christ or the church or the authority of Scripture is the only true and valid way. This was the danger present in Girolamo Savonarola's insistence on the exclusive rightness of his doctrine. George Eliot was looking for a more foundational, experiential, and holistic way of engaging the great questions of good and evil, sin and redemption, life and death.

c. Spirituality: the Mystery beneath the Real

Religion is not just about human feeling and action, and it is not reducible to morality. It also has the aspect of reverence, the capacity to acknowledge and relate to the reality of the unseen, to what I have been calling the mystery beneath the real – a mystery associated with deep love, musical harmony, the sense of losing oneself in a greater whole, the intuition that the universe is a perpetual utterance of the One Being. This is the divine mystery, which is found not above and beyond the real but beneath and within it. But what it is in and for itself exceeds our capacity to think and know. It is like an inexhaustible fountain, an influx in the darkness before there is any vision to interpret. We certainly cannot find in our own natures, or in all the world's mythico-religious systems, a key to the divine mystery. At best, the narrator of 'Janet's Repentance' tells us, we fill up 'the margin of ignorance which surrounds our knowledge with the feelings of trust and resignation. Perhaps the profoundest philosophy could hardly fill it up better.'[20] An intensive sort of spirituality characterizes several of George Eliot's figures – Dinah, Romola, Dorothea – but there is a hesitancy to give it a label such as 'mysticism' that might turn it into something arcane or reduce it to a history-of-religions category.[21]

Instead of 'mysticism,' the better term is probably 'spirituality,' and indeed something of the classical Catholic model of spiritual formation is reflected in the religious journey of both the author and her heroines. We have seen that Maggie Tulliver found a guide to life in Thomas à Kempis, and that Dorothea Brooke was compared with St. Theresa of Avila. George Eliot was clearly familiar with both of these authors, and there may have been others whom she read, such as Catherine of Siena and St. John of the Cross. In all of these figures, as in George Eliot herself and many of her fictional characters, a growth in spiritual discernment occurs, a deepening recognition of suffering and ambiguity in life, a willingness to submit to the patient pedagogy of wisdom, and a determination to connect spirituality and practice. This is not an unrestrained mystical enthusiasm but a disciplining of mind and heart in service of the divine mystery. Mature faith is the fruit of struggle with darkness and temptation, including the temptation to a simplistic overbelief or no belief. The mode of apprehension is neither literal nor dialectical but sacramental.

A certain hesitancy, or reserve, in the face of the sacred is characteristic of George Eliot. While Edgar Tryan and Dinah Morris were able to speak of God as a suffering, sympathetic, empowering, ever-present friend, the chief characters in the later novels seem reluctant to utter the name of the Holy One. They and the authorial voice employ circumlocutions such as 'the Unseen Love,' 'the Highest Good,' 'the Perfect Right,' 'the Infinite Sorrow,' 'the Supreme Unity' – rather like the circumlocutions for the divine name found in the literature and faith of Israel. When reference is made to the divine power, unity, or omnipresence, we are reminded that no totalizing system can capture its complexity or unpack its mystery. Another kind of circumlocution is suggested by the remark in *Daniel Deronda* that divinity is often mediated to us through the judgment of another person – an other 'who brings to us with close pressure and immediate sequence that judgment of the Invisible and Universal which self-flattery and the world's tolerance would easily melt and disperse. In this way our brother may be in the stead of God to us.'[22] By faithfully exercising such a judgment in relation to Gwendolen, Daniel Deronda was in the stead of God to her. He never directly uttered the name of God, but the judging and transforming power of the Invisible became visible through him. The mystery of God comes forth through the mysteries of redemption.

How do we know that it is truly the mystery of God that comes forth? Or that the mystery beneath the real is not simply the sheer meaninglessness and absurdity of a purposeless universe? Or that it is really God whose stead is taken by a faithful friend? This raises again the question of how George Eliot's position with respect to religion differs from that of a purely Feuerbachian theory of projection, the 'raw' Feuerbach with which she is usually associated. At this point I find an insight of John Hick to be helpful. He acknowledges, as I think we must, that religious experience is in fact a human projection or construction shaped to a considerable extent by particular cultural and historical contexts. But he goes on to point out that all the great religious traditions share the basic conviction that genuine religious experience is not *simply* human projection but is at the same time a cognitive and affective *response* to a transcendent reality other than ourselves that engenders a transformation from self-centeredness to reality-centeredness (which is what religions call 'salvation' or 'redemption'). The criteria present in the great traditions for distinguishing authentic from illusory or destructive responses to the Real focus upon observable 'fruits' in human life – qualities such as love, compassion, faithfulness, hope, self-denial, suffering for the sake of others, social mission, spiritual discernment, connectedness with reality.[23] These are the spiritual qualities characteristic of George Eliot's heroines and heroes, and of many ordinary folk in her stories as well. There is something about the way they live, their 'spirituality,' that tells us that for them religion is not an illusion but a response to something of overwhelming importance. The judgment of the Invisible and Universal – which demands of persons a transition from self-centeredness to reality-centeredness – is scarcely something attributable to our self-flattery and the world's tolerance. Authentic belief does not yield worldly prizes; rather it orients us to something 'that lies outside personal desires, that includes resignation for ourselves and active love for what is not ourselves.'[24] George Eliot had a deep sensibility to religious experience: she knew how and why religious people experience a divine redemptive power and presence.

It is of course possible to offer a naturalistic as opposed to a religious interpretation of religious experience, to reduce religion to a purely human construct that allegedly serves psychological and social needs. There is no way of *proving* either interpretation, no non-circular way of establishing fundamental positions. 'All meanings, we know, depend on the key of interpretation.'[25] We must make basic assumptions and test them against lived experience to determine how persuasive they are. Is it the case that the human problem is simply one of a social and psychological pathology that can be remedied by getting rid of false religious consciousness? Or is it an ontological problem rooted in the inability of human beings to find security and fulfillment in any finite object? Are humans hopelessly lost in a situation of anxiety and meaninglessness? Or is something like redemptive transformation going on in the midst of suffering, cruelty, and despair by means of which that which founds and secures human life actually comes forth? Through the creation of her fictional worlds, George Eliot was drawn beyond Feuerbachian reduction to a much more profound engagement with religious truth. Her 'cooking'[26] of Feuerbach yielded something that can genuinely nourish theological reflection.

In the final analysis Feuerbach's own construal of human experience remains flat, one-dimensional, and uninteresting. The simple 'reversal' of theological predicates into humanistic ones not only lacks imagination but also fails to appreciate the rich complexity and multidimensionality of the world in which we live. The reversal is naively optimistic for it assumes that alienation and evil will disappear once it is recognized that the human species itself is the rightful object of veneration, the source and end of all love. Feuerbach lacked a sense of the tragic and thus had no real understanding of the religious awareness of guilt and forgiveness, sin and redemption.[27] His theory is too predictable, too unnuanced, too prosaic, too insensitive to intended religious meanings. How pretentious to suppose that one has found, in Casaubon-like fashion, the key to all religious mythologies! Possibly George Eliot had Feuerbach, or Strauss, or a composite of theologians in mind when she created the character of Casaubon in *Middlemarch*.[28] While Casaubon thought he had discovered the key to all religious mythologies in a primordial revelation, Feuerbach found it in a primordial psychic projection and Strauss in a primordial divine-human unity. George Eliot was suspicious of all such totalizing theories, all proposals about the 'essence' of something.[29]

What Feuerbach lacked above all else was poetic sensibility – an appreciation for mystery, an attention to the concrete and particular, an ability to see and articulate the surprising connections (as well as differences) between things, an apprehension of both deep conflicts and new possibilities. George Eliot possessed it in abundance. And without poetry religion is impossible.

3. The Mystery of God and the Mysteries of Redemption

a. Redemptive Transformation

Thus we arrive at what I regard as the central problematic facing postmodern theology, namely how to speak meaningfully of God's presence and action in the world today,[30] and it is at this point that the linkage implicit in George Eliot's fiction between the idea of God and the idea of redemption proves helpful. A similar linkage is found in the recent work of the theologian Edward Farley. Farley argues that God's concrete reality is not thinkable. Rather what we are able to think and experience is the way that God comes forth as God in the facticity of redemption. 'Redemption' or 'redemptive transformation' means the various processes by which human beings are turned away from idolatrous, alienating, destructive attachments and moved in the direction of goods such as courage, freedom, compassion, and justice. The word 'God' has meaning in actual religious communities in connection with some sort of experienced redemption; and, because God is the power that brings about the redemption, a conviction of the reality of God emerges along with a grasp of the meaning of God. Only the infinite, eternal horizon toward which humans are oriented can found their being in such a way as to free them from idolatrous attachments to finite and temporal objects; and, because such a liberation is actually experienced, the eternal horizon must be real. This does not establish what it is in and for itself; rather it gives us a 'symbolics,' a network of significations for 'bespeaking' God, not a definition of God's nature and attributes. God is never directly conceived and experienced but rather 'appresented' in and through the symbolics of redemption. Farley identifies his approach with an 'anti-attribute tradition' or a negative theology that goes back to Pseudo-Dionysius and Maimonides, appears again in the classical Reformers and liberal Protestant theology (Friedrich Schleiermacher), and is exemplified by contemporary Jewish theology (Franz Rosenzweig, Martin Buber, Emmanuel Levinas) and recent continental philosophies of religion (Nicholas Berdyaev, Gabriel Marcel, Paul Ricoeur).[31] Is it too much to suggest that George Eliot in her own way belongs to this tradition?

Farley specifies certain 'ciphers' that emerge from ways that redemption is experienced in the realms of human agency, the interhuman, and the social. In the sphere of human agency these are the ciphers of founding, empowerment, and courage. Thereby the corrupted human passions for existence, others, and the real are transformed toward 'an authentic vitality of subjectivity, agapic freedom toward others, and wonder in the face of the real.' In the sphere of the interhuman it is the cipher of reconciling love. The only thing that can break interhuman alienation is the power of repentance and forgiveness. In the sphere of the sociopolitical it is the cipher of justice, which aims toward a social redemption beyond all competing interests and political agendas. Farley also identifies ciphers of creativity and holiness, which are closely related to ciphers of redemption. The holy gathers and shatters all other ciphers. What is truly holy and awesome about God is not an unfathomable abyss but an unfathomable reconciling, liberating love.[32]

The redemptive coming forth of God as God does not take place by way of a divine-human immediacy that bypasses language, institutions, history. Being-founded is not a supernatural inter-vention in a human psyche; rather it occurs only in connection with something that alters language, calls forth new communities, resymbolizes tradition. As a facticity, redemption takes place in and through the historical. The 'through-which' of redemption is the historical mediation of new stories, altered symbolics, new intersubjectivities, changed historical memories, charismatic figures, new communities and traditions.[33]

What I find interesting is that George Eliot's fiction describes the 'through-which' of redemption in terms very similar to those used by Farley. In her novels we encounter characters whose stories are changed: they experience being-founded (for example, Edgar Tryan, Dinah Morris), acquire a new courage for life (Janet Dempster, Maggie Tulliver), repent and are forgiven (Hetty Sorrell, Gwendolen Harleth), engage in acts of love and mercy (Romola de' Bardi, Dorothea Brooke), strive to build communities of justice (Felix Holt, Daniel Deronda). A superabundant love is at work in these stories, despite all the ambiguities, limitations, and tragic conflicts that are woven into them.

George Eliot once defined the tragic as the terrible difficulties created by the conflict between individual interests and the necessities of the general human condition. Under these circumstances, 'piety' and the 'will of God' consist in combining renunciation with resistance, a willing submission to fate with the resolve to over-come evil insofar as possible ('Promethean effort towards high possibilities').[34] In so doing human beings find the wherewithal to survive, even to flourish, and life goes on, but fragmentarily, ambiguously, brokenly. Redemption is occurring in a not-yet-redeemed world. These are marks of George Eliot's meliorism and realism. 'Never to bear and bruise one's wings against the inevitable but to throw the whole force of one's soul towards the achievement of some possible better.'[35] The task of practical wisdom is to say, not 'This is good, and I will have it,' but 'This is the less of two unavoidable evils, and I will bear it.'[36] The very unattainability of moral perfection offers an all the more urgent reason 'for at least diminishing the pressure of evil, for worshipping the goodness and the great endeavors that are at least a *partial* salvation, a *partial* redemption of the world.'[37]

For George Eliot, partial redemption seemed more achievable in the realms of human agency and the interhuman than in the realm of the social, which is preeminently the realm of the tragic, the realm where the clash between the individual and the general accomplishes little by way of changing fundamental structures. She was deeply aware of ethnic, creedal, gender, and class divisions, but her novels portray very little progress toward a more just society. For example, in *Daniel Deronda*, Gwendolen was able to become a better person, but the 'spirit of arrogance and contemptuous dictatorialness'[38] of the English upper classes remained undiminished. Just this is the dilemma of modern-day Theresas, we are told in *Middlemarch:* they lacked a 'coherent social faith and order' in which their reforming zeal could achieve concrete results. So in spite of the 'incalculably diffusive' effects of Dorothea's goodness, life in Middlemarch went on pretty much as before.[39] Perhaps this is just the point: the effects of her goodness were diffused across a multitude of individuals but not concentrated upon specific social reforms, such as her frustrated desire to build better cottages for tenant farmers. Even the more overtly political novels, *Romola* and *Felix Holt*, offer little hope of a transformation of the social order. But individuals are not thereby exempted from social responsibility. They are enjoined to place the public good above private interests. Thus Romola found her place among suffering Florentines, and Felix among the working poor. Political reforms such as the franchise will help, but only if individuals learn to use them responsibly. The 'great yearning' for justice that is within us can actually move human beings to act responsibly – it has an efficacious power; but it is an illusion to think that the kingdom of justice will ever be established as a political fact.

The stories of Milly Barton, Maynard Gilfil, Edgar Tryan, Janet Dempster, Dinah Morris, Adam Bede, Maggie Tulliver, Silas Marner, Romola de' Bardi, Felix Holt, Dorothea Brooke, Daniel Deronda, and Gwendolen Harleth follow a common basic pattern despite important differences. Through various sorrows and sufferings – their own and/or those of others – some kind of redemptive transformation takes place. God is experienced as present and engaged in this process in some fashion. Mr. Gilfil told Caterina that God sees and judges us whole, knowing the underlying goodness that is in most of us. Janet found that God not only offers forgiveness but also gives strength to do the right. Dinah felt that she was part of the divine presence, that it was the divine pity beating in her heart. Maggie found the clue of life in an imitation of Christ and sensed that the Unseen Pity would be with her to the end. Silas came to believe in a goodness greater than he could comprehend in spite of trouble and wickedness. Romola became a fellow worker in the history of redemption, which she discovered is not a miraculous history of special effects but depends rather on individual human beings who see the good and do it in concrete circumstances. Dorothea believed that by striving for the unattainable, unknowable good, human beings are part of the divine power against evil. Daniel learned that, through his acts of kindness toward Mirah and Gwendolen, he found a pathway that was a sign of the divine omnipresence in which everything dwells. Gwendolen resolved, in the light of the judgment of the Invisible and Universal that Deronda brought to bear on her, to live and be better, indeed to be one of the best of women who make others glad that they were born.

How do we know that these beliefs, feelings, apprehensions of divinity are genuine, that they are not simply projections of human desires or indications of the resilience and resourcefulness of humanity? The answer that George Eliot hints at is similar to the one adduced by Farley: only that which is infinite and eternal can free human beings from idolatrous attachments to finite and temporal objects. Any other source, even the Feuerbachian human species-essence, would itself be an idol and could not offer genuine redemption. Thus those who are mediators of divine redemption have the sense of being 'channeled,' 'called,' 'subdued,' 'laid upon,' and 'led on' by a gratuitous power not at their disposal. It is not simply they – finite, fragile, sinful human beings – who are speaking and acting, but God speaking and acting through them. In the language of traditional theology, they are 'inspired,' filled by the Holy Spirit. If redemption is really experienced, then the activity and reality of God are experienced. But what are this activity and reality?

b. God: Divine Sympathy, Suffering, Omnipresence

Farley argues that because we are not privy to the divine activity itself we have need of a speculative paradigm that employs metaphors. He proposes that we think of God as 'the influential power (efficacy) of human empathy.' This paradigm assumes that Scripture does not give us a direct, determining, unopposable divine causality. Rather 'God's redemptive activity concurs with the independence and responsiveness of worldly entities.' The metaphor that governs the paradigm is that of divine 'empathy.'

> If redemption means a founding that imparts courage to anxious and idolatrous agents, a reconciling love imparted to human relations, and an emancipating norm of justice for oppressed groups, that which redeems is a kind of compassion, an acting on behalf of needy others. And if the meaning of the event of Jesus as Christ is that the divine empathy and the empathy of Jesus are so united that Jesus embraces the suffering necessary to embody a universalizing as–such relation, then the empathy of God is also a pathos, a 'fellow-feeling' that suffers because its creativity inevitably moves the world in the direction of complex and intensified experiencings and therefore in the direction of intensified suffering.[40]

By a 'universalizing as–such relation,' Farley means that Jesus described and embodied a relationship to God that is simply 'as such,' an absolute relationship, a matter of direct trust, without resentment, calculation, preoccupation with status, cultic and moral paraphernalia, etc.; it is an 'innocent' life of faith and trust in God.[41]

Farley notes that the terms 'empathy,' 'sympathy' ('fellow-feeling'), 'compassion,' and 'love' are often used synonymously despite semantic shades of difference. Empathy, he says, is a transcendentally-based capacity to perceive the other in its experiencing. Sympathy is not just a perception but a participation in the life of the other. Compassion is a participation in the *suffering* of the other. Love is an unqualified suffering self-impartation of one's being to or for the sake of the other. The terms move from the more abstract and universal to the concrete and particular. These distinctions tend to collapse or merge when applied to the divine activity, and Farley intends the expression 'divine empathy' to include all of these features.[42] George Eliot's preferred encompassing metaphor, as we have seen, is 'sympathy' ('the one poor word which includes all our best insight and our best love'),[43] which is functionally equivalent to Farley's 'empathy.' It is not by accident that all of her stories are love stories, for it is in love relationships that pathos for and suffering with the other (*sym-pathos*) is at its most intense and concrete. These stories are reverberations of the cosmic love story.

How is the divine empathy/sympathy/suffering actually exercised so as to be efficacious in the world?[44] Is it simply the Creativity that disposes the world, the force or energy (*nisus*) that pushes it toward novelty and greater intensity of suffering (Bergson, Whitehead)? Or is the God who redemptively comes forth as God a Thou, a 'face' of empathetic suffering (Buber, Levinas)? Is God substance or subject? Farley wants to affirm both, but he avoids Hegel's speculative way of integrating subject and substance under the category of 'Spirit.' For him it is a matter of two distinct, unsynthesizable appresentations of divinity. On the one hand, something *disposes* or *pushes* the world toward synthesis, cooperation, novelty, offering relevant graded possibilities to each occasion of experience. An eros toward beauty is implanted in world processes. On the other hand, something works to *draw* worldly entities out of their self-preoccupation and isolation into the realm of the other. It is empathy with the other's suffering that draws the self out of itself; and it is in the face of the suffering other that the face of God, the divine Thou, is encountered. Human empathy has an efficacious or influential character. 'To experience another's sympathetic participation in one's grief . . . is to be affected in one's being.' Divine empathy is similarly efficacious; it is the one and only thing that is concerned for the mutual enhancement of all entities and enlarges the sympathy of all.

God as Thou makes its own empathetic suffering available to entities. As entities grasp the vulnerable beauty of others in their environment, they are at the same time grasping and experiencing the mystery at work in that beauty, a suffering Thou whose empathy bestows on others a pathos that draws entities out of themselves . . . The pathos of the other simply cannot of itself penetrate the entity's self-orientation until or unless it is connected to the Pathos in which everything takes place.[45]

The similarities between Farley's theology of God and George Eliot's theological intuitions should be evident. In these similarities she is close to Farley's theological mentor, Friedrich Schleiermacher. As far as we know she never read a word of Schleiermacher, but it is worth reflecting on the fact that both she and Schleiermacher were influenced by Spinoza in an early stage of their intellectual development. She would have agreed that the reality of God is not thinkable, and that the divine mystery manifests itself, if at all, through the mysteries of redemption. The relationship to God is one not of cognition but of feeling – the feeling of simple trust and dependence.[46] She criticized the dualistic antithesis of God and world, which requires special and exceptional acts of God in the world. Rather God acts, if at all, through natural, historical, and human processes. She oscillated between thinking of divinity on the one hand as an active, sympathetic presence and suffering, a Thou that indwells and empowers specific individuals in concrete circumstances; and on the other hand as a generalized omnipresence, a cosmic and moral lawgiver, a transpersonal substance or highest Good that indwells and disposes everything.[47] The oscillation reflects the fact that she never resolved the tension between a Hegelian philosophy of subject or spirit (*Geist*) and a Spinozistic philosophy of substance. These are the two great options for thinking about divinity that have appeared in the history of religions in a diversity of forms: God as personal subject and as cosmic power or process. Whether they are ultimately reconcilable or incompatible is one of the undecidable questions. We cannot know what God is in and for godself.

In so far as the second way of thinking about God prevailed in her later novels, George Eliot was drawn closer to Spinoza and Schleiermacher theologically. An interesting variation on this approach is the testimony to wisdom found at the end of Felix Holt's address to working men.[48] The wisdom that stands outside of human beings is the wisdom of nature and of God, and the work of history is the stupendous yet patient pedagogy by which wisdom builds her home within the human heart, bringing about a re-orientation to love and justice. Wisdom is the power by which God's rule of the world is accomplished pedagogically, not imperi-ously. It (or she) is both an impersonal power that drives us and yet a personified power that draws us. This dual characteristic is found in the figure of Wisdom in Hebrew Scripture, and in fact the figure mediates between the two approaches. Wisdom is personified inso-far as she becomes incarnate in human faces and voices, but what is incarnate is not a divine person but a divine power.

The first way of thinking was more characteristic of the early novels, and it was anticipated by George Eliot's *Westminster Review* essay of 1855.[49] There, as we have seen, she argued that we need the sympathetic presence of a friend in order to have the courage and strength to act under difficult circumstances. The sympathy thus experienced is efficacious; it actually strengthens us. But human friends are often weak and not steadfast; we need also a divine friend who will pour new life into our languid love and empower our vacillating resolve. The divine friendship is not given to us directly but through the mediation of human friends. God is manifest in the flesh – not just the flesh (or face) of Jesus, but also the flesh (and faces) of countless human beings. God may appear in the face of a friend who helps or judges us, or in the face of a friend who suffers and is in need. The concrete encounter with suffering and needy others is what finally draws human beings out of their predominant egoism and self-centeredness, and when the divine pathos is seen in those human faces the effect is all the more powerful.

George Eliot's stories illustrate these ideas in very compelling, moving ways. The suffering death of Milly Barton and the anguish of Amos Barton broke the cold-heartedness of the parishioners of Shepperton, and they gave their pastor solace. Janet Dempster found in Edgar Tryan a friend who mediated to her the reality of divine, uplifting strength, and she saw in his compassionate, dying face the face of God. The madonna-like face of Dinah Morris manifested the loving, sympathetic presence of God to those in need, such as Lisbeth Bede when her husband died, and Hetty

Sorrel when she faced the gallows. Dinah knew that sorrow is part of love and that true love does not seek to throw it off because it heightens pathos and intensifies experience. Thus humanity needs a suffering God, and such a God is found in the Man of Sorrows, who is one with the infinite love itself. Dinah's sermon set forth the idea of divine friendship espoused in the *Westminster Review* treatise.[50] God is not remote and lofty but has come near and is our friend – above all in the words and deeds of Jesus, who was just like God and whose love for the poor is the same love that God has for us. God is always there as our friend, more steadfastly than any human friend, and God's friendship is what enables us to hold up when pain and troubles come or when we face our own death. It is not that God grants us special favors, for example, exemptions from the laws of cause and effect; rather God is just *there* through thick and thin.

Dinah was the greatest witness to the sympathetic, suffering presence of God in George Eliot's fiction, but the idea did not come to an end with her story. Maggie Tulliver learned the truth of renunciation from Thomas à Kempis's theology of the cross, and she gave her own life in an effort to rescue others from the flood. Silas Marner discovered the divine friendship in the face and hand of a little child, who led him out of self-preoccupation into a life of love and sympathy. Romola was turned away from self-preoccupation by the arresting face and voice of Savonarola, from whom she learned to think of God through the image of the cross – 'the image of a Supreme Offering, made by Supreme Love, because the need of man was great.'[51] She in turn befriended the sick and hungry in pestilence-ridden places and also her husband's lover, the hapless Tessa and her children; as such she became a visible madonna, a madonna with a face. Dorothea Brooke, who strove to be part of the divine power against evil, served this role in her sympathy for Tertius Lydgate, who thought she had a heart large enough for the Virgin Mary; and Dorothea was shocked out of her own jealousy and egoism by an awareness of Rosamond's great need. The 'dominant spirit of justice' came upon her during her night of self-mortification, and she resolved that her own irremediable grief should make her more rather than less helpful. By emptying herself of her own desires, she received a greater abundance: Rosamond gave back to Dorothea what she had given up, and in this way Rosamond too for a moment became a media-trix of grace. Daniel Deronda, by responding sympathetically to the needs of Mirah, Mordecai, and Gwendolen, found a pathway into the divine life. We are told that he was 'in the stead of God' to Gwendolen, and she was finally able to overcome her own selfishness when she saw the face of her drowning husband and fully appreciated the anguish Deronda suffered on her behalf.

These later stories are told against the backdrop, not so much of an active, suffering, empowering divine Face, but rather of an all-inclusive Omnipresence, a Whole that contains and preserves every part as a part. George Eliot found the latter idea expressed in Jewish mysticism, but the former is very much present there as well (although God's face cannot be seen directly).[52] It is notable that metaphors of 'drawing' and 'growing' are used by Mordecai of the Omnipresence, as though it were a personal Presence. Romola in particular struggled with the question whether it is possible to experience a personal Presence. As she drifted despairingly at sea with thoughts of death, 'memories hung about her like the weight of broken wings that could never be lifted – memories of human sympathy which even in its pains leaves a thirst that the Great Mother has no milk to still.'[53] This is one of the few gendered references to divinity in George Eliot's fiction, and the gender is female. But even the Great Mother's milk cannot always slake the thirst of human beings. At this point in her life Romola felt orphaned and alone. Later, however, she concluded that these negative thoughts could not be founded in the truth of things: it was 'impossible that it had not been a living spirit, and no hollow pretence, which had once . . . kindled a new life in her.'[54]

Connected with the idea of God are questions of divine provi-dence and theodicy, which, as we have seen, George Eliot was concerned with in all her novels but especially in *Romola, Middle-march,* and *Daniel Deronda*. Edward Farley in addressing these questions argues that the activity of God takes place in connection with unpredictable human responses and adamant resistance. God is an ongoing empowering of entities but not with predetermined outcomes and without overcoming the tragedy of the world, which on his reading arises from the fact that conflict, frustration, and non-fulfillments are built into organic, historical, psychological existence as conditions of the very possibility of finite beings. Farley goes further and suggests that God godself is implicated in the tragic character of world process. God does not promote *evil* if evil means not tragedy but resistance to empathy. But divine activity intensifies suffering in order to have entities that themselves can exist empathetically. By fostering union and cooperation, God tragically draws the world toward greater intensities of both sorrow and joy.[55]

This interpretation accords well with George Eliot's insight that true divine providence works against the interests of individuals and cuts across normal human passions. Far from serving our self-interests and personal agendas, providence demands of us something more, pushes us to the limits of human possibilities. Rather than adjusting the laws of cause and effect to what suits us best, it creates a moral universe in which deeds yield inexorable consequences. It presents possibilities for good and evil, and it empowers individuals to make something good of these opportunities; but individuals must be receptive to this empowerment and are responsible for the decisions they make. Providence is the divine pedagogy, the work of wisdom in history. Whether this constitutes an actual theodicy in George Eliot's case – a justification of the goodness and righteousness of God in face of evident evil – is a complex matter. If theodicy amounts to a rational 'explanation' of the ways of God, she would reject it.[56] She once wrote: 'The fact that in the scheme of things we see a constant and tremendous sacrifice of individuals is, it seems to me only one of the many proofs that urge upon us our total inability to find in our own natures a key to the Divine Mystery.'[57] She experimented with various possibilities in her writings, formulating ideas of remarkable interest to postmodern theology, but she never arrived at a solution that seemed to her truly satisfactory. For this reason her ultimate stance in relation to the question of God was agnostic. She did not arrive at a *visio beatifica* but remained on a pilgrimage to the end.

4. Judaism and Christianity

We have noted that toward the end of her career George Eliot was attracted to Judaism, and that throughout her adult life she appreciated the importance of affirming a diversity of religious views and traditions among which there should prevail what she called 'separateness with communication.'[58] Separateness is important because each religion has its own distinctive cultural and historical genius. It is only in the web of history, with all its specificity and contingency, that great ideas are conceived, born, and matured into distinctive contributions to the wider human community. Without their religio–cultural–ethnic determinacy these ideas lose their power; they become abstractions.[59] Communication is important because all religions constitute pathways toward an ultimate, incomprehensible, unattainable divine Unity, and because conflicts and rivalries between religions can generate highly destructive forms of human aggression. The author was attracted to Lessing's great ideal of religious tolerance, but this did not mean for her a religious indifferentism.

The genius of a religion may also indicate a point of vulnerability. So it is with Judaism and Christianity. The genius of Judaism, suggests Farley, has been its 'capacity to preserve an authentic faith and life before God while existing in cultural environments hostile to that faith.' It has had the resources to resist the corrupting elements of an alien culture, but at the price of limiting its faith to a particular people, of tying together too closely religion and ethnicity. The genius of Christianity, by contrast, has been 'its way of carrying the faith of Israel into any and all societal and cultural frameworks without an ethnic *sine qua non*.'[60] This capacity is related to the figure of Jesus, who as the 'incarnation' of divine empathy instantiated an absolute, as-such relationship to God, independent of Torah and nationhood, and thus brought about a universalizing of the faith of Israel. But the universalizing has come with a price, namely the risk of cultural assimilation at one extreme, and of institutional imperialism and doctrinal dogmatism at the other. While George Eliot did not pose the issue in quite these terms, they are not incompatible with her way of thinking.

She was opposed to efforts by Christians to convert Jews, and she believed that for Judaism to flourish once again and to maintain its distinctive identity it must have a national homeland, or at least an 'organic center' to which Jews everywhere in the world could relate. She was attracted, as we have seen, to the spirituality of Judaism, its communal ethos combined with an ethical universalism, its sense of the divine presence in the whole of creation, its hesitancy to utter the name of God. By avoiding the triumphalism and absolutism of much Christian theology, it not only is less dangerous to other religions but also more realistic about history: the messianic age has not come and redemption here and now is partial, ambiguous, unfinished, tragic. Moreover, Judaism has (in the words of Mordecai) a mission to serve as the 'heart' of humanity, to work for equality and freedom and be a 'covenant of reconciliation.'[61]

But George Eliot did not convert to Judaism. She maintained an association with Christianity through both the Church of England and Unitarianism, although hers was a nonconformist, noncreedal, nonpracticing form of Christian belief. The question must have occurred to her: what constitutes the distinctive genius of Christianity? What is the appropriate role of Christ in Christianity? Is it possible to reaffirm Christ after an engagement with biblical criticism, feminism, Unitarianism, and Judaism? These are questions that she largely avoided. She could not return to the Jesus-piety of her youth after Strauss had demonstrated the extensive presence of mythical elements in the gospel stories about Jesus, and after both Strauss and Feuerbach had exposed the metaphysical difficulties in the classical doctrine of the two natures of Christ. In some respects for her the Jesus-figure was displaced or supplemented by the madonna-figure – an undeniably human figure, sublime yet sensuous, one whose face was filled by the glory of God but also by motherly love and care.

Yet George Eliot remained strongly attracted to the Man of Sorrows. She saw in his story the mythos and pathos of the human story, and his story hovered in the background of the stories of her great heroines and heroes, many of whom exemplified an *imitatione Christi*. She attended to the symbolism attached to the beginning of the story at Christmas (the child of promise who leads us into a new life) and the ending of the story at Easter (the cross of renunciation and suffering).[62] She once hinted at how the interpretation of the identity of Jesus as both divine and human (the traditional christological problem) might be reconstructed so as to make sense to persons who live in the age of modernity and postmodernity. It is a reconstruction that enhances communication between Christianity and Judaism because it offers a picture of Jesus that is not anti-Jewish (even if it is not itself a Jewish interpretation).

'Who *was* this man?' Dinah Morris asked in her sermon on the Hayslope green.

> Was he only a good man – a very good man, and no more? . . . He was the Son of God – "in the image of the Father," the Bible says; that means, just like God, who is the beginning and end of all things . . . So then, all the love that Jesus showed to the poor is the same love that God has for us . . . He has showed us what God's heart is, what are his feelings toward us.[63]

To say that Jesus was 'the Son of God' does not mean that he had a divine nature miraculously conjoined with human nature; he was not a god in human flesh. Rather it means that he was 'just like God,' and he was just like God in his love, his deep compassion and sympathy for those in need. His love was *the very same love* that God has for us; it showed us what God's heart and feelings are. This identity of divine and human love in Jesus is what for Christians sets him apart from other human beings, but it intensifies rather than diminishes his humanity, and thus it also connects him with every human being. 'Is not the Man of Sorrows . . . one with the Infinite Love itself – as our love is one with sorrow?'[64] Jesus showed that love and sorrow, joy and suffering, are necessarily connected because love for the other draws one out of oneself into the pathos and suffering of the other. The utmost intensity of love, as in God's love for us, entails the utmost suffering. This connection, which is a Jewish as well as a Christian insight,[65] is one that human beings experience in their daily lives, and it is rooted in the divine mystery itself. It is the mystery beneath the real.

Notes

1. George Eliot's Religious Pilgrimage

1. I will follow the accepted practice of citing the pen name 'George Eliot' in full, not simply as 'Eliot,' which implies a surname. In the notes I use the abbreviations 'GE' for George Eliot and 'GHL' for George Henry Lewes.

2. See, for example, E. S. Shaffer, *Kubla Khan and the Fall of Jerusalem: The Mythological School in Biblical Criticism and Secular Literature, 1770–1880*, Cambridge: Cambridge University Press 1975, chap. 6; Thomas Vargish, *The Providential Aesthetic in Victorian Fiction*, Charlottesville: University Press of Virginia 1985, chap. 4; and Mary Wilson Carpenter, *George Eliot and the Landscape of Time: Narrative Form and Protestant Apocalyptic History*, Chapel Hill: University of North Carolina Press 1986. Carpenter traces in great detail the biblical imagery and number symbolisms employed in GE's novels, but her approach to the texts is not theological; in fact, it is anti-theological. By contrast, Valerie A. Dodd, in *George Eliot: An Intellectual Life*, New York: St. Martin's Press 1990, notes GE's wide exposure to theology and her continuing interest in religion, but finally offers an aesthetic rather than a theological interpretation. The most recent biographies – Frederick R. Karl, *George Eliot: Voice of a Century*, New York: W. W. Norton & Co. 1995; Rosemary Ashton, *George Eliot: A Life*, London: Hamish Hamilton 1996; Penguin Books 1997; Kathryn Hughes, *George Eliot: The Last Victorian*, New York: Farrar, Straus and Giroux 1999 – offer very little on the subject of religion. William S. Peterson notes this deficit in his review of Ashton in *The New York Times*, 27 July 1997. He refers to 'Eliot's life-long search for some larger meaning in the cosmos,' and suggests that it would be helpful if the next biographer would tell us not only about 'Eliot the beleaguered woman' but also about 'Eliot the beleaguered religious skeptic.' Unfortunately, the next biographer,

Hughes, does not; she assumes that GE's religion reduces to a Feuer-bachian humanism and at best serves a psychological function, a substi-tute perhaps for the lack of maternal love.

3. Basil Willey, *Nineteenth Century Studies*, London: Chatto & Windus 1955, p. 238.

4. Gordon S. Haight (ed.), *The George Eliot Letters*, 9 vols., New Haven: Yale University Press 1954–6, 1978, 1.6 (to Maria Lewis, 18 Aug. 1838): henceforward *Letters*. The letters are a major source for this chapter. Not only are many of the letters epistolary masterpieces, but they reveal the author's wit, charm, and humanity. In the lofty phrases of a precocious twenty-one-year old she proclaims that the Lord's voice 'is to be heard in every note of the scale to which His dealings in the Kingdom of Grace and of Providence are set; from the still and gently drawing whispers of His Spirit in the soul to the deep-toned and almost stunning thunder of his power when whole nations, while falling a sacrifice on the shrine of His incensed justice, subserve at the same time the designs of His compassion by putting others in fear that they may know themselves to be but men.' But then she comes back to earth with the following comment: 'Both this and many other defects in my letter are attributable to a very mighty cause – no other than the boiling of currant jelly' (1.59 [to Maria Lewis, 20 July 1840]).

5. *Letters*, 6.216 (to Dr. Joseph Frank Payne, 25 Jan. 1876).

6. *Letters*, 5.31 (8 May 1869).

7. *Letters*, 4.95 (to Barbara Bodichon, 26 Nov. 1862).

8. *Daniel Deronda* (1876), edited by Terence Cave, London: Penguin Books 1995, chap. 63, p. 749. Because the novels are published in differ-ent editions, I cite chapter numbers (the same in all editions) followed by page numbers (for the particular edition indicated) – e.g. 63.749.

9. Ibid., 60.725.

10. See Dodd, *George Eliot,* pp. 194–7, 286–7; and the introduction by Jane Irwin to her edition of *George Eliot's Daniel Deronda Notebooks*, Cambridge, Cambridge University Press 1996, pp. xxxvi–xxxviii.

11. *Letters*, 1.6, 9–10, 12, 14, 16–17, 34, 38, 44, 48, 63, 102–3 (these are letters mostly written to Maria Lewis, GE's former boarding school teacher, between 1838 and 1841).

12. See Gordon S. Haight, *George Eliot: A Biography*, London: Penguin Books 1986, pp. 18–29; and Ashton, *George Eliot*, pp. 19–32.

13. *Letters,* 1.128 (to Robert Evans, 28 Feb. 1842). 'While I admire and cherish much of what I believe to have been the moral teaching of Jesus himself, I consider the system of doctrines built up from the facts of his life and drawn as to its materials from Jewish notions to be most dis-

honourable to God and most pernicious in its influence on individual and social happiness.' A month later she repented of her 'impetuosity' and strove to put an end to this little 'holy war' by resuming church attendance with the proviso that she would hold her own opinions (see *Letters*, 1.134 [to Abijah Hill Pears, 31 Mar. 1842]). Alienation from her own family on religious matters (as described in all the biographies) certainly played a role in both the sympathetic and the unsympathetic representations of religion in GE's novels.

14. The Unitarian chapel in Hampstead was within walking distance of where GE and GHL lived from 1863 to 1878. A letter from Catharine T. Herford to *The Guardian*, 2 July 1980, written in response to letters questioning the propriety of placing a memorial to GE in Westminster Abbey on the hundredth anniversary of her death, states the following: 'George Eliot was no atheist, even if her parish church was closed to her. My mother – living in Hampstead until her marriage in 1886 and brought up as a member of the Rosslyn Hill (Unitarian) Chapel – used to tell us that she remembered the author attending the chapel more Sundays than not, and finding there a spiritual home denied in other recognised communities.' I am indebted to David Pailin for confirming the details of this letter, to which reference is made in Dodd, *George Eliot*, p. 86.

15. 'Evangelical Teaching: Dr. Cumming', *Westminster Review*, Oct. 1855, in *Selected Essays, Poems and Other Writings*, ed. A. S. Byatt and Nicholas Watten, London: Penguin Books 1990, p. 41.

16. Ibid., pp. 43–65.

17. Paul Ricoeur, 'Religion, Atheism, and Faith,' in Alasdair MacIntyre and Paul Ricoeur, *The Religious Significance of Atheism*, New York: Columbia University Press 1969, p. 60.

18. *Letters*, 1.126 (to Abijah Hill Pears, 28 Jan. 1842). See also 1.143–4 (to Francis Watts, 3 Aug. 1842). Mary Sibree wrote to her brother John on 28 Oct. 1842 that 'Miss Evans . . . seemed more settled in her views than ever, and rests her objections to Christianity on this ground, that Calvinism is Christianity, and that granted, that it is a religion based on pure selfishness' (*Letters*, 1.151 n. 42).

19. *Letters*, 1.206 (Caroline Bray to Sara Sophia Hennell, 14 Feb. 1846). The Christ-image was a cast of Thorwaldsen's *Risen Christ*, and the picture an engraving of Delaroche's *Christ*. Both were in her study at Foleshill. Other letters from GE to Sara Sophia Hennell indicate that she had ceased to relish her work on the translation (*Letters*, 1.185 [6 Apr. 1845]), and that she came to regard much of Strauss's treatment of the betrayal, passion, crucifixion, and resurrection of Jesus as tedious or taste-

less – e.g., his interest in anatomical details of the crucifixion, or in the legend concerning the 'bursting asunder' of Judas (*Letters*, 1.207 [4 Mar. 1846]). But when the work was finished she wrote: 'I do really like reading our Strauss – he is so klar und ideenvoll but I do not know *one* person who is likely to read the book through, do you?' (*Letters*, 1.217–18 [GE to Sara Sophia Hennell, 20 May 1846]). The matter of 'coldbloodedness' is discussed in this and the immediately preceding letter. Strauss himself referred in his Preface to the first edition (1835) to the *Kaltblütigkeit* with which 'criticism undertakes apparently dangerous operations.' In the published translation this was reduced to 'insensitivity,' although GE preferred 'sang froid.' On her later contacts with Strauss, whom she regarded as a rather melancholy figure, see Haight, *George Eliot*, pp. 150–1, 261. On her work on the translation, see my editorial introduction to David Friedrich Strauss, *The Life of Jesus Critically Examined*, trans. from the 4th German edition (1840) by George Eliot, Philadelphia: Fortress Press 1972; London: SCM Press 1973, pp. xlvii–xlix.

20. See Strauss, *The Life of Jesus Critically Examined*, pp. xxii–xxxvi, 287–96, 584–96, 757–84. In the third edition (1838), Strauss retracted his portrayal of the message and person of Jesus in apocalyptic terms, and re-presented him as one filled with the greatest intensity of God-consciousness possible for a single individual. On this basis he argued that Jesus was the essential figure by whom the idea of divine-human unity was and continues to be revealed to humanity as a whole. This 'mediating' Christology brought him into proximity with Schleiermacher, of whom he had been critical in the earlier editions, and also to some extent with Hegel and theological Hegelians such as F. C. Baur. But this and other changes introduced marked tensions into the underlying philosophical perspective of the work, which remained that of a monistic pantheism, and his fundamental impulse was to resist any attempt to mediate between the orthodox doctrines of faith and modern 'scientific' knowledge. Strauss was a disjunctive rather than a mediating thinker, and consequently he was much more effective at criticism than at reconstruction. Thus in the fourth edition of 1840 he restored most of the original readings from the first and second editions of 1835–6, having inflicted considerable damage on his credibility. (See pp. xxxvi–xlvii, 797–802.) Charles Hennell had arranged to translate the fourth edition on the assumption that it was the latest and most authoritative, although the other editions were in his possession and he was partially aware of the variations between them. Had Mary Ann Evans translated the third rather than the fourth edition, a strangely compromised version of Strauss's work would have become known in English.

21. Ibid., p. 781.

22. Ibid., pp. 777–8.

23. *Letters*, 2.153 (29 April 1854). GE was tempted, in fact, to sanitize Feuerbach for an English audience, but in the end made only a few changes (see *Letters*, 2.137, 142, 154, 157). U. C. Knoepflmacher quotes only the 'everywhere agreeing' part of this statement and sets forth what has now become widely accepted dogma: 'This agreement [with Feuerbach] is everywhere exemplified in [GE's] novels. Feuerbach and the "Higher Criticism" had taught her that Christianity was a fable, a beautiful fiction which contained only a "Religion of Humanity," teaching the perennial truth of human love and selflessness. In her own fiction, begun two and a half years later, she sought to recreate this "truth" with something of the fierce intensity which marked her evangelical upbringing.' *Religious Humanism and the Victorian Novel: George Eliot, Walter Pater, and Samuel Butler*, Princeton, N.J.: Princeton University Press 1965, pp. 53–4. On Knoepflmacher, see further below, n. 76.

24. See Kathryn Bond Stockton's discussion of 'Cooking Feuerbach' in *God between Their Lips: Desire between Women in Irigaray, Brontë, and Eliot*, Stanford: Stanford University Press 1994, pp. 186–92. Stockton argues that GE read a 'spiritual materialism' out of (or into) Feuerbach's work. God on this reading is neither a purely spiritual being nor the material essence of the cosmos but that which stands between and unifies the material and the spiritual – a Hegelian idea that appears also in Derrida and Irigaray. Whereas Feuerbach moved away from this dialectical insight to a strict philosophical materialism, GE held on to it in her vision of a mystery *beneath* (not above or detached from) the real. While my interpretation differs from Stockton, I find her insight helpful. My view is that what emerges in GE's fiction has more the character of a material spirituality than of a spiritual materialism. The two phrases together bring out the dialectical character of the relationship between the spiritual and the material as GE understood it.

25. *Letters*, 2.421 (to Sara Sophia Hennell, 17 Jan. 1858). While the remark is aimed at a very negative article about 'The Religious Weaknesses of Protestantism' published in the *Westminster Review*, it could apply as well to Feuerbach.

26. See Ludwig Feuerbach, *The Essence of Christianity* (1841), trans. George Eliot, New York: Harper Torchbooks 1957, esp. chaps. 1, 4, 7, 15, 20, 24. The following is a typical statement of Feuerbach: 'The clearest, most irrefragable proof that man in religion contemplates himself as the object of the Divine Being, as the end of the divine activity, that thus in religion he has relation only to his own nature, only to himself . . . is

the love of God to man, the basis and central point of religion . . . How can the worth of man be more strongly expressed than when God, for man's sake, becomes a man, when man is the end, the object of the divine love?' (p. 57). This egocentric preoccupation with the worth of man, his self-contemplation and self-reconciliation, contrasts sharply with GE's understanding of religion as self-renunciation and reorientation to a mystery that transcends self.

27. See Dodd, *George Eliot*, pp. 181–90. The materialism underlying Feuerbach's philosophy became clearer in later works, such as *Principles of the Philosophy of the Future* (1843), trans. Manfred H. Vogel, Indianapolis: Bobbs-Merrill Co. 1966. Van A. Harvey, in *Feuerbach and the Interpretation of Religion*, Cambridge: Cambridge University Press 1995, argues that in works after 1845, culminating in *Theogonie* (1857), Feuerbach developed a different critique of religion, which sees the object of religion to be all-encompassing nature, the sum of forces from within and without that impinge upon the self and upon which human beings know themselves to be helplessly dependent. In contrast to customary religious attempts to escape this reality, Feuerbach proposed a religion that would embrace nature and worship it, attuning itself to the natural rhythms of life and death. In this he hearkened back to a theme found in his earliest work, *Thoughts on Death and Immortality* (1830). Had GE been familiar with these ideas, she would have found them unattractive. On Hegel's critique of projectionist theories of religion, see *Lectures on the Philosophy of Religion*, ed. Peter C. Hodgson, vol. 1, Berkeley and Los Angeles: University of California Press 1984, pp. 71–3, 136–7, 288–324.

28. Dodd, *George Eliot*, pp. 115–20; Haight, *George Eliot*, pp. 301, 506. Dodd writes: 'Fascinated though she was by systems, she ultimately, however, felt the repugnance of a sceptic for them. She steadfastly refused to be identified with the English Positivists . . . It was characteristic of her eclecticism that, during the period when she was reading Comte, she also turned to the works of Hegel, who, like Comte, explored the link between a new logic and the historical process, but from a very different viewpoint' (p. 120). According to Haight GE insisted that she could not submit her intellect or soul to the guidance of Comte and that she was never a Comtist, although because they were a 'poor unfortunate sect' she would not renounce them (pp. 301–2). GE's interest in positivist philosophy may have been stimulated by GHLs enthusiasm for it (Ashton, *George Eliot*, p. 106). She told Sara Sophia Hennell that she regarded Comte as a great but one-sided thinker (*Letters,* 3.439 [12 July 1861]); and to Mrs. Peter Taylor she noted that Comte does not deny an

'Unknown Cause,' but only that 'such a conception is the proper basis of a practical religion' (*Letter*, 4.367 [30 May 1867]). For portrayals of GE as a card-carrying positivist, see Bernard J. Paris, *Experiments in Life: George Eliot's Quest for Values*, Detroit: Wayne State University Press 1965; and T. R. Wright, *The Religion of Humanity: The Impact of Comtean Positivism on Victorian Britain*, Cambridge: Cambridge University Press 1986, pp. 173–201.

29. Wright, *The Religion of Humanity*, p. 21.

30. Auguste Comte, *Auguste Comte and Positivism: The Essential Writings*, ed. Gertude Lenzer, Chicago: University of Chicago Press 1975, p. xxi. For Comte's discussion of the religion of humanity and the theory of the Great Being, see the selections from his *System of Positive Polity* (1851–4) in this anthology, pp. 381–9, 448–58. On his view of women, see pp. 372–80.

31. In *Daniel Deronda,* the narrator comments: 'We are all apt to fall into this passionate egoism of imagination, not only towards our fellow-men, but towards God' (69.796).

32. Edith Simcox reported in her *Autobiography* that GE thought 'the weak point in Utilitarianism . . . lay not in their taking human welfare as the standard of right but in their trying to find in it the moral *motive*' (*Letters*, 9.217). Simcox, a brilliant young woman, became pathologically attached to GE, whom she worshipped as a goddess. Later she was a leader in the trade union and women's movements. Extracts from her *Autobiography* that bear on GE are printed in vol. 9 of the *Letters*.

33. John Hick's description of the basic characteristic of religion fits George Eliot aptly. See *An Interpretation of Religion: Human Responses to the Transcendent*, New Haven: Yale University Press 1989, p. 14.

34. *Letters*, 8.27 (GE's draft for John Chapman to James Martineau, 29 Aug. 1851). GE became editor of the *Westminster Review* in 1851.

35. *Letters*, 3.293 (to Mrs. Richard Congreve, 5 May 1860).

36. *Letters*, 1.277 (to Sara Sophia Hennell, 9 Feb. 1847).

37. Dodd, *George Eliot*, chaps. 2–7, 9–12.

38. Dodd, *George Eliot*, pp. 249–53; Haight, *George Eliot*, pp. 69, 172–3, 199–200; Dorothy Atkins, *George Eliot and Spinoza*, Romantic Reassessment, No. 78, Salzburg: Salzburg Studies in English Literature, 1978, chaps. 1–2. Atkins focuses on the interaction of freedom and determinism in George Eliot's novels. While this is a very helpful study, I think it overstates the case by giving a tightly Spinozistic reading of *Adam Bede* (chap. 3). GE's translation of Spinoza's *Tractatus* has never been published, but her translation of the *Ethics* appeared in 1981, edited by Thomas Deegan. GE herself remarked that Spinoza's thought is

extremely difficult, and that before his work is published in English translation it needs to be interpreted and explained in an accessible way (*Letters*, 1.321 [to Mr. and Mrs. Charles Bray, 4 Dec. 1849]). For a recent study of Spinoza, see Richard Mason, *The God of Spinoza: A Philosophical Study*, Cambridge: Cambridge University Press 1997, especially the introduction and chaps. 1, 2, 7 for matters mentioned in this paragraph.

39. Dodd, *George Eliot*, p. 253.

40. *Letters*, 5.31 (8 May 1869).

41. See *Letters*, 1.102–3 (to Maria Lewis, 12 Aug. 1841); 1.121 (to Maria Lewis, 13 Nov. 1841); 1.123 (to Martha Jackson, 16 Dec. 1841); 1.133 (to Abijah Hill Pears, 13 Mar. 1842); 1.136 (to Francis Watts, 11 Apr. 1842); 1.255 (to John Sibree, 8 Mar. 1848); 2.154 (to Sara Sophia Hennell, 7 May 1854). In the last letter she indicates her difficulties with Section 4 of the Appendix to Feuerbach's *Essence of Christianity*, where he makes precisely this distinction.

42. Her familiarity with the *Lectures on the Philosophy of World History* would have come through her friendship with John Sibree, who translated this work into English in the late 1840s. An allusion to the philosophy of history is found in *The Mill on the Floss* (1860), ed. A. S. Byatt, London: Penguin Books 1979, book 6, chap. 3, p. 494: 'The happiest of women, like the happiest of nations, have no history.' Cf. G. W. F. Hegel, *Lectures on the Philosophy of World History. Introduction: Reason in History*, trans. H. B. Nisbet with an introduction by Duncan Forbes, Cambridge: Cambridge University Press 1975, pp. 78–9: 'History is not the soil in which happiness grows. The periods of happiness in it are the blank pages of history.' GE alluded to Hegel's *Aesthetics* in a letter to Sibree, 8 Mar. 1848 (*Letters*, 1.247–8). Darrel Mansell argues that George Eliot incorporated two aspects of Hegel's theory of tragedy into her novels: that tragic conflict is between two relative forces of good (the individual protagonist and the general life of society) rather than between good and evil principles; and that the resolution of tragic conflict entails a reestablishment of the common social fabric, thus enabling life to go on after the heroic struggle to transcend or change it. Tragedy is moral in George Eliot's view if evil does not prevail, but a relative good. See 'A Note on Hegel and George Eliot,' *The Victorian Newsletter* 7, Spring 1965, pp. 12–15. Of course George Eliot became indirectly acquainted with Hegel's thought through her translations of Strauss's *Life of Jesus* and Feuerbach's *The Essence of Christianity*; but Strauss and Feuerbach were both left-wing Hegelians who gave a slanted version of his philosophy. GHL was directly familiar with Hegel, had con-

siderable appreciation for his thought, and wrote several articles and book chapters about him (see *Letters,* 5.118, 122, 169; 9.10–11). His earliest piece, a lengthy review of Hegel's *Vorlesungen über die Aesthetik*, Berlin 1835, in *The British and Foreign Review* 13, 1842, pp. 1–49, provides a survey of Hegel's life and thought, summarizes Hegel's view of the connection between art and religion (a view adopted by Lewes himself), and excerpts a passage in which Hegel expresses appreciation for the realism of Dutch painting. GE was surely acquainted with this review by the time she began living with Lewes. On various Hegel references in her and Lewes's writings, see Anthony McCobb, *George Eliot's Knowledge of German Life and Letters*, Romantic Reassessment, No. 102.2, Salzburg: Salzburg Studies in English Literature 1982, pp. 15–16, 114–16.

43. I discuss this similarity to Schleiermacher in chap. 8.

44. *Letters,* 1.230–1 (to Sara Sophia Hennell, 18 Feb. 1847).

45. *Letters,* 5:447–8 (to John Walter Cross, 19 Oct. 1873).

46. See Raimon Panikkar, *The Cosmotheandric Experience*, Maryknoll, N.Y.: Orbis Books 1993.

47. *Letters,* 3.366 (26 Dec. 1860).

48. See the description of Thias Bede's gradual descent into alcoholism in *Adam Bede*, chap. 4, and the critique of gambling as a form of amusement in *Daniel Deronda*, chap. 1. Alcohol is also a central theme in the third of the *Scenes of Clerical Life*, 'Janet's Repentance,' and the issue of gambling recurs in several of the novels. Rosemary Ashton says there may be a hint of alcoholism in GE's own extended family (*George Eliot*, p. 179).

49. 'Life, though a good to men on the whole, is a doubtful good to many, and to some not a good at all. To my thought, it is a source of constant mental distortion to make the denial of this a part of religion, to go on pretending things are better than they are.' *Letters,* 4.183 (to Caroline Bray, 18 Mar. 1865).

50. See GE's reviews in 1851 of works by R. W. Mackay and W. R. Greg (*Selected Essays*, pp. 271, 293–4). Here the influence of Spinoza is especially felt (Dodd, *George Eliot*, pp. 94–5, 250–3).

51. This is a central theme of all the novels, especially *Adam Bede*, *Middlemarch*, and *Daniel Deronda*. To a despairing friend she wrote, 'The progress of the world – which you say can only come at the right time – can certainly never come at all save by the modified actions of the individual beings who compose the world.' *Letters,* 6.98–100 (to Mary Elizabeth Ponsonby, 10 Dec. 1874).

52. *Adam Bede* (1859), edited with an introduction by Stephen Gill,

London: Penguin Books 1985, chap. 17, p. 178.

53. *Letters,* 4.158 (to Sara Sophia Hennell, 13 July 1864); cf. 4.183 (to Caroline Bray, 18 Mar. 1865).

54. *Letters,* 4.499 (to Clifford Allbutt, 30 Dec. 1868).

55. *Letters,* 6.98–9 (to Mary Elizabeth Ponsonby, 10 Dec. 1874).

56. See *The Poems of George Eliot*, Cambridge: Cambridge University Press 1887, pp. 387–90.

57. GE was quite severe in denouncing the 'degrading folly' and 'odious trickery' of spiritualism. See *Letters,* 3.359 (to Sara Sophia Hennell, 13 Nov. 1860), 5.48–9 (to Harriet Beecher Stowe, 11 July 1869), 5.281 (to Harriet Beecher Stowe, 24 June 1872).

58. *Letters,* 3.231 (6 Dec. 1859). An extensive discussion of the meaning of future life and immortality is found in the letters, and it is evident that GE's views changed over time: see 1.12, 27–8, 31–2, 125–6, 135–6, 143–4, 240; 4.135, 158; 8.69–70. The idea of impersonal immortality is expressed in some of her poems: 'The Legend of Jubal' (1869), 'The Death of Moses,' and 'Oh May I Join the Choir Invisible' (1867). See *Poems*, pp. 306, 437, 441–2. On Alfred North Whitehead's doctrine of objective immortality, see *Process and Reality*, New York: Macmillan 1929, pp. 89, 94, 527–33.

59. *Adam Bede,* 3.40. The 'three concords' may be a reference to the Lutheran Formula of Concord, or to the three ancient creeds acknowledged by all Anglicans: Apostles', Nicene, and Athanasian (see p. 550, n. 7).

60. Ibid., 17.181–4.

61. Hence her critique of the 'oracular' species of novels in 'Silly Novels by Lady Novelists' (*Westminster Review*, Oct. 1856), *Selected Essays*, pp. 148–56. To Joseph Frank Payne she wrote: 'I become more and more timid – with less daring to adopt any formula which does not get itself clothed for me in some human figure and individual experience, and perhaps that is a sign that if I help others to see at all it must be through the medium of art' (*Letters,* 6.217 [25 Jan. 1876]).

62. *Letters,* 6.89 (to Harriet Beecher Stowe, 11 Nov. 1874).

63. *Selected Essays*, p. 41.

64. *Letters,* 1.267 (to the Brays and Hennells, 8 June 1848); cf. also 1.35, 72, 116.

65. *Letters,* 1.162 (to Sara Sophia Hennell, 9 Oct. 1843).

66. *Letters,* 7.346 (to Mrs. Elma Stuart, 11 Dec. 1880).

67. *Letters,* 3.111 (to Charles Bray, 5 July 1859).

68. *Letters,* 3.227 (5 Dec. 1859). In an article on 'Progress: Its Law and Cause,' Herbert Spencer wrote: 'After all that has been said, the ultimate

mystery of things remains just as it was . . . The sincere man of science
. . . alone truly *sees* that absolute knowledge is impossible. He alone *knows*
that under all things there lies an impenetrable mystery' (*Westminster
Review* 67 [Apr. 1857], pp. 484–5; quoted in *Letters,* 2.341 n. 1). GE
referred to this article in a letter to Sara Sophia Hennell, 5 June 1857
(*Letters,* 2.341), remarking that 'there was more feeling in it than we
generally get in his writing.' On Spencer, see further below, n. 77.

69. Jennifer Uglow, in *George Eliot,* London and New York: Virago/
Pantheon Pioneers 1987, uses this phrase in the title of her chapter on
Adam Bede, but she does not analyze it.

70. Peter Mudford, in his editorial introduction to *Silas Marner, The
Lifted Veil, Brother Jacob,* London: Everyman Library 1996, says that
George Eliot's sense of mystery was closely associated with her love of
music, and that she associated musical harmony with human sympathy
(p. xx). A journal entry describes how she was caught up in the singing of
the Mass in the Nürnberg Frauenkirche: 'How the music that stirs all
one's devout emotions blends everything into harmony – makes one feel
part of one whole, [in] which one loves all alike, losing the sense of a
separate self' (Haight, *George Eliot,* p. 256). To John Sibree she wrote:
'No mind that has any *real* life is a mere echo of another. If the perfect
unison comes occasionally, as in music, it enhances the harmonies. It
is like a diffusion or expansion of one's own life to be assured that its
vibrations are repeated in another, and words are the media of those
vibrations. How can you say that music must end in silence? Is not the
universe itself a perpetual utterance of the One Being?' (*Letters,* 1.255 [8
Mar. 1848]).

71. *Adam Bede,* 3.39.

72. Ibid., 17.179–80.

73. G. W. F. Hegel, *Aesthetics: Lectures on Fine Art,* trans. T. M.
Knox, Oxford: Clarendon Press 1975, pp. 597–600.

74. See Dodd, *George Eliot,* pp. 101–5, 295–8.

75. Review of R. W. Mackay, *The Progress of the Intellect* (*Westminster
Review,* Jan. 1851), in *Selected Essays,* pp. 270, 281–3.

76. U. C. Knoepflmacher emphasizes the seriousness of the impact of
natural science on GE's thinking. See his *Religious Humanism and the
Victorian Novel,* chap. 2. His interpretation is that in the light of scientific
empiricism she abandoned any further possibility of religious faith in a
transcendent reality. Instead, she found in Feuerbach's love-oriented
humanism a means of softening the harshness of Darwinian evolutionary
theory. But this soft humanism required a moral tradition to give it back-
bone, and this she discovered in the neglected Hebraic roots of Western

culture. Thus her turn to Judaism in her last novel had little to do with its religion and much to do with its cultural resilience. Tradition becomes for Knoepflmacher the God-substitute GE needed to undergird an ethical humanism. Such an interpretation leads to a complex and distorted reading of the novels. The simpler and more persuasive hypothesis is that GE attempted to reconstruct a religious worldview in the light of the cultural and scientific challenges of her time.

77. Herbert Spencer's version of evolutionary theory represented such a determinism, but in other respects he modified Darwin's approach and attempted to work out a connection between morality, social policy, and the struggle for survival. He allowed for the existence of an incomprehensible, unknowable power or force from which everything derives (see above, n. 68), and he gave a mechanistic explanation of how life has progressed by the adaptation of inner relations to outer ones. GE was well-acquainted with Spencer from the early 1850s to the end of her life, and while influenced by him she was repelled by many of his theories, especially his later antifeminism and his views on race and nationality. See Nancy L. Paxton, *George Eliot and Herbert Spencer: Feminism, Evolutionism, and the Reconstruction of Gender*, Princeton, N.J.: Princeton University Press 1991.

78. For this interpretation I am partly indebted to John P. McGowan, *Representation and Revelation: Victorian Realism from Carlyle to Yeats*, Columbia: University of Missouri Press 1968, chap. 6 ('The Development of George Eliot's Realism'). Gordon Haight and Valerie Dodd point to the influence of John Ruskin's aesthetic theory on George Eliot's visionary realism: see Haight, *George Eliot*, pp. 239–40, and Dodd, *George Eliot*, pp. 295–8. If she knew anything of Hegel's philosophy of art, she would have found resources there as well. See Stephen Houlgate, 'Hegel and the "End" of Art,' *The Owl of Minerva* 29, fall 1997, pp. 1–21.

79. *Daniel Deronda*, 33.380.

80. *Adam Bede*, 3.39. The idea of the presence of God will be examined more fully in the chapter on *Adam Bede*. In an early letter GE spoke of the 'hallowed Sheckinah' of God's Spirit, and it is clear that this is a theme she originally derived from the Hebrew Bible (*Letters*, 1.72 [to Maria Lewis, 27 Oct. 1840]).

81. F. W. H. Myers reported a conversation with George Eliot in 1873 in which she pronounced the words 'God, Immortality, Duty,' and remarked 'how inconceivable was the *first*, how unbelievable the *second*, and yet how peremptory and absolute the *third*. Never, perhaps, have sterner accents affirmed the sovereignty of impersonal and unrecompensing Law . . . I [Myers] seemed to be gazing . . . on vacant seats and empty

halls – on a sanctuary with no Presence to hallow it, and heaven left lonely of a God' (*Century Magazine* 23 [Nov. 1881], pp. 62–73; quoted in Haight, *George Eliot*, p. 464). This account was written from recollection eight years after it occurred, and it is difficult to know how much credence to give it. Rosemary Ashton doubts its veracity, believing that it is couched in overwrought language GE would not have used and that it turns her into the evangelist of a gloomy rationalism (*George Eliot*, pp. 333–4). God, while in the strict sense 'inconceivable' (as the apophatic tradition has always insisted), may nonetheless be necessary for the idea of duty. In *Middlemarch*, the epigraph to chapter 80 quotes Wordsworth's *Ode to Duty*, where God and duty are linked rather than divided. In *Daniel Deronda*, which GE began to write shortly after this conversation, she seems to be preoccupied, in the Jewish parts, with precisely the question of a hallowing presence. See also below, chap. 7, n. 35.

82. See Uglow, *George Eliot*, pp. 112–13.

83. 'The fact that in the scheme of things we see a constant and tremendous sacrifice of individuals is, it seems to me only one of the many proofs that urge upon us our total inability to find in our own natures a key to the Divine Mystery. I could more readily turn Christian and worship Jesus again than embrace a Theism which professes to explain the proceedings of God. But I don't feel at all wise on these matters.' *Letters*, 2.403 (to Charles Bray, 15 Nov. 1857). Rosemary Ashton confirms that GE's stance was agnostic, not atheistic (*George Eliot*, pp. 82–3). In a review of a book by Harriet Martineau and H. G. Atkinson, which espoused atheism, she wrote: 'While science teaches us that we are profoundly ignorant of *causes* and *realities*, it becomes us not to dogmatize upon what we *cannot* know . . . In plain language: as it is confessed we cannot have direct immediate knowledge of God, so neither can we know that he is not' (*Leader*, 1 March 1851, p. 202; quoted in Ashton, *George Eliot*, p. 83).

84. *Letters*, 3.231 (to François d'Albert-Durade, 6 Dec. 1859).

85. *Selected Essays*, pp. 66–7. The validity of the interpretation offered below is confirmed for me by a similar passage found in 'Janet's Repentance:' 'The act of confiding in human sympathy, the consciousness that a fellow-being was listening to her with patient pity, prepared [Janet's] soul for that stronger leap by which faith grasps the idea of the Divine sympathy.' *Scenes of Clerical Life* (1857–8), ed. Jennifer Gribble, London: Penguin Books 1998, 'Janet's Repentance,' 25.336. Human sympathy serves as an analogy by which to understand the divine sympathy, but the latter, in the context of this story, clearly is not an illusory projection of the former. The Divine Presence was for Janet a palpable

reality (25.337), the source of the strength by which her life was transformed.

86. E.g. *Letters*, 1.231 (see above, n. 44).

87. *Letters*, 5.448 (19 Oct. 1873).

88. *Letters*, 6.98 (to Mary Elizabeth Ponsonby, 10 Dec. 1874).

89. *Daniel Deronda*, 32.367.

90. Alan Mintz points out that many of GE's heroines and heroes are also preoccupied with the question of vocation. See *George Eliot and the Novel of Vocation*, Cambridge, Mass.: Harvard University Press 1978.

91. See *Letters*, 1.14, 18–19, 36–7, 48, 109, 113, 116.

92. While reading the proofs of Feuerbach she wrote to Caroline Bray: 'My troubles are purely psychical – self-dissatisfaction and despair of achieving anything worth the doing . . . We are all islands . . .' (*Letters*, 2.155–6 [19 May 1854]).

93. Journal, 31 Dec. 1857 (in John Walter Cross [ed.], *George Eliot's Life as Related in Her Letters and Journals*, 3 vols., New York: Harper & Brothers 1885, 1.346). On 2 Jan. 1858 she added that she values the favorable responses to *Scenes* 'as grounds for hoping that my writing may succeed, and so give value to my life; as indications that I can touch the hearts of my fellow-men, and so sprinkle some precious grain as the result of the long years in which I have been inert and suffering. But at present fear and trembling still predominate over hope' (Cross, *George Eliot's Life*, 2.2).

94. She wrote this to Barbara Bodichon upon the completion of *Adam Bede* (*Letters*, 3.64 [5 May 1859]). Gordon Haight describes the difficulties GE faced in starting each new novel; see, e.g., *George Eliot*, pp. 350–1. In her journal for 19 June 1861 she wrote: 'This is the last entry I mean to make in my old book, in which I wrote for the first time at Geneva in 1849. What moments of despair I passed through after that – despair that life would ever be made precious to me by the consciousness that I lived to some good purpose! It was that sort of despair that sucked away the sap of half the hours which might have been filled by energetic youthful activity; and the same demon tries to get hold of me again whenever an old work is dismissed and a new one is being meditated' (Cross, *George Eliot's Life*, 2.222).

95. *Letters*, 4.158–9 (to Sara Sophia Hennell, 13 July 1864).

96. *Letters*, 4.158 n. 5.

97. Haight, *George Eliot*, p. 447.

98. Journal, 26 Feb. 1859 (Cross, *George Eliot's Life*, 2.66).

99. Haight, *George Eliot*, pp. 447–54, 465, 493–6.

100. 'I was once told that there was nothing out of myself to prevent

my becoming as eminently holy as St. Paul . . .' (*Letters*, 1.7 [to Maria Lewis, 18 Aug. 1838]).

101. See Haight, *George Eliot*, p. 264. References to the painting occur in several of the novels. In *Adam Bede*, Dinah Morris is depicted in terms that clearly reflect the Madonna figure herself (2.24, 26.281); in *Middlemarch*, Dorothea Brooke is compared with Saint Barbara, who also appears in the painting (10.88); and in *The Mill on the Floss*, Raphael's rendering of the 'mysteriously divine child' in such a way that we cannot explain why we feel it to be divine is offered as an example of the inexhaustible mystery of human nature (5.1.400). Thus three of the four major figures in the painting are introduced into GE's fictional world.

102. The evidence for this is scattered throughout the *Letters*. On her involvement with the Unitarians, see above, n. 14. Ashton acknowledges the evidence, but interprets it as a matter of remaining 'interested in forms of worship,' perhaps also of 'longing for spiritual comfort and support,' but without any wavering from a conversion to unbelief (*George Eliot*, p. 276).

103. *Letters*, 5.448 (to John Walter Cross, 19 Oct. 1873). We can only surmise what the 'reasons' were – perhaps a consideration for Lewes, who was not a religiously oriented person (Ashton, *George Eliot*, p. 101), or the desire not to make a public display. In his edition of *George Eliot's Life as Related in Her Letters and Journals*, Cross, who became her husband in 1880 (a year and a half after Lewes's death), notes that her catholicity of judgment and wide sympathy made it 'exceedingly difficult to ascertain, either from her books or from the closest personal intimacy, what her exact relation was to any existing religious creed or to any political party. Yet GE's was emphatically a religious mind. My own impression is that her whole soul was so imbued with, and her imagination was so fired by, the scientific spirit of the age – by the constant rapid development of ideas in the Western world – that she should not conceive that there was, as yet, any religious formula sufficient nor any known political system likely to be final' (3.307).

104. *Letters*, 3.429, 442; 4.213–14; 6.163; 7.274; Haight, *George Eliot*, chap. 15.

105. *Letters*, 1.25–26; 2.185; 3.111.

106. *Letters*, 6.89 (11 Nov. 1874).

107. *Letters*, 4.472 (to Clifford Allbutt, Aug. 1868).

108. *Letters*, 6.217 (to Dr. Joseph Frank Payne, 25 Jan. 1876).

109. Cross reports GE told him that, 'in all that she considered her best writing, there was a "not myself," which took possession of her, and that she felt her own personality to be merely the instrument through

which this spirit, as it were, was acting' (Cross, *George Eliot's Life*, 3.306).

110. Although I use the word 'fiction' in the title, my treatment is limited to the novels. I do not discuss 'The Lifted Veil' (1859), a short story written in a first-person stream-of-consciousness technique; or the allegorical short story, 'Brother Jacob' (1860, pub. 1864), which anticipated certain themes of *Silas Marner*; or the fictional essays contained in *The Impressions of Theophrastus Such* (1879). Nor do I consider GE's poetry, including the poetic drama *The Spanish Gypsy* (1868). The short stories and the essays in *Theophrastus Such* (with the exception of the last essay on modern Judaism) do not contribute to an understanding of GE's views on religion. The novels constitute the great bulk of the fiction, and I employ the term 'fiction' because I am attempting in this study to draw out some connections between theology and fiction.

2. *Unspoken Sorrows, Sacred Joys:* Scenes of Clerical Life

1. *Letters*, 2.406–10 (Journal, 6 Dec. 1857). Information on the historical background of the stories is provided by Oliver Lovesy in *The Clerical Character in George Eliot's Fiction*, English Literary Studies, Victoria, B.C.: University of Victoria 1991, introduction and chap. 1. His interest is in the rhetorical study of character in a literary-historical framework, and he offers a taxonomy of clerical types that are found not only in *Scenes* but in GE's other novels as well. He avoids theological questions entirely.

2. *Letters*, 2.269 (6 Nov. 1856). See Haight, *George Eliot*, chap. 8.

3. Thus my approach differs sharply from that of U. C. Knoepflmacher, who is convinced that GE, like her alleged mentor Feuerbach, set out to demolish the theological aspects of religion in order to advance her humanist fundamentals. Whatever theology lingers in the stories is sentimental nonsense. Since on this view religion simply entails otherworldliness, and since the idea of an otherworldly salvation is an illusion, the task of the novelist is to force human beings to come to terms with the harsh realities of everyday existence, but without losing their trust in the possibility of justice, love, and other moral ideals. It is difficult to see how these 'conflicting impulses' can be reconciled, and Knoepflmacher judges GE's attempts at doing so in *Scenes of Clerical Life* to be unsuccessful. Unlike Melville, 'she shrank from the full terror of accounting for the nature of evil in a universe without design.' See *George Eliot's Early Novels: The Limits of Realism*, Berkeley and Los Angeles: University of California Press 1968, chaps. 1–3, esp. pp. 1, 42, 88. From my perspective the tensions perceived by Knoepflmacher are introduced by his failure to recognize that GE was in fact experimenting with the reconstruction of a

religion oriented to this-worldly redemption.

4. *Letters,* 2.362 (12 July 1857).

5. Journal, 19 Dec. 1857, in Cross, *George Eliot's Life,* 1.345.

6. Journal, 2 Jan. 1858 (Cross, *George Eliot's Life,* 2.2).

7. GE told John Cross that she chose this name because 'George' was Mr. Lewes's Christian name, and 'Eliot' was 'a good mouth-filling, easily pronounced word' (Cross, *George Eliot's Life,* 1.310). She used the name when she first began corresponding with Blackwood. Following intense speculation, after the publication of *Adam Bede,* it became widely known who the author really was, but by then Marian Evans had become 'George Eliot.'

8. He was modeled on the Rev. John Gwyther, curate of Chilvers Coton, 1831–41, whose sermons GE heard (Haight, *George Eliot,* p. 211). Shepperton is the fictionalized Chilvers Coton, near Nuneaton in Warwickshire, the Milby of 'Janet's Repentance.'

9. *Scenes of Clerical Life,* ed. Jennifer Gribble, London: Penguin Books 1998. 'The Sad Fortunes of the Rev. Amos Barton,' chap. 1, pp. 7, 9–10 (hereafter cited in-text by chapter and page number). Each of the three 'Scenes' has its own chapter numbers. A curate was a deputy to the rector or vicar who was responsible for a parish and who paid his assistant whatever he chose from his own 'living' or stipend.

10. See Ludwig Feuerbach, *Principles of the Philosophy of the Future,* p. xix (Vogel's Introduction). This aspect of the Feuerbachian critique of religion was further developed by Karl Marx.

11. He was modeled on the Rev. Bernard Gilpin Ebdell, vicar of Chilvers Coton, who christened Mary Ann Evans in 1819. Cheveral Manor is based on Arbury Hall, where her father was agent or estate manager. But the plot of the story is entirely fictional. See Haight, *George Eliot,* pp. 220–1.

12. 'Janet's Repentance,' 13.278. This theme is revisited in *Daniel Deronda,* where Grandcourt breaks his spirited wife Gwendolen as a trainer does a horse.

13. The term 'superabundance' is used of Mr. Jerome's garden. It was 'one of those old-fashioned paradises' that contained 'a superabundance of everything that a person retired from business could desire to possess himself or to share with friends' (8.248). Mr. Jerome, the old Dissenter, through his loyal support of Mr. Tryan and his generosity to those in need, himself manifested something of the superabundance to which his garden, with its 'charming paradisiacal mingling of all that was pleasant to the eyes and good for food,' attested. Nature was for GE a reflection of the divine mystery, and nature metaphors abound in her writing, as in the

passages cited here.

14. *Letters*, 2.347 (11 June 1857).

15. The language of repentance, which seems to me not wholly appropriate, is suggested by a passage from the parable of the lost sheep quoted by the narrator: 'It was probably a hard saying to the Pharisees, that "there is more joy in heaven over one sinner that repenteth, than over ninety and nine just persons that need no repentance"' (Luke 15.7 KJV) (22.314). The narrator observes that 'certain ingenious philosophers' must take offence 'at a joy so entirely out of correspondence with arithmetical proportion.' Jeremy Bentham and the Utilitarians sought a calculus for determining 'the greatest good of the greatest number,' a calculus that is insensitive to concrete human need when it is encountered. Emotion, by contrast, is 'obstinately irrational: it insists on caring for individuals . . . This is the inherent imbecility of feeling, and one must be a great philosopher to have got quite clear of all that, and to have emerged into the serene air of pure intellect, in which it is evident that individuals really exist for no other purpose than that abstractions may be drawn from them – abstractions that may rise from heaps of ruined lives like the sweet savour of a sacrifice in the nostrils of philosophers, and of a philosophic Deity' (ibid.). Mr. Tryan's God is not a philosophic Deity who demands sacrifices but an empathic God who rejoices over every sinner who repents and who 'has drunk the cup of our suffering to the dregs' (18.304). This statement may reflect GE's reluctance to embrace pantheism, although the philosophical position described here is closer to rationalism and deism than to pantheism.

16. 'Janet's Repentance,' 18.299–303. It is difficult for me to grasp how, in light of such statements, Knoepflmacher can conclude that Mr. Tryan, while ostensibly an evangelical Christian, is in fact 'a spokesman for George Eliot's modern humanist "essence,"' modeled on Comte's account in the *Catechisme Positive* of the conversations of a woman with a priest of the new secular faith (*George Eliot's Early Novels*, pp. 81–2).

17. Thomas A. Noble, *George Eliot's Scenes of Clerical Life*, New Haven: Yale University Press 1965, p. 90 and chap. 3.

18. Rosemary Ashton, *George Eliot*, pp. 168, 177–8.

19. Kathryn Hughes, *George Eliot*, p. 185.

20. *Letters*, 2.425–6 (Jane W. Carlyle to George Eliot, 21 Jan. 1858). See also the letters GE received from Charles Dickens (2.423–4, 18 Jan. 1858), who guessed that the author was a woman; and from the Rev. Archer Gurney, who praised the author's 'true independence which seems to mark a real supremacy of intellect' (Cross, *George Eliot's Life*, 1.324–5, 14 May 1857).

3. Feeling the Divine Presence: Adam Bede

1. Various attempts have been made – from feminist, humanist (Feuerbachian), and psychoanalytic perspectives – to deconstruct GE's sympathetic portrayal of Dinah as a religious figure. See: Bernard J. Paris, 'George Eliot's Religion of Humanity,' *English Literary History* 29, Dec. 1962, pp. 418–43; Knoepflmacher, *George Eliot's Early Novels*, chap. 4; Elizabeth Deeds Ermarth, 'George Eliot's Conception of Sympathy,' *Nineteenth Century Fiction* 40, June 1985, pp. 23–42; Mary Wilson Carpenter, *George Eliot and the Landscape of Time*, chap. 2; Dorothea Barrett, *Vocation and Desire: George Eliot's Heroines*, London and New York: Routledge 1989, chap. 3; Elaine J. Lawless, 'The Silencing of the Preacher Woman: The Muted Message of George Eliot's *Adam Bede*,' *Women's Studies* 18, 1990, pp. 249–68. Oliver Lovesy's interest in Dinah in *The Clerical Character in George Eliot's Fiction* is principally to locate her in relation to two other clerical types in the story, Mr. Irwine and Adam Bede (whom Lovesy regards as a heroic, secular priest), thus deflecting attention from Dinah in her own right. Kathryn Hughes in her recent biography, *George Eliot*, devotes two or three sentences to Dinah Morris while discussing the other characters in some detail. Dinah's religion is reduced to an 'intense soul-searching manifest in acts of practical charity of which the Feuerbachian narrator so obviously approves' (p. 201). Frederick Karl is even more dismissive: he regards Dinah as 'anti-life in many of her pronouncements' (*George Eliot*, p. 270). To accept these interpretations as valid, one has to insist on a subtext of subversive meaning over against the plain and evident sympathy with which Dinah and her ministry are presented by the author, and as a consequence the story is mutilated almost beyond recognition. This is pointed out in an unpublished paper by Ellen Ott Marshall, 'Dinah Morris: A Constructive Proposal for the Meaning of Christianity in the Nineteenth Century' (1997).

2. Gordon S. Haight, *George Eliot*, p. 249. See GE's journal entry for 30 Nov. 1858, published in *Letters*, 2.502–5; and reprinted as Appendix 1 to *Adam Bede*, ed. Stephen Gill, London: Penguin Books 1985, pp. 540–3. The reference to Dinah as 'the "preacher-woman"' is found in chap. 2, p. 21. (The pagination of the latest printing of the Gill edition differs from earlier printings; citations are to the current version. Subsequent references to chapter and page numbers are cited in-text.)

3. GE recognized this problem and tried to rectify it, with only partial success; see *Adam Bede*, Appendix 1, p. 542.

4. *Letters*, 2.502–5 ('History of Adam Bede', Journal, 30 Nov. 1858);

3.174–6 (to Sara Sophia Hennell, 7 Oct. 1859); *Adam Bede,* Appendix 1, pp. 540–1. In addition to the experiences of her aunt, GE read Robert Southey's *Life of Wesley* and attended to details of historical background from the *Gentleman's Magazine* of 1799 (Haight, *George Eliot,* pp. 249–50). The accuracy of her portrayal of a woman lay preacher at the time is confirmed by recent studies of the role of women in the Wesleyan movement: Paul Wesley Chilcote, *John Wesley and the Women Preachers of Early Methodism,* Metuchen, N.J.: Scarecrow Press 1991; Earl Kent Brown, *Women of Mr. Wesley's Methodism,* New York: The Edwin Mellen Press 1983; and Deborah M. Valenze, *Prophetic Sons and Daughters: Female Preaching and Popular Religion in Industrial England,* Princeton, N.J.: Princeton University Press 1985. Valentine Cunningham, in *Everywhere Spoken Against: Dissent in the Victorian Novel,* Oxford: Clarendon Press 1975, chap. 7, provides detailed information on the Dissenting or Nonconformist context of *Adam Bede.* But he believes that GE ultimately sacrificed her religious sympathies to a Feuerbachian humanism; see below, n. 28.

5. *Letters,* 3.63 (5 May 1859). Bodichon was in Algiers at the time.

6. *Letters,* 2.505; *Adam Bede,* Appendix 1, p. 543.

7. Journal, April 1858 (Cross, *George Eliot's Life,* 2.16–17). See Haight, *George Eliot,* chap. 9.

8. See above, chap. 1, and Cross, *George Eliot's Life,* 2.42 (Journal, Dresden, 1858).

9. The Catholic sensibility is partly traceable to the influence of Comteanism, which appropriated many Catholic symbols into its secularized religion. In fact the Sistine Madonna was taken by the positivists as a symbol of humanity and thus as an object of worship. See Wright, *The Religion of Humanity,* p. 196. While some of the male characters in *Adam Bede* (Arthur Donnithorne, Seth Bede) show an inclination to worship Dinah Morris, George Eliot does not present her in that light, and she must have been aware of the deeply ambivalent attitude of positivism toward women. Dinah is not placed on a pedestal but is down on the stony road along with struggling fellow beings. She, like the Christ whom she figures, is a *mediator* of redemption, not the source of redemption. Dinah indeed compares herself to the bush that, when it burns with the divine presence, is not itself the object of attention but is eclipsed by the brightness of the Lord (8.92).

10. *Adam Bede,* 2.16–20. Hayslope is the fictionalized version of Ellastone, a village on the Staffordshire–Derbyshire border where GE's father worked as a young man. Snowfield is based on Wirksworth, a former mining town on the Derbyshire moors, where Mary Ann Evans

visited her Aunt Elizabeth. See Uglow, *George Eliot*, p. 100. The nearest large town is Derby – the Stoniton where Hetty was arrested and tried. The novel makes much of the contrast between the 'rich undulating district of Loamshire' (Staffordshire) and the barren hills and cold grey stone of Stonyshire (Derbyshire) (*Adam Bede*, 2.19). The latter was Dinah Morris's chosen place of work, where the need was greatest, but in the course of the story she was drawn to the former.

11. GE reported that GHL 'was so delighted with the presentation of Dinah and so convinced that the readers' interest would centre on her, that he wanted her to be the principal figure at the last. I accepted the idea at once, and from the end of the third chapter worked with it constantly in view.' *Letters*, 2.504; *Adam Bede*, Appendix 1, p. 541–2. Dinah is absent from the middle part of the novel (chaps. 17–44), having returned to Snowfield, but she reappears to assume the central role in the last part (chaps. 45–55). During her absence the story focuses on Adam, Hetty, Arthur, the Poysers, and other good folk of Hayslope such as the schoolmaster Bartle Massey and the rector Adolphus Irwine. Hetty's crisis, flight, and trial are rendered in fine detail. During her absence Dinah was not forgotten. Seth thought often of Dinah and received an important letter from her (chap. 30); Hetty remembered Dinah's promise to be a friend in need (chap. 37); and it was recognized by all that only Dinah could help Hetty after her arrest (chap. 40).

12. The influence of Hegel's aesthetic theory may be felt here. According to Hegel, beauty consists in the harmony of content and form, soul and body (G. W. F. Hegel, *Aesthetics: Lectures on Fine Art*, trans. T. M. Knox, Oxford: Clarendon Press 1975, pp. 74–5).

13. *Adam Bede*, chap. 45. Dinah did more than offer Hetty forgiveness. She shared her shame and suffering, brought about her repentance, and gave her strength to endure. Perhaps this is partly what GE intended by the epigraph from Wordsworth placed on the title page of the first edition:

> And when
> I speak of such among the flock as swerved
> Or fell, those only shall be singled out
> Upon whose lapse, or error, something more
> Than brotherly forgiveness may attend.
>
> (The Excursion [1814], book 6, lines 651–8)

See p. 1 of the Penguin edition and the editor's note, p. 548. We are reminded from 'Janet's Repentance' that something more than forgiveness is required – not just for Hetty, of course, but for all erring human beings.

14. *Westminster Review*, Oct. 1856. See *Selected Essays*, pp. 140–63. In discussing this matter I draw upon the paper by Ellen Ott Marshall cited in n. 1.

15. *Selected Essays*, p. 149.

16. Friedrich Schleiermacher's concept of the 'feeling of utter (or simple or absolute) dependence' (*Gefühl der schlechthinnige Abhängigkeit*), which is set forth in *The Christian Faith* (1821–2, 1830), is precisely what GE is representing here, but without any direct knowledge of Schleiermacher's theology. She was directly familiar with Feuerbach, but Feuerbach's version of religious feeling evacuates it of reference to anything other than itself. Schleiermacher's key insight is that the *whence* of the feeling of *utter* or *absolute* dependence must be God. Such a feeling cannot be evoked by a relationship to self or world. Utter dependence on oneself would assume the sort of human autonomy that is an illusion, and utter dependence on the world would result in a determinism that cancels all human freedom (see Schleiermacher, *The Christian Faith*, ed. H. R. Mackintosh and J. S. Stewart, Edinburgh: T&T Clark 1928, §§ 4–5). Thus my contention is that GE was actually closer to Schleiermacher's than to Feuerbach's understanding of religious feeling. I discuss Edward Farley's characterization of the religious relationship as an 'as-such' relationship in chap. 8 below.

17. *Adam Bede*, p. 555, n. 1 to chap. 11.

18. Similarly, Bartle Massey shared bread and wine with a grief-stricken Adam on the morning of Hetty's trial (ibid., chap. 42).

19. Mr. Irwine's words are not from the Bible. We are told that he preferred to quote from Sophocles and Theocritus (ibid., 5.70).

20. *Adam Bede*, 2.26–8. For further discussion of this passage, see below, chap. 8, p. 175.

21. In the light of Dinah's strong and consistent emphasis on the *this-worldly* presence of God, it is a mystery to me how U. C. Knoepflmacher can conclude that Dinah believed 'in an otherworldly Divine Presence,' a belief that, we are assured, George Eliot does not share, even though 'she does very much partake of the young preacher's fervent desire to impose love and purpose on an actuality which displays a "strange deadness to the Word."' But the 'Word' in question is not the Word of God but the word of man. A complex hermeneutic is required to reconcile this reading with what the text actually says. See *George Eliot's Early Novels*, chap. 4, esp. p. 104.

22. *Adam Bede*, 30.329–30. Edward Farley quotes this passage in the epigraph to chap. 19 of *Divine Empathy: A Theology of God*, Minneapolis: Fortress Press 1996. I find intriguing similarities between Farley's theo-

logy of divine empathy and George Eliot's religion of divine sympathy. In the final chapter I will show how Farley's categories provide a vehicle for unpacking some of the theological implications of George Eliot's fiction.

23. Carpenter, *George Eliot and the Landscape of Time*, p. 40.

24. '"God himself is dead," it says in a Lutheran hymn, expressing an awareness that the human, the finite, the fragile, the weak, the negative are themselves a moment of the divine, that they are within God himself, that finitude, negativity, otherness are not outside of God and do not, as otherness, hinder unity with God.' Hegel, *Lectures on the Philosophy of Religion*, vol. 3, 1985, p. 326. This Hegelian ontology of divine suffering, as opposed to the Feuerbachian notion that humans simply read suffering into God out of their own need, is closer to GE's intention in my view.

25. The Reverend Adolphus Irwine was quite a different clerical type than Dinah. He was not an insensitive man, but he did not, as Dinah did, go immediately to comfort Lisbeth Bede when he learned of the death of her husband. From a doctrinal point of view he was tolerant, even lax. He lacked theological enthusiasm, taking more interest in custom, liturgy, and church history than in divinity. His 'mental palate,' we are told, 'was rather pagan;' he preferred to quote from Sophocles and Theocritus than the Bible (see chap. 5, esp. pp. 69–70). A typical representative of the genteel clergy, he nonetheless was open to Dinah's ministry, and after the arrest of Hetty he was a stabilizing force, counseling Adam not to seek vengeance and working to obtain a pardon for Hetty. See Oliver Lovesy's comparison of Dinah and Irwine in *The Clerical Character in George Eliot's Fiction*, pp. 38–47.

26. *Adam Bede*, 52.511; 54.532. Marriage carries with it its own distinctive pathos in virtue of the intense bond it can create between two human beings. When Adam said, 'Then we'll never part any more, Dinah, till death parts us,' the narrator comments: 'What greater thing is there for two human souls, than to feel that they are joined for life – to strengthen each other in all labour, to rest on each other in all sorrow, to minister to each other in all pain, to be with each other in silent unspeakable memories at the moment of the last parting?' (54.531).

27. See Carpenter, *George Eliot and the Landscape of Time*, pp. 52–3. My interpretation of this linkage differs from Carpenter's. Rather than introducing a subversive subtext into the story, I regard it as linking Dinah with the kind of suffering assumed by Christ. The biblical Dinah suffered twice at the hands of patriarchy. The Canaanite, Shechem, fell in love with Dinah and they agreed to marry. But Dinah's brothers reviled her and refused to give their consent unless Shechem and his kinsmen were circumcised. The Canaanites agreed to this, in the interest of

harmony with the Jews, but while they were still in pain the brothers of Dinah attacked, killed all the males, plundered the city, and took their wives. Thus Jacob and his sons had to leave the land of Canaan.

28. I am helped in these reflections on the ending by Terrence W. Tilley's discussion of *Adam Bede* in *The Evils of Theodicy*, Washington, D.C.: Georgetown University Press 1991, chap. 8. GE does not in his view offer a false theodicy, a phony justification of evil, but rather shows 'the depths of unacknowledged, unconfessed, and permanent evil' as well as 'a way to the good of reconciliation.' Tilley's study is one of very few that reads the novel from a theological perspective and finds in it religious resources of value. By contrast, Valentine Cunningham offers the following judgment about the ending: 'The result is less a concession wrung from the reader that, after all, Dinah's words about, and faith in, God are a mistaken and now untenable gloss on what is essentially human sympathy, than the feeling that all that has gone before is wasted . . . The ending must, then, be construed as George Eliot's wrenching away from the novel her emotional support, her sympathy with Dinah, and the imposition, in intellectual allegiance to Feuerbach, of the humanizing reinterpretation' (*Everywhere Spoken Against*, pp. 169–70). Such a distorted conclusion results from the assumption that GE simply surrendered her earlier evangelical sympathies to a Feuerbachian ideology. Despite his disappointment with the ending, Cunningham believes that GE stood out among Victorian novelists as one who treated 'Dissenters with enormous compassion and with a notable measure of fairness' (p. 9). On Dinah's return to 'the orthodox role of wife and mother,' Rosemary Ashton remarks that 'feminists then and now have been frustrated by [GE's] limiting end choices for her heroines.' Ashton speculates that the explanation lies in a combination of realism and a desire not to alienate readers (*George Eliot*, pp. 206–7). This is virtually Ashton's only mention of the role of Dinah in the novel.

29. For this idea I am indebted to an unpublished paper by Kirsten A. S. Mebust, 'The End of Suffering: An Eschatology of Word and Presence in *Adam Bede*' (2000). The proposal for a counter-apocalyptic intuition, as opposed to either apocalyptic or anti-apocalyptic, comes from Catherine Keller, *Apocalypse Now and Then: A Feminist Guide to the End of the World*, Boston: Beacon Press 1996, chap. 7.

30. Haight, *George Eliot*, p. 339; cf. pp. 272–80. There were several journal entries to this effect during the next few years as George Eliot struggled with the demons of creativity. See Cross, *George Eliot's Life*, 2.203, 222, 225–7, 231, 240, 243, 279, 290.

4. *The Clue of Life:* The Mill on the Floss, Silas Marner

1. *The Mill on the Floss*, ed. A. S. Byatt, London: Penguin Books 1979, bk. 1, chap. 6, p. 100. Since the chapters are renumbered in each of the seven books of this novel, to provide a reference to other editions it is necessary to cite both book and chapter number as well as page number (e.g., 1.6.100).

2. *Mill*, 6.14.597. Dorothea Barrett interprets the novel in very different terms than the ones proposed here. She views Maggie as 'the other possible Marian Evans who never left home, never broke the ties most sacred to her, never discovered the George Eliot in herself. The only end that George Eliot can see for such a life is frustration, a deathlike life, or death itself come early.' Using a psychosexual hermeneutic, she argues that the novel is centrally concerned with 'the internal war between opposing elements in one personality' and 'the external war between men and women.' The latter war was played out as Maggie struggled to achieve self-identity over against the dominant males of her life: her father, her brother Tom, Philip Wakem, and Stephen Guest. The relationship between Tom and Maggie, according to Barrett, included significant elements of abuse and incest. Neither she nor (as far as I can tell) other critics attend to the religious aspects of Maggie's struggle. See *Vocation and Desire*, chap. 4, esp. pp. 53, 71.

3. See Byatt's introduction and notes to *Mill*, pp. 38, 672–3 n. 16; and *Mill*, 1.5.94. U. C. Knoepflmacher connects the name of the river with the idea of historical-temporal 'flux,' and he believes that the ending of the story represents an unresolved tragedy that required another novel, *Silas Marner*, to overcome. See *George Eliot's Early Novels*, chap. 6. My own analysis of the tragic dimension of the story differs from Knoepflmacher's. Mary Wilson Carpenter's interpretative key is not 'tragedy' but 'apocalyptic,' and she draws connections between *Mill* and *Romola*. See *George Eliot and the Landscape of Time*, pp. 54–60.

4. See Haight, *George Eliot*, pp. 302, 305. Dorlcote Mill was drawn from GE's memory of Arbury Mill, near her birth place. There are many autobiographical touches in her depiction of Maggie and of Maggie's relationship to her brother Tom Tulliver, who had some of the characteristics of GE's estranged brother Isaac Evans.

5. *Mill*, 7.5.648–9. Focusing on this climactic passage, David Carroll argues that Maggie is characteristic of GE's heroines in that she faces an impasse in which opposing claims are so finely balanced that any decision, resolution, and closure become impossible. This, he argues, 'is a privileged moment towards which the whole narrative has been moving and

it announces that the search for a coherent view of the world has finally broken down.' There is no scheme of meaning; coherence dissolves into incoherence; and life is made up of a never-ending conflict of interpretations: this is the reality GE is attempting to convey to her readers. See *George Eliot and the Conflict of Interpretations: A Reading of the Novels*, Cambridge: Cambridge University Press 1992, pp. 1–4, 136. However, Carroll precisely overlooks the fact that Maggie burned Stephen's letter and resolved to inform him that they must part forever. Moreover, she knew instantly what to do when the flood came, and she died in a noble attempt at rescue. The novel does not, therefore, end in a state of irresolved tension and meaningless incoherence. Maggie *acts,* as do all of GE's heroines and heroes – Dinah Morris, Silas Marner, Romola de' Bardi, Felix Holt, Dorothea Brooke, Daniel Deronda – something new happens, a kind of redemption is achieved, and life goes on. The reality of the conflict of interpretations points to the ambiguity of situations but does not imply an existentially meaningless or static world. It is from the latter philosophical perspective that Carroll judges the ending of *The Mill on the Floss* to be 'melodramatic' and 'mythic,' at tension with its predominant narrative logic (pp. 137–9). By contrast, I believe that the narrative logic of the story requires the sort of ending that it has been given, an ending that is sad and realistic, yet also hopeful.

6. Jacques Bénigne Bossuet was a seventeenth-century French Catholic bishop. A brilliant controversialist, he attacked the Quietists, the Jesuits, and the Protestants, the latter in his *Histoire des variations des Église protestantes* (1688).

7. See *Mill,* 4.3.382 and the editorial note, p. 681 n. 91. Included among them was John Keble's *The Christian Year* (1827), a collection of poems celebrating the Christian calendar to which GE alluded on several occasions in her writings.

8. Thomas à Kempis was a fifteenth-century Augustinian monk. GE acquired a copy of *De Imitatione Christi* in early 1849, during her father's final illness. 'Verily its piety has its foundations in the depth of the divine-human soul,' she wrote to Sara Sophia Hennell (*Letters*, 1.278 [9 Feb. 1849]); and she gave her copy to Sara in 1851 (1.278 n. 9). She was reading Thomas à Kempis again in 1859 as she wrote *The Mill on the Floss* (*Letters*, 3.205 [Journal, 18 Nov. 1859]).

9. Presumably the inner Teacher, named by theological tradition as Christ and/or the Holy Spirit. GE did not articulate a theory of inspiration, but one seems to be implicit in her writing. God does not act in the world by outer, external, supernatural means, but through the inner witness of the Spirit, the witness of Spirit to spirit.

10. Insofar as the portrayal of Maggie is autobiographical, we may assume that George Eliot herself experienced the need for renunciation, and that she too threw some pride and impetuosity into it. As a very young woman she was attracted to a religious asceticism. Later she found it necessary to renounce the antagonism and 'negative propagandism' toward genuine religious faith that she indulged during the years following her break with evangelical Christianity. She found herself oscillating between asceticism and sensuality. She may have had a sexual relationship with a man whom she knew she could not marry, John Chapman. Perhaps there is a bit of Chapman (the London publisher for whom she worked in the early 1850s) in Stephen Guest, and of G. H. Lewes (her life-partner) in Philip Wakem. She felt driven to produce fiction that would be genuinely beneficial for humanity, and she chastised herself for her procrastination and failures. In later years she had to resist the temptations of fame and wealth.

11. *Letters*, 3.339 (28 Aug. 1860).

12. *Letters*, 3.360 (Journal, 28 Nov. 1860). 'The reader who vaguely remembers *Silas Marner* as a distasteful, saccharine high-school text may be every bit as startled upon rereading this fine novel as by taking a second look at that other children's classic, *Gulliver's Travels*.' Thus writes U. C. Knoepflmacher at the beginning of his surprisingly favorable assessment of the story. He also identifies some connections between *The Mill on the Floss* and *Silas Marner,* believing that the latter novel overcame artistic and conceptual difficulties encountered earlier. 'Through the medium of a "legendary tale," [GE] reconciled the incongruities which had arisen, to greater or lesser degrees, in all of her former fictional attempts to find the ideal in the "real."' See *George Eliot's Early Novels*, pp. 221–37. On Knoepflmacher's thesis, see further below, n. 20.

13. *Letters*, 3.382 (24 Feb. 1861).

14. *Silas Marner: The Weaver of Raveloe*, edited with an introduction by David Carroll, London: Penguin Books 1996, chap. 1, quotation from p. 14. Hereafter cited in-text by chapter and page numbers.

15. Ashton, *George Eliot*, p. 251.

16. Angels led Lot and his family away from the doomed cities of Sodom and Gomorrah (Gen. 19.1–25); and John Bunyan depicted the City of Destruction at the beginning of *The Pilgrim's Progress*. See the editor's note, *Silas Marner*, p. 192 n. 13.

17. *Silas Marner*, 14.131. Cf. Isa. 11.6: 'The wolf shall live with the lamb, the leopard shall lie down with the kid, the calf and the lion and the fatling together, and a little child shall lead them.'

18. William Wordsworth, 'Michael,' lines 146–8 (1836 edition). See

the editor's note, *Silas Marner*, p. 184 n. 1.

19. Perhaps it can be argued that in *Silas Marner* GE dwelt on the figure of the child in the great Madonna paintings to which she was attracted, whereas in other novels, notably *Adam Bede* and *Romola*, she focused on the Madonna herself. To be sure, in *Silas Marner* the gender roles are reversed: the child is female, and the parent male. Cf. the reference in *The Mill on the Floss* (5.1.400) to Raphael's rendering of the 'mysteriously divine child.'

20. Knoepflmacher believes that in *Silas Marner* GE achieved a break-through that enabled her to move beyond the barren antithesis between reason and faith, natural explanation and supernatural causality, empirical fact and impenetrable mystery, that had in his view plagued her earlier novels. She did this 'by fusing the laws of observed experience with the poetic justice of a fairy tale.' The insight that emerged from this fusion is simply 'that all belief, natural and supernatural, stems from man's ele-mental need to confide in somebody other than the self.' Even though the fusion represents a fairy-tale solution – 'reconciliation through fable' – it was presumptively sufficient to overcome 'the philosophical nihilism which [GE] had merely resisted in her earlier fiction.' See *George Eliot's Early Novels*, chap. 7, esp. pp. 249–51, 255–6, 258. While appreciating Knoepflmacher's reading, I do not agree that GE attained this fusion only for the first time in *Silas Marner*. From the beginning she was attempting to work out a this-worldly, non-supernaturalistic interpretation of reli-gion, and she succeeded at it already in the earlier novels. Knoepflmach-er's version of the 'insight' attained in *Silas Marner* is thin, namely that belief arises from the elemental need to confide in somebody other than oneself. The resolution is provided not by a fairy tale but by the Christmas story, whose meaning is much richer, namely that we are led out of ourselves not by our own need but by the needy, vulnerable other.

5. *The Kingdom of Justice:* Romola, Felix Holt

1. Haight, *George Eliot*, pp. 343–51. The historical and geographical detail in the novel is extraordinary.

2. Cross, *George Eliot's Life*, 2.255. See 2.203, 225–7, 231, 240, 243.

3. *Romola*, edited with an introduction by Dorothea Barrett, London: Penguin Books 1996, p. vii. In-text references are to chapter and page numbers of this edition. *Romola* was first published in serial form in 1862–3 in *Cornhill Magazine*, which offered a far greater sum for the novel than GE's Edinburgh publisher, John Blackwood, could afford. Later she regretted the decision and returned to Blackwood for her

subsequent works. See Haight, *George Eliot*, pp. 355–61.

4. *Romola*, pp. xii–xiv (Barrett's Introduction). The success of *Romola* as historical fiction has been much debated. It reflects the mid-nineteenth century setting in which it was written as much as that of late fifteenth-century Florence. GE's interests were larger than that of writing a good historical romance; she was engaged with fundamental existential, political, and religious questions with which human beings struggle in all ages and places. At the beginning of the Proem (pp. 1–2) reference is made to 'the broad sameness of the human lot, which never alters in the main headings of its history – hunger and labour, seed-time and harvest, love and death.' For example, religious superstition has not changed. People could not be certain that, behind the names given to the Unseen Powers, 'there was no angry force to be appeased, no intercessory pity to be won' (p. 5); thus, when the old Roman god Mars was deposed by the patron saint of Florence, San Giovanni, he was treated with respect and placed on a high tower near the River Arno in the belief that if he were damaged the city would suffer (8.81). Now the saint, John the Baptist, was annually paraded about in a religious festival, his ascetic image ironically crowned with the symbol of Florentine wealth, the mint where gold florins were made (8.89). We are told that the Republic was especially zealous about keeping its religious festivals in times of trouble (8.84). And in times of plenty the wealthy lavished money on themselves and had no fear of the masses who licked the hands of masters. 'This world . . . seemed to be a handsome establishment for the few who were lucky or wise enough to reap the advantages of human folly: a world in which lust and obscenity, lying and treachery, oppression and murder, were pleasant, useful, and when properly managed, not dangerous' (21.208). In all of this, the author is commenting on her own time and place as much as on that of the story.

5. Thus I read the novel more in ethical than in apocalyptic terms, as compared with Mary Wilson Carpenter in *George Eliot and the Landscape of Time*, chap. 3. Carpenter believes that GE appropriated the 'scheme of the Apocalypse' as set forth in the book of Revelation, but that she revised it 'into a post-Christian and postpatriarchal vision of humanity. Romola progresses toward a new age governed by a Comtean conception of "feminine" values, values that emphasize devotion to the community but that also encompass a degree of female independence and autonomy unparalleled in any of GE's other novels' (pp. 61–2). I affirm the feminist reading, but I believe that for GE the feminine values were also the values of the religion of the cross, and that her vision should be regarded as post-Christian not in a negative but in a positive sense, i.e., as revi-

sionary Christian. Comte himself did not advocate an independent social
or political role for women; rather the proper place for women was in
marriage and family life. Carpenter devotes considerable attention to
structural features of the narrative, which incorporate complex elements
of the apocalyptic scheme, but in the final analysis her reading is also
more ethical than it is apocalyptic, focusing on the image not of the 'kingdom of justice' (as I do) but of 'a women's community guided only by a
spirit of charity' (p. 63). Yet the apocalyptic elements, when demythologized, are important, for they remind us that the human condition is not
purely ethical, that we are confronted with forces of destiny and history
that we do not control, and that even the highest ethical accomplishments
are ambiguous.

6. The dream (chap. 15) proved to be a true prophecy of coming
events. Romola was distressed but did not heed the warning. No explanation is provided of how Dino could have foreseen Romola's fate, but
Tito's attempt to dismiss the dream with a psychological interpretation
(chap. 17) receives no support from the narrator. The story contains other
dreams and visions (e.g. of the prophetess Camilla Rucellai, who foresaw
the death of Romola's godfather, chap. 52), and many coincidences of
time and place that seem to go beyond normal probabilities. Such dreams
and coincidences do occur in real life, but their effect is exaggerated,
perhaps, by the genre of romance with which GE is experimenting in this
novel. There is no suggestion of a direct supernatural causality; rather
opportunities are provided for the realization of good through the working of natural causes and human initiative.

7. Carpenter suggests that GE 'struggled to produce a visionary
history of Woman clothed with the sun of righteousness;' she wanted 'to
find in her text the face of a female self not yet born – the face of a *legitimate* prophetess' – legitimate as compared with the assumed 'illegitimacy'
of her 'attempt to re-write the culminating prophetic text of Christianity
as female prophecy' (*George Eliot and the Landscape of Time*, pp. 102–3).

8. See Felicia Bonaparte, *The Triptych and the Cross: The Central
Myths of George Eliot's Poetic Imagination*, New York: New York University Press 1979, p. 20. In a letter to Alexander Main in 1871, GE
acknowledged that he had correctly guessed the derivation of the name
and that the second 'o' in 'Romola' should be pronounced as short rather
than long (*Letters*, 5.174). In a later letter she clarified the pronunciation
further: 'according to the Italian usage [it] is Rōmŏla' (*Letters*, 9.215). See
also Carpenter, *George Eliot and the Landscape of Time*, p. 200, n. 16.

9. 'What,' thought Tito, 'was the end of all life, but to extract the
utmost sum of pleasure?' (11.115). His outlook on life was atheistic as well

as amoral because he had no fear of the divine nemesis and no regard for the divine law that binds the heart inwardly (11.116). His attitude toward religious symbols was utterly cavalier. In this as in other respects he was the complete opposite of Romola.

10. See Bonaparte, *The Triptych and the Cross,* chap. 1, esp. pp. 18–25, and chaps. 2, 3, 6, 7, 9.

11. See Dorothea Barrett's Introduction to *Romola,* pp. xiv–xv. Barrett extends her analysis further in *Vocation and Desire,* chap. 5. I do not deny that Comtean motifs appear in *Romola* and the other novels, notably the appropriation of the madonna figure. But in my view the Comtean dogma is not present, and Romola does not conform to the role of wife and mother to which Comte consigned women. GE offers an original religious construction that cannot simply be reduced to the variety of influences that contributed to it.

12. Barrett's Introduction to *Romola,* pp. xv–xvi. Carpenter's version of the tripartite scheme is that 'Romola first lives in an "age of the father" guided by her father, then in an "age of the son" guided first by the false son Tito and then by Savonarola's teaching of the true Son, and finally in an "age of the spirit," in which the institution of Christianity has withered away and Romola lives in a women's community guided only by a spirit of charity' (*George Eliot and the Landscape of Time,* p. 63). I agree that the three stages of Romola's life can be seen to correspond to Joachim's trinitarian interpretation of history. But I find no evidence in the text for the claims that the institution of Christianity has withered away and that the 'spirit' in question is only a human spirit, not the divine Spirit. Romola continued to model her life on the cross, understood not as a substitutionary atonement but as a concrete manifestation of the suffering love of God. She maintained a small institutional symbol in her home, an altar. The community in which she lived was not exclusively a women's community: her household included the boy Lillo, and she continued to participate in the larger community of Florence. To be sure, she was a this-worldly rather than an other-worldly madonna, but that is the whole point of GE's reinterpretation of the Christian doctrine of redemption. Rosemary Ashton offers a judgment similar to that of Barrett and Carpenter: Romola's progress is 'an odyssey from unbelief, through flirtation with mysticism, to a kind of respiritualized secular humanism' (*George Eliot,* p. 276). The religion of the cross becomes 'mysticism' on this reading, and the humanitarianism of the last phase is judged to be secular, though 'respiritualized.' The respiritualization does not seem to be a matter of recognizing the presence of the sacred in the midst of the secular. Such judgments are skewed by the assumption that Comte and

Feuerbach lay behind everything GE wrote about religion. Ashton also mentions Spinoza, but Spinoza cannot be used to support a secular reading of the novels.

13. *Romola*, chap. 68. GE's interest in Judaism first surfaced in 'The Lifted Veil,' published in 1859, but it was more explicitly developed in *Romola*. On Jewish themes in the novel, see William Baker, *George Eliot and Judaism*, Romantic Reassessment, No. 45, Salzburg: Salzburg Studies in English Literature 1975, chap. 5.

14. *Romola*, 67.549. Cf. Luke 17.20–1: 'The kingdom of God cometh not with observation: neither shall they say, Lo here! or, lo there! for, behold, the kingdom of God is within you' (KJV).

15. *Romola*, 21.209; 24.226–9. The sermon on the coming of the day of vengeance that Savonarola preached in the cathedral of Florence (chap. 24) offers a striking contrast to the sermon of Dinah Morris on Hayslope green. Here was a God of anger, vengeance, and punishment rather than of love, friendship, and fellow suffering. Here was a Catholic form of accusation and consolation not so dissimilar from the evangelical piety of John Cumming. Here was an appeal to visions and miracles as proof of divinely sanctioned authority – an appeal that proved to be the Frate's undoing, for he was unwilling to risk the miracle of trial by fire (chap. 65), and the people turned against him. Yet the narrator's analysis of Savonarola's preaching does not produce a wholly negative judgment but rather a complex, mixed picture: 'there were strains that appealed to the very finest susceptibilities of men's natures, and there were elements that gratified low egoism, tickled gossiping curiosity, and fascinated timorous superstition' (25.234). The sermon itself, notes GE, 'is not a translation, but a free representation of Fra Girolamo's preaching in its more impassioned moments' (see p. 611 n. 6 to chap. 24).

16. *Romola*, 71.574–5. David Carroll argues that these words mean Savonarola became a martyr to the destruction of his religious belief, and that it was GE's intention in her treatment of the reformer to show that such beliefs are a mythical hypothesis that will inevitably be superseded. See David Carroll, 'George Eliot Martyrologist: The Case of Savonarola,' *From Author to Text: Re-reading George Eliot's Romola*, ed. Caroline Levine and Mark W. Turner, Aldershot: Ashgate 1998, pp. 104–21.

17. *Felix Holt, the Radical* (1866), ed. Lynda Mugglestone, London: Penguin Books 1995, pp. x–xii (Introduction by Mugglestone). In-text references are to chapter and page numbers of this edition.

18. Haight, *George Eliot*, pp. 395–7.

19. It is not clear whether Treby is modeled on any particular town. Stoke-on-Trent and the adjacent Newcastle-under-Lyme in North

Staffordshire would be the most obvious candidates for Treby Magna and Little Treby.

20. The Radical Party consisted of those who wanted to make thorough or radical changes to the Constitution, inspired originally by the French Revolution. After the Reform Bill of 1832 was passed, advocates of violent change were drawn into the Chartist movement and the Radicals became less revolutionary. They never formed a distinct party in the House of Commons and subsequently were simply the advanced section of the Liberal Party.

21. *Felix Holt*, chap. 4. Rufus Lyon's portrayal provides another mini-scene of clerical life. He may have been based on GE's recollections of Francis Franklin, a Baptist minister and father of the Miss Franklins whose school she attended from 1832 to 1835, and whom she is reported to have greatly admired at the time. See *Felix Holt*, pp. 511–12, ed. n. 1 to chap. 4. Valentine Cunningham believes that another influence in his construction was that of John Sibree, who would have been the source of the political reforming aspect of Rufus's character, while Franklin contributed to his Puritan temper. Despite what he regards as her 'manipulation' of Dinah Morris and Rufus Lyon, he concludes that GE had 'a very unique compassion for and insight into the Nonconformist spirit' and 'an authentic grasp of some aspects of Nonconformist history and historical process.' See *Everywhere Spoken Against*, chap. 7, esp. pp. 183–6, 189.

22. Cf. Ps. 37.30–1: 'The mouths of the righteous utter wisdom, and their tongues speak justice. The law of their God is in their hearts; their steps do not slip.'

23. *Felix Holt*, 16.184. These words anticipate the concluding words of *Middlemarch*. See below, p. 120.

24. *Felix Holt*, chap. 26. The epigraph to the chapter quotes from Shakespeare's *Henry V*:

> Consideration like an angel came
> And whipped the offending Adam out of her;
> Leaving her body as a paradise
> To envelope and contain celestial spirits (1.1.28–31).

GE has silently converted 'him' and 'his' in this passage, referring to Henry V, to 'her'.

25. *Felix Holt*, chap. 49. Esther's dark night of the soul anticipated a similar night experienced by Dorothea in *Middlemarch*. See below, p. 115.

26. 1 Cor. 9.16: 'For though I preach the gospel, I have nothing to

glory of: for necessity is laid upon me; yea, woe is unto me, if I preach not the gospel' (KJV).

27. The reference is to the Root and Branch Petition of 1640, which demanded the abolition of the episcopal system 'with all its dependencies, roots, and branches.' The phrase itself is based on Mal. 4.1. Mr. Lyon's introduction of the term allowed Felix to play on the meaning of 'radical,' namely 'root' (*radix*). See *Felix Holt*, p. 531 n. 5 to chap. 27.

28. GE's views about extending the franchise to women were ambiguous. Although conventional views of women's roles are powerfully challenged in *Felix Holt*, no suggestion is made that women should participate in the electoral process. The author apparently believed that women must be educated and assume a different role in society before they could vote responsibly.

29. On the matter of both women's suffrage and class interests, GE may have been influenced by Herbert Spencer, although she was basically opposed to his theories about gender and class. These matters were being widely discussed during the 1860s. See Paxton, *George Eliot and Herbert Spencer*, chap. 7.

30. This view is remarkably Hegelian. In the *Phenomenology of Spirit* Hegel spoke of the 'enormous labor of world history' as the 'pedagogical progress' of the Spirit toward its own self-actualization. He emphasized that the length of this path has to be patiently endured, and that each moment must be lingered over. See the selection from the Preface to *Phenomenology of Spirit* in *G. W. F. Hegel: Theologian of the Spirit*, ed. Peter C. Hodgson, Minneapolis: Fortress Press; Edinburgh: T&T Clark, 1997, pp. 98–9.

6. *Widening the Skirts of Light:* Middlemarch

1. See Haight, *George Eliot*, pp. 421–2.

2. Thomas H. Johnson (ed.), *The Letters of Emily Dickinson*, 3 vols., Cambridge, Mass.: Harvard University Press 1965, 2.506. The phrase 'mysteries of redemption' does not occur in *Middlemarch*, but Dickinson may have been thinking of Matt. 13.11 or Luke 8.10: 'Unto you it is given to know the mysteries of the kingdom of God: but to others [I speak] in parables; that seeing they might not see, and hearing they might not understand' (KJV).

3. The novel was first published in eight two-monthly parts between December 1871 and December 1872.

4. *Letters*, 5.296 (4 Aug. 1872). See Haight, *George Eliot*, chap. 13.

5. *Letters*, 5.168 (24 July 1871).

6. *Middlemarch* (1871–2), ed. Rosemary Ashton, London: Penguin Books 1994, chap. 6, pp. 59–60; chap. 11, p. 95; chap. 15, p. 141; chap. 36, p. 346; Finale, p. 832. Subsequent references to chapter and page numbers of this edition are cited in-text. Mary Wilson Carpenter believes that the web imagery derives 'from an apocalyptic vision whose possibilities George Eliot now exploits in a witty formal design.' In accord with her interests, Carpenter focuses her discussion on the structural intricacies of the work. See *George Eliot and the Landscape of Time*, chap. 4 and p. 105.

7. Carpenter believes that the name signifies the transposition of 'the exalted melodies and universal harmonies of apocalyptic symphony into a "lower" key – the simpler rhythms of a "middle march," of a musical comedy rather than an oratorio, of an earthly rather than a heavenly music.' See *George Eliot and the Landscape of Time*, p. 104.

8. The idea of being *in medias res* is taken up again at the beginning of *Daniel Deronda* (the epigraph to chap. 1).

9. The piety of GE's youth and her restless quest for a worthy vocation are powerfully represented in Dorothea. While not sharing her heroine's beauty, she, like Dorothea (9.80), had a rich, sensuous voice (see Cross, *George Eliot's Life*, 3.302).

10. *Middlemarch*, 10.88. Saint Barbara's repose is captured by Raphael in his *Sistine Madonna*, a painting which gave GE artistic representations of not one but two of her characters, Dinah Morris and Dorothea Brooke. Raphael put Saint Barbara, who was martyred in the third century, into the picture because she was revered by Pope Julius II, who commissioned the painting. The tower in which she was confined is visible in the background of the painting.

11. Carpenter provides a fascinating discussion of the varied imagery of 'keys' in this novel – not only Casaubon's key to all mythologies, but Dorothea's key to her mother's jewel box, her acquisition of the keys to Lowick, the key to Featherstone's caskets that Mary Garth refused to give to the dying old man, the keys to the Stone Court brandy chest, etc. Keys presumably unlock some treasure or hidden meaning for which the characters are always searching but which they are never quite finding. Carpenter concludes that the apocalyptic harmonies of *Romola* are transposed in *Middlemarch* into the 'key' of a Romantic musical comedy – 'a key that postulates the existence of a kind of quincunxial web, and prophesies, if it does not perform, the harmony of humanity.' Yet the author knows that all such harmonies remain but fragments of an inexhaustible web. See *George Eliot and the Landscape of Time*, pp. 120–30. Compare my discussion below of the image of events of history as random scratches on the surface of polished steel.

12. He was also in need of human companionship, for he was an isolated, lonely man, but he was incapable of giving or receiving affection. He had spiritual hungers that could not be expressed, much less satisfied (chap. 29). Dorothea recognized his need and tried in vain to break through his shell.

13. Whole chapters of this novel are filled with Middlemarch gossip, rumors, innuendos, prejudices, rivalries, etc. This is the pithiest summary: 'To be candid, in Middlemarch phraseology, meant, to use an early opportunity of letting your friends know that you did not take a cheerful view of their capacity, their conduct, or their position . . . Then, again, there was the love of truth – a wide phrase, but meaning in this relation, a lively objection to seeing a wife look happier than her husband's character warranted, or manifest too much satisfaction in her lot . . . Stronger than all, there was the regard for a friend's moral improvement, sometimes called her soul, which was likely to be benefited by remarks tending to gloom . . . On the whole, one might say that an ardent charity was at work setting the virtuous mind to make a neighbor unhappy for her good' (74.741). What a complicated apparatus in place of the simple love of neighbor!

14. This saying of Jesus as found in the synoptic tradition (e.g. Matt. 16.25) adds 'for my sake' after 'lose their life.' I think George Eliot would have been be more likely to add, 'for the sake of all suffering human beings in the world.' The losing, emptying, giving up is for her more cosmic than christic. Of course, the addition of 'for my sake' is probably attributable to the synoptic tradition rather than to Jesus. The version in Mark 8.35 adds not only 'for my sake' but also 'for the sake of the gospel,' or substitutes the latter for the former, demonstrating the fluidity of the tradition and its tendency to embellish.

15. *Middlemarch*, 81.797. The reflections about marriage in this novel are intriguing. When she entered into it, Dorothea was utterly naive, thinking of it solely in terms of spiritual communion (2.22). Later the narrator comments that in marriage 'we begin by knowing little and believing much, and we sometimes end by inverting the quantities' (20.195). Rosamond could never understand that the conditions of marriage demand 'self-suppression and tolerance' (75.753). In the Finale, marriage is described as 'the beginning of the home epic – the gradual conquest or irremediable loss of that complete union which makes the advancing years a climax, and age the harvest of sweet memories in common' (Finale, 832). It is a different type of epic from that of Saint Theresa. It is ironic that, of several famous Victorian marriages, only the union of George Eliot and George Henry Lewes, which was not legally a

marriage at all, was successful. See Phyllis Rose, *Parallel Lives: Five Victorian Marriages*, New York: Alfred A. Knopf 1983.

16. On the theme of vocation in *Middlemarch*, see Barrett, *Vocation and Desire*, chap. 7; and Mintz, *George Eliot and the Novel of Vocation*. Mintz argues that GE exposes the tension between two conflicting ideas of vocation that arose out of secularized versions of older Protestant ideas about a worldly calling: 'the impulse toward self-aggrandizing ambition and the impulse toward selfless contribution to society.' Often these impulses are combined in a single character, who has to resolve the conflict one way or another (p. 2).

17. GE revised the penultimate paragraph of the novel for the second edition. In the first edition she placed the responsibility for Dorothea's alleged 'mistakes' partly on the Middlemarch society that had condoned her marriage to a sickly older man and justified an inferior education for women. Critics pointed out that Middlemarch society had not in fact condoned the marriage, and that Dorothea had disregarded numerous warnings. See *Middlemarch*, pp. 852–3 n. 282. The second edition simply remarks on the struggle of a 'young and noble impulse' amidst 'the conditions of an imperfect social state' (Finale, 838). David Carroll believes that by this revision GE acknowledged 'that she had overbalanced in exonerating Dorothea from blame at the expense of Middlemarch. The saint is also a Quixote.' See *George Eliot and the Conflict of Interpretations*, p. 254. But Quixote though she may be, the conclusion stands: despite her own weaknesses and illusions, and despite the limited opportunity for anything like 'ardent deeds' afforded by her particular social context, Dorothea's 'unhistoric acts' *did* contribute to the greater good. All of GE's 'saints' are partly Quixotic, for their ideals and visions exist in a state of tension with hard reality, yet they work to transform reality as best they can. They are fragile and vulnerable human beings who struggle with temptations and illusions.

18. *Letters*, 1.228 (26 Nov. 1846). On the theme of anonymity and the linkage to the Emmaus story, see Henry Ally, *The Quest for Anonymity: The Novels of George Eliot*, Newark: University of Delaware Press 1997, pp. 13–14. This is an answer to the question posed (but not answered) by Rosemary Ashton as to 'why Dorothea has to end up living a hidden life' (*George Eliot*, p. 327). There were publicly visible women in George Eliot's time, including herself, of course, but the heroines of her novels are not of this type. They share the anonymity that is the more common human fate.

19. *Middlemarch*, 39.392. When Dorothea pressed Will about *his* religious belief, he answered: 'To love what is good and beautiful when I see

it. But I am a rebel: I don't feel bound, as you do, to submit to what I don't like' (39.392). She pointed out that if he likes what is good, that comes to the same thing, and she was content with the answer. But the reader senses that their religious sensibilities are quite different and will never be reconciled.

20. Perhaps in the background of the imagery of light and darkness is the passage in the first chapter of the Gospel of John: 'The light shines in the darkness, and the darkness did not overcome it' (John 1.5). Darkness did not overcome the light, nor did the light overcome or eliminate the darkness; rather it shines in the midst of darkness, and the best that can be hoped for is an extending of its borders (or 'skirts'), not a final triumph.

21. John Walter Cross observed that George Eliot was, in her own words, neither an optimist nor a pessimist but a 'meliorist.' *George Eliot's Life*, 3.309–10.

22. Knoepflmacher, *Religious Humanism and the Victorian Novel*, pp. 102–4; cf. all of chap. 3. The reference to 'ethics heightened' is from Matthew Arnold, *Literature and Dogma: An Essay towards a Better Apprehension of the Bible*, London 1873, p. 21.

23. Prayer rarely appears directly in any of GE's stories. Her characters frequently engage in introspective reflection, but we do not hear them directing petitions to God or conversing with the divine. Dinah Morris prayed for a blessing at the beginning of her sermon (*Adam Bede*, chap. 2), and again with Hetty in the prison (chap. 45). But in both cases these prayers were for the benefit of others, not herself. They were a mode of indirect communication with fellow humans, not of direct communication with God. GE was wary of the latter. As for Dorothea, we are told early on (*Middlemarch*, 1.9) that she sometimes 'knelt suddenly down on a brick floor by the side of a sick labourer and prayed fervidly as if she thought herself living in the time of the Apostles.' There appears to be a slight discrepancy between this passage and Dorothea's statement that she now rarely prayed; but in any event the prayer mentioned here was not for her own benefit, which confirms the main point. One remark of the narrator bears directly on prayer. After arranging for Raffles to have some brandy along with his opium, knowing that it would hasten his death, 'Mr Bulstrode rose and spent some time in prayer. Does any one suppose that private prayer is necessarily candid – necessarily goes to the roots of action? Private prayer is inaudible speech, and speech is representative: who can represent himself just as he is, even in his own reflections?' (70.710).

24. I am thinking of Hegel's famous image of the weft and warp of

history. See Hegel, *Lectures on the Philosophy of World History. Intro-duction: Reason in History*, p. 71. It is conceivable that George Eliot was familiar with this image through the translation by John Sibree. Hegelian motifs are discernible in her philosophy of history as well as in her theory of tragedy.

7. Finding the Pathways: Daniel Deronda

1. Rumors began circulating in Middlemarch that Will Ladislaw had Jewish ancestry (or if not Jewish some other sort of 'cursed alien blood,' e.g., Corsican or Gypsy) (*Middlemarch*, 71.719). It was assumed stereo-typically that Will's maternal grandfather was Jewish because he was a pawnbroker, whereas the story makes it clear that he was a member of a Calvinist Dissenting church (61.615–16). Others may have assumed that Will's paternal grandfather was Jewish because he was a Polish musician. In any event, Will was different and, according to yet other rumors, 'crack-brained' (46.462).

2. See Anne E. Patrick, 'George Eliot's Final Experiment: Power and Responsibility in *Daniel Deronda*,' *Morphologies of Faith: Essays in Religion and Culture in Honor of Nathan A. Scott, Jr.*, ed. Mary Gerhart and Anthony C. Yu, Atlanta: Scholars Press 1990, pp. 321–42 (323–6). Daniel's name obviously reminds us of the prophet Daniel, to whom God gave 'knowledge and skill in every aspect of literature and wisdom; Daniel also had insight into all visions and dreams' (Dan. 1.17). Mirah was named after a sister of the fifteenth-century chronicler Rabbi Joseph ben Joshua ha-Cohen ben Meir; and Mordecai, according to Haight, was inspired by Emanuel Deutsch. See Haight, *George Eliot*, p. 489. The biblical Mordecai was the adoptive father of Esther and a man of great wisdom.

3. Many critics did not grasp the connection between the two plots and indicated a decided preference for the English parts of the story. Jewish leaders praised the novel and expressed appreciation to George Eliot for having written it. See *Letters*, 6.275, 314, 317, 379. I am not persuaded by U. C. Knoepflmacher's contention of a sharp break between the alleged anti-religious humanism of the prior novels and GE's 'suspension of dis-belief to make belief once again possible' in *Daniel Deronda*. He thinks she was motivated by a concern about the weakening of values and con-victions by the scientific humanism of the era, but he judges that her attempt to renovate religion in the Deronda half of the novel to be 'an undeniable failure.' See *Religious Humanism and the Victorian Novel*, chap. 4. By contrast, I read *Daniel Deronda* as the culmination of a steady trajectory of concern about religious questions. The notion that GE un-

expectedly only at the end of her literary career introduced God-concepts and God-oriented figures is not defensible.

4. The old Anglo-Saxon kingdom in southern England whose capital was Winchester (the Wanchester of the story).

5. The story actually opens *in medias res,* in September 1865, when Daniel Deronda observed Gwendolen at the roulette table in Leubronn. But then a flashback returns the narrative to late October 1864 and provides the background to the chance encounter of the two protagonists. The variation of time sequence and the use of double plot give the novel an alluring mystery and complexity. See Barbara Hardy's discussion of these matters in the introduction to her edition of *Daniel Deronda,* London: Penguin Books 1967, pp. 23–9.

6. *Daniel Deronda,* ed. Terence Cave, London: Penguin Books 1995, chap. 11, p. 134. Chapter and page references to this edition are cited hereafter in-text.

7. Several references occur to the British colonies in the West Indies and in particular to the brutal crushing of a rebellion in Jamaica in October 1865 (29.331). Conversation about the latter in November 1865 forms the chronological midpoint of the novel. Gwendolen's maternal grandfather acquired his wealth as a West Indian plantation owner (3.24).

8. The condition of Jews in England did improve during the nineteenth century. The authorial voice acknowledges this by referring to 'the poverty and contempt which were the common heritage of most English Jews seventy years ago' (40.504). But, as Terence Cave points out (pp. xx–xxi), prejudice and patronizing tolerance toward Jews was still widespread in the 1860s and 1870s. Among the cultured elite, the tolerance often took the form of the Comtean evolutionist belief that individual races will eventually die out or fuse into a universal religion – a view that GE may once have shared but came to reject as a consequence of her study of the history of religions. Emanuel Deutsch's project for the development of Jewish settlements in Palestine was already being discussed in the late 1860s. GE met Deutsch in 1866 and was deeply impressed by him. In the epigraph to chapter 42, the novelist quotes the Jewish historian Leopold Zunz: 'If there are ranks in suffering, Israel takes precedence of all the nations.'

9. *Daniel Deronda,* 36.451. Mary Wilson Carpenter points out that New Year's Day is also the Feast of the Circumcision, commemorating the circumcision of Jesus. Circumcision entails the inflicting of pain for the sake of being sealed in the covenant of redemption. Thus Daniel not only urged Gwendolen to seek 'the higher, the religious life,' but also to 'take the present suffering as a painful letting in of light.' Believing that

GE may be alluding in this passage to a poem by John Keble on the circumcision of Christ, Carpenter suggests that 'the encounter between
Daniel and Gwendolen becomes an emblem of the bond between the circumcision made with hands and the circumcision made without hands.
Daniel's advice to Gwendolen confers the spiritual heritage of the Jew on
the Christian.' See *George Eliot and the Landscape of Time*, pp. 151–2.

10. Deronda's friend Hans Meyrick commented ironically on the
'theological' nature of his conversations with Gwendolen, whom Hans
delighted in calling 'your Vandyke duchess' (45.564, 52.645). Earlier Sir
Hugo remarked, 'You are always looking tenderly at the women, and talking to them in a Jesuitical way.' He warned him against flirting with
Gwendolen, but Deronda was sure that he had never flirted (32.360–1).
The fact is that he and Gwendolen had flirted from the first moment they
laid eyes on each other. When Sir Hugo said, 'I hope you are not playing
with fire, Dan,' the young man naively insisted that no fire was present
(36.453–4). Deronda remembered these words the next time he met
Gwendolen: she clung to him and he began to sense the coming of 'some
painful collision' in his life (45.564).

11. *Daniel Deronda*, 38.477; see the editor's annotation, p. 833 n. 6. See
also Jane Irwin (ed.) *George Eliot's Daniel Deronda Notebooks*, Cambridge:
Cambridge University Press 1996, pp. 167–70.

12. Critics have wondered how Daniel could have been unaware of his
Jewish identity if he had been circumcised shortly after birth. He learned
from his mother, Leonora Halm-Eberstein, that he had been given up for
adoption at two years of age after his father died (chap. 51). Perhaps this
simply represents a lapse on GE's part. Yet we are told that the Princess
hated being a Jew, and she could plausibly have decided not to have had
her son circumcised so that he could pass for an 'English gentleman.' In
fact, her determination was that he should not know he was a Jew. Daniel
was named for his Italian grandfather, Daniel Charisi. His father's
surname was also Charisi, but when his mother gave him to Sir Hugo for
adoption, she chose a 'foreign name' for him from another branch of the
family: Deronda. 'The Jews have always been changing their names,' she
said (51.637–38). The family came in fact from a line of Spanish Jews,
some of whom settled in Genoa after being driven from their homes
during the Inquisition (50.620, 63.748; cf. *Romola*, chap. 68).

13. *Daniel Deronda*, 69.804. David Carroll comments that this is 'the
heroine's first religious experience, a glimpse of the true relationship
between the self within its own horizon and a plurality of other horizons,
the most sophisticated expression of which is Mordecai's vision of the
divine unity. From the pulsations of the self, the [divine] influxes in the

darkness, the mysterious seed-like images, has emerged this embryonic moral being, the self and the world stabilising at last into a world-view which is Gwendolen's own.' See *George Eliot and the Conflict of Interpretations*, p. 312. This statement nicely links Gwendolen's religious experience not only with Mordecai's vision but also with Daniel's sense that the religious feeling evoked in him by the Hebrew liturgy in Frankfurt (see below) was like 'a divine influx in the darkness, before there was any vision to interpret' (32.368).

14. *Daniel Deronda*, 69.807. E. S. Shaffer provides a brilliant psychological analysis of the emotional liaison between Daniel and Gwendolen, which comes to a culmination, she believes, in their mutual assumption of moral responsibility and their passage in this scene through a crucifixion-and-resurrection-type experience. But Shaffer, who accepts Feuerbach's view that theology is an unconscious, esoteric pathology, believes that for GE the premises of moral responsibility are not religious but atheistic, a will-to-believe in the face of ultimate meaninglessness or absurdity. See Shaffer, *Kubla Khan and the Fall of Jerusalem*, chap. 6, esp. pp. 253–91.

15. See the introduction to her edition of *Daniel Deronda*, p. 29.

16. *Daniel Deronda*, 70.808. The idea is also suggested by the title to Book VIII (the last book of the novel), 'Fruit and Seed.' The final words of the quotation hint at GE's doctrine of subjective immortality. Consider also the last words of the dying Mordecai to Daniel and Mirah: 'Death is coming to me as the divine kiss which is both parting and reunion – which takes me from your bodily eyes and gives me full presence in your soul. Where thou goest, Daniel, I shall go. Is it not begun? Have I not breathed my soul into you? We shall live together' (70.811).

17. This was one of Hegel's earliest insights. See Richard Kroner's introduction to Hegel's *Early Theological Writings*, trans. T. M. Knox, Chicago: University of Chicago Press 1948, p. 9.

18. See Jane Irwin's introduction to her edition of *George Eliot's Daniel Deronda Notebooks*, pp. xxviii–xliii. Correspondence from August 1873 reveals that GE and GHL visited synagogues in Frankfurt and Mainz, purchased books on Jewish subjects, and read Leopold Kompert's stories of life in the ghetto (*Letters*, 5.424, 425 n. 8, 427 n. 4). GHL made the rather hyperbolic statement to John Blackwood that 'only learned Rabbis are so profoundly versed in Jewish history and literature as she is' (*Letters*, 6.196 [1 Dec. 1875]). GE also had to battle against her own earlier prejudice against Judaism, triggered in part by Disraeli's racial theories. In a letter to John Sibree, while acknowledging the superiority of Hebrew poetry, she attributed the mythological and historical husk of the Bible to the Jews and the ethical kernel solely to Jesus (*Letters*, 1.246–7 [11 Feb.

1848])). On GE's relation to Judaism, see also Baker, *George Eliot and Judaism*; and Alice Shalvi (ed.), *Daniel Deronda: A Centenary Symposium*, Jerusalem: Jerusalem Academic Press 1976.

19. Haight, *George Eliot*, pp. 407, 469–71. Deutsch was born in Silesia and was educated by his uncle, a rabbi, and at the University of Berlin. In 1855 he came to London to work at the British Museum. An expert in languages, he had various radical ideas and wrote a famous article on the Talmud. GE was deeply touched by his painful death of cancer in 1873.

20. *Letters*, 6.301–2 (29 Oct. 1876).

21. This is the theme of her last essay, 'The Modern Hep! Hep! Hep!,' *The Impressions of Theophrastus Such*, ed. D. J. Enright, London: Everyman Library 1995, pp. 135–55. 'Hep! Hep! Hep!' was the Crusaders' war cry: it is said to have stood for the phrase 'Hierosolyma est perdita' (Jerusalem is lost). A reference to it occurs at the beginning of chap. 33 of *Daniel Deronda*.

22. Haight, *George Eliot*, pp. 473–4. Poor health prevented it.

23. Reference is made at the end of chapter 20 to a Society for the Conversion of Jews.

24. Alan Mintz describes Deronda's struggle to find a vocation and the evolution of his personal history into a redemptive calling such that his person and his work finally became one and the same. Mintz believes that the possibility of assuming a vocation of transcendent importance can be predicated only on the grounds of religious hope, and he concludes that in *Daniel Deronda* 'religion has indeed been smuggled back in after its varied displacements in George Eliot's earlier work.' *George Eliot and the Novel of Vocation*, chap. 7 and pp. 167–8. Whether religion was actually displaced in the earlier work is a matter of contention. Mintz does not further discuss the religious aspects of the novel.

25. It is noteworthy that Gwendolen derived no benefit from the liturgy and sermon that she heard every Sunday. Church was for her only part of a larger round of 'inexplicable social fashions,' and she was cut off from anything resembling pastoral care or religious fellowship (48.604). Her uncle, the Rector, Mr. Gascoigne, was eager to assure that his niece was well-married, but he had no capacity for ministering to the hunger of her soul.

26. This is the reading of the Cabinet edition of 1878. The first edition of 1876 reads: 'A man is bound to thank God, as we do every Sabbath . . .' David Kaufmann called GE's attention to the inaccuracy. Barbara Hardy wonders whether her feminism played a role in first converting the daily recital to a weekly one, and then (having to accept the daily recital) in limiting the duty to Jewish men. See the Hardy edition (which follows

the reading of 1876), p. 899 n. 5 to chap. 46; and the Cave edition (which follows the reading of 1878), p. 838 n. 7 to chap. 46.

27. See Ps. 104.1–4.

28. There are references just preceding the quoted passage to 'the dire clash of civil war,' to 'grey fathers' looking for the corpses of their sons, and to girls who 'forget all vanity to make lint and bandages which may serve for the shattered limbs of their betrothed husbands' (69.803).

29. Mary Wilson Carpenter points out that GE incorporated into *Daniel Deronda* a rich panoply of images from 'the Apocalypse of the Old Testament,' i.e., the book of Daniel. These images provide a hermen-eutical key to many of the allusions of the novel and especially to its use of numerological schematisms, which GE employed in other novels as well. 'The text of *Daniel Deronda*,' writes Carpenter, 'emerges as George Eliot's last apocalyptic interpretation – an interpretation of the landscape of time as a common landscape of exile. Homelessness, disinheritance, and alienation, she suggests, are the universal condition unless bridged by a prophetic vision that perceives invisible connections and reinterprets ancient texts by the dim light of our common "night-school"' (*George Eliot and the Landscape of Time*, p. 153; see the whole of chap. 5). Carpenter believes that GE intended to rewrite the prophetic vision in such a way that history would be seen to be 'not a divine scheme but the product of human interpretation.' She is principally interested in how historical meaning is continually reconstructed by such interpretations. She does not grasp the possibility that the 'divine scheme' might be actualized through such constructions, and she overlooks the centrality of the idea of God and of 'pathways' to God in Mordecai's prophetic vision. For Carpenter, GE's version of this vision is simply that of a human com-munity in which religious differences are reconciled. I find Carpenter's detailed exegesis and her tracking of allusions to be helpful, but they do not in my judgment yield the anti-theological interpretation she favors. It is as though there is to be found at the center of the extraordinary reli-gious imagery evoked by George Eliot only a black hole, not an encom-passing living presence. (On the distinction between a 'living spirit' and a 'hollow pretence,' see *Romola*, 71.572.) If the ultimate referent of reli-gious language is presumed to be empty, one wonders why such language should continue to be employed.

30. Aristotle, *Poetics*, 1456a.

31. Thomas Vargish does not seem to recognize that GE is engaged in both a critique of the conventional doctrine of providence and a recon-struction that is oriented to the possibility of redemptive transformation in an ambiguous and tragically conflicted world. He thinks that she rather

takes the idea of providence and converts it into a literary device designed
to achieve certain aesthetic effects in the construction of plot. Providence
is simply a mythological representation of social process and context. See
Vargish, *The Providential Aesthetic in Victorian Fiction*, chap. 4.

32. Carroll, *George Eliot and the Conflict of Interpretations*, p. 289.

33. In her edition of *Daniel Deronda*, p. 897 n. 6. On the *Sefer Yetzirah*,
see Aryeh Kaplan, *Sefer Yetzirah: The Book of Creation*, York Beach,
Maine: Samuel Weiser Inc. 1990, introduction, chap. 1, and appendix 2;
and Leonard R. Glotzer, *The Fundamentals of Jewish Mysticism: The Book
of Creation and Its Commentaries*, Northvale, New Jersey: Jason Aronson
Inc. 1992, introduction and chap. 1. References to the *Sefer Yetzirah* are
found in Irwin, *George Eliot's Daniel Deronda Notebooks*, pp. 133, 456.
The latter reference notes that 'the design is to exhibit a system whereby
the universe may be viewed methodically in connection with the truths
given in the Bible, showing from the gradual & systematic development of
the Creation, & from the harmony which prevails in all its parts that One
God produced it & that he is over all. The alphabet is used as a key to
mystical meanings, along with the numbers which it also stands for.'

34. See Ps. 91.9: 'Because thou hast made the LORD, which is my
refuge, even the Most High, thy habitation' (KJV).

35. *Daniel Deronda*, 60.724–5. The grandfather, Daniel Charisi, also
said: 'Let us bind ourselves with duty, as if we were sons of the same
mother . . . Let us bind love with duty; for duty is the love of law; and law
is the nature of the Eternal' (60.722). This statement is relevant to the
question whether or not GE linked God and duty; see above, chap. 1
n. 81.

36. This vision may have a Hegelian provenance with its dual emphasis on the separate identity of a people and the sublation of differences in
an encompassing whole. See Baker, *George Eliot and Judaism*, chap. 7.
Whether GE acquired these ideas directly from Hegel, or whether they
were mediated through certain nineteenth-century Jewish scholars
(Heinrich Graetz, Michael Sachs, Franz Delitzsch, Salomon Munk,
Moritz Steinschneider) whom she read and who were influenced by
Hegel, is uncertain. Hegel pointed to the dilemma of a people, the Jews,
who had lost their state, their national identity; and he was attracted to the
mystical symbolism of the Kabbalah. For him Judaism was the religion
that first obtained insight into the great truth of the divine unity.

37. Irwin, *George Eliot's Daniel Deronda Notebooks*, pp. 173–4, 454.
Her knowledge of the Kabbalah derived principally from the work of
Christian David Ginsburg and Heinrich Hirsch Graetz.

38. My reflections in the last several paragraphs have been assisted by

two essays by Anne E. Patrick, 'George Eliot and Difference: Ambiguities of Genre, Gender, and Religion in *Daniel Deronda*,' *Papers of the Nineteenth Century Theology Working Group*, ed. Marcia Bunge and Gerda Schmidt, Berkeley: American Academy of Religion 1990, pp. 1–16; and 'George Eliot's Final Experiment: Power and Responsibility in *Daniel Deronda*.'

39. Rosemary Ashton, *George Eliot*, pp. 347–8. Kathryn Hughes's judgment sounds like a copy of Ashton's. Regarding Deronda and the other Jewish characters as 'hard to like,' she writes: 'Jewish history is as bloody and shameful as Christianity's. There is no reason to believe that a Jewish nation would run its affairs any better than Catholic Spain or Protestant Sweden. Eliot was herself famously agnostic, so it is hard to see why anyone should take her endorsement of the religiously committed life seriously. Finally, and most important, why can nothing be done to regenerate society from within?' (*George Eliot*, pp. 321–2).

40. Ashton, *George Eliot*, pp. 348–9.

8. George Eliot and Postmodern Theology

1. In this chapter I summarize and draw together a variety of themes from the previous chapters. Apart from specific quotations, ideas that have been discussed before are not referenced again.

2. *Letters*, 2.269 (GHL to John Blackwood, 6 Nov. 1856).

3. *Daniel Deronda*, 58.706. The contrast is with 'peaceful authorship,' which breathes 'the air of fields and downs.' Since the reference of the latter is to the authorship of the ineffective Rector of Pennicote, Mr. Gascoigne, the contrast is ironic or playful; but I suspect that GE was less than impressed by critics who recycle the same stale air; and at the same time she may have longed for a peaceful authorship.

4. Footnoted references in the preceding chapters to some of the recent critical literature demonstrate the extent to which this is the case. Friedrich Schleiermacher identified the 'cultured among its despisers' as the audience to whom he addressed his *Speeches on Religion* (1799). Another example of an anti-religious interpretation and its forced conclusions is provided by Helena Granlund in *The Paradox of Self-Love: Christian Elements in George Eliot's Treatment of Egoism*, Stockholm: Almqvist & Wiksell International 1994. GE, she writes, 'points to the dehumanizing effects of lower egoism and to the necessity of a highest good beyond self and her choice of words shows her awareness of the basic Christianity of this view. At the same time she arranges her wording so as to give a human definition of this highest good beyond self. In

spite of this re-definition, however, she returns to the traditional terms of divine, holy, sacred, when approaching the subject, on occasion borrowing substance and authority from religion to support her denial of this authority. Were it not for the well-known facts of her private life, her well-documented apostasy and subsequent atheism, we would be hard put to pronounce with certainty upon Eliot's belief' (p. 166). Yes, indeed! Granlund is aware that the alleged apostasy and atheism introduce pronounced tensions into her thesis, but she sticks with it partly because she cannot imagine a reconstruction of Christian theology that would free it from its 'supernatural elements.' This is why, when Dinah says that she felt herself to be a part of the Divine Presence, Granlund assumes that GE cannot really be intending a God-reference but only a 'human definition' of the highest good (p. 155). In order to avoid 'the absurdity of having her heroines worship themselves,' GE had to introduce 'a Christian writing convention' (p. 163). In other words, God-talk is a mask to conceal the fact that not only the 'lower egoist' but also the 'higher egoist' really makes his or her own self, or human selves, the highest good and center of existence. This is a strange conclusion for a dissertation that set out to show that 'Eliot's treatment in her novels reflects the Augustine [sic] paradox that the choice of self leads to the destruction of self, whereas the choice of non-self leads to the fulfilment of self' (Abstract, p. ii). A far simpler conclusion would be that when GE wrote 'God' she meant God, not a 'writing convention.' At the end, however, Granlund seems doubtful of her conclusion. She began by quoting Nietzsche's judgment that GE was inconsistent because she repudiated Christian faith while insisting on Christian morals (pp. 1, 169). Yet Granlund believes that in *Daniel Deronda* there is a hint of an objective reality behind or beneath the phenomenon of religious experience (pp. 173–4). It is astonishing that Granlund finds this 'hint' only at the end of GE's fictional journey, for it is there from the beginning.

5. This theme is found in several of Ricoeur's recent essays. See 'The Hermeneutic Function of Distanciation,' 'Philosophical Hermeneutics and Biblical Hermeneutics,' 'What Is a Text?,' 'The Model of the Text,' and 'Imagination in Discourse and in Action,' all of which are collected in Paul Ricoeur, *From Text to Action: Essays in Hermeneutics, II,* trans. Kathleen Blamey and John B. Thompson, Evanston, Ill.: Northwestern University Press 1991, chaps. 3, 4, 5, 7, 8.

6. Ibid., p. 83.

7. *Letters,* 4.104 (23 Aug. 1863). In her Journal for 29 July 1863 GE wrote: 'On our return we found a letter from Frederick Maurice – the greatest, most generous tribute ever given to me in my life' (Cross, *George*

Eliot's Life, 2.259). Cross notes that he was unable to find this letter, and it is not included in Haight's edition of the *Letters*.

8. H. Richard Niebuhr's Foreword to the Harper Torchbook edition of Ludwig Feuerbach, *The Essence of Christianity*, trans. George Eliot, New York: Harper & Brothers 1957, p. ix.

9. Paul Lakeland, *Postmodernity: Christian Identity in a Fragmented Age*, Minneapolis: Fortress Press 1997, pp. 8–12, 42–3, 45.

10. John B. Cobb, Jr., in an unpublished paper, 'Revisioning Ministry for a Revisioned Church' (1992).

11. *Scenes of Clerical Life*, 'Janet's Repentance,' 10.265.

12. *Letters*, 3.366 (to Barbara Bodichon, 26 Dec. 1860).

13. *Letters*, 6.216 (to Dr. Joseph Frank Payne, 27 Jan. 1876).

14. Paul Ricoeur, 'Religion, Atheism, and Faith,' in *The Religious Significance of Atheism*, p. 60.

15. 'Janet's Repentance,' 16.293. Compare the exhortations against which Gwendolen Harleth rebelled: 'We must resign ourselves to the will of Providence'; 'there is benefit in all chastisement if we adjust our minds to it' (*Daniel Deronda*, 21.232, 26.289).

16. *Adam Bede*, 17.178.

17. *Romola*, 67.549.

18. *Letters*, 1.162 (to Sara Sophia Hennell, 9 Oct. 1843); 7.346 (to Mrs. Elma Stuart, 11 Dec. 1880).

19. *Scenes of Clerical Life*, 'The Sad Fortunes of the Rev. Amos Barton,' 3.36.

20. 'Janet's Repentance,' 22.315.

21. When Will Ladislaw characterized Dorothea's religion as a 'beautiful mysticism,' she replied: 'Please not to call it by any name. You will say it is Persian, or something else geographical' (*Middlemarch*, 39.392).

22. *Daniel Deronda*, 64.763.

23. See John Hick, *A Christian Theology of Religions: The Rainbow of Faith*, Louisville: Westminster John Knox Press 1995, pp. 28, 50, 78–9, 102–3. Gordon Kaufman makes a similar point, arguing that, while the symbol God must be understood as a product of the human imagination, this does not mean that it is merely imaginary. All other symbols that we use (such as 'tree,' 'I,' 'world,' or 'light-year') have also been created by the human imagination, and this fact does not imply their falsity or emptiness. The question for Kaufman is whether the symbol 'God' 'continues to do the work for which it was created, whether it can continue to function significantly in human life.' Kaufman's working definition of God is as follows: 'by "God" we mean that reality, *whatever it might be*, orientation on which evokes our human moral and creative powers (that

is, our distinctively human powers), encouraging their development and enhancement by promising significant human fulfillment (salvation) in the future.' With the exception of the appeal to the future, this definition expresses a view similar to that of George Eliot. For both Kaufman and GE, God can be understood to be the ultimate mystery and point of reference for human life without being reduced to a merely human function or illusion. See Gordon D. Kaufman, *In Face of Mystery: A Constructive Theology*, Cambridge, Mass.: Harvard University Press 1993, pp. 39–40, 79, and the whole of Part I on 'theology as construction.'

24. *The Mill on the Floss*, 4.3.385–6.

25. *Daniel Deronda*, 6.57.

26. See above, chap. 1 n. 24.

27. This is true of Feuerbach's early writings, those with which GE was familiar. Later, after the publication of *Theogonie* in 1857, he developed a much more pessimistic interpretation of the human condition, which went beyond tragedy to fatalism (see above, chap. 1 n. 27).

28. One of GE's contemporaries, Eliza Lynn, thought that the original of Casaubon was Dr. R. H. Brabant, an eccentric physician who dabbled in theology, was acquainted with Strauss and other German theologians, and helped to arrange the translation of *Das Leben Jesu*, which was to be undertaken by his daughter Rufa, with whom Mary Ann Evans was acquainted. After Rufa married Charles Hennell, Mary Ann visited Dr. Brabant for several weeks and allowed herself to become rather too intimate with him. When Rufa found the translation work to be too difficult, Mary Ann it took it over, early in 1844. Lynn wrote in her memoirs that Dr. Brabant 'never got further than the introductory chapter of a book which he intended to be epoch-making, and the final destroyer of superstition and theological dogma.' See Haight, *George Eliot*, pp. 47–53. Thus Dr. Brabant provides a possible linkage between Casaubon and Feuerbach: like Casaubon he could never get beyond the beginnings of a grandiose project, and like Feuerbach that project would expose the illusions of theology.

29. Feuerbach wrote not only an 'essence of Christianity,' but also an 'essence of religion' and an 'essence of faith according to Luther.'

30. See my book, *Winds of the Spirit: A Constructive Christian Theology*, Louisville: Westminster John Knox Press; London: SCM Press 1994, chap. 5. In that book I explore a more Hegelian way of responding to this question, while in the present chapter I am tracing George Eliot's approach, which is closer to Spinoza and Schleiermacher than to Hegel. I do not attempt here to adjudicate between these approaches but rather find value in both.

31. Edward Farley, *Divine Empathy: A Theology of God*, Minneapolis: Fortress Press 1996, chaps. 1, 4–7. Farley argues that a negative theology also presupposes and requires an affirmative theology.

32. Ibid., chaps. 9–10.

33. Ibid., pp. 176, 256.

34. 'Notes on "The Spanish Gypsy" and Tragedy in General' (*c.* 1868), in Cross, *George Eliot's Life*, 3.30–5.

35. *Letters*, 4.499 (to Clifford Allbutt, 30 Dec. 1868).

36. *Felix Holt*, 'Address to Working Men,' p. 495.

37. *Letters*, 4.158 (to Sara Sophia Hennell, 13 July 1864).

38. *Letters*, 6.301–2 (to Harriet Beecher Stowe, 29 Oct. 1876).

39. *Middlemarch*, Prelude and Finale, pp. 3, 838.

40. Farley, *Divine Empathy*, p. 295. I am providing in this and the following paragraphs a summary of chap. 19.

41. Ibid., pp. 264–5.

42. Ibid., pp. 295–6.

43. *Adam Bede*, 50.488.

44. Farley, *Divine Empathy*, pp. 297–9, and chap. 20.

45. Ibid., pp. 304–5.

46. This is most powerfully illustrated by GE in the figure of Dinah Morris. See above, chap. 3 n. 16.

47. This second way of understanding God anticipates the position espoused by James M. Gustafson: '"God" refers to the power that bears down upon us, sustains us, sets an ordering of relationships, provides conditions of possibilities for human activity and even a sense of direction.' *Ethics from a Theocentric Perspective*, vol. 1, Chicago: The University of Chicago Press 1981, p. 246. Gustafson is reluctant to employ personal or anthropomorphic metaphors of God. John Hick argues that the two ways of thinking about God – the one acknowledging the ultimate ineffability of the divine nature, the other speaking of God for devotional and liturgical purposes as a personal presence with human-like qualities – are present in all the great religious traditions and cannot be synthesized; each in its own way is valid. *A Christian Theology of Religions*, p. 59.

48. *Felix Holt*, p. 498. Wisdom and love, according to Schleiermacher, are the most adequate attributes of the divine life. Wisdom designates the causal efficacy of God's love vis-à-vis the world.

49. 'Evangelical Teaching: Dr. Cumming,' *Westminster Review*, Oct. 1855, in *Selected Essays*, pp. 38–68.

50. *Adam Bede*, 2.26–33.

51. *Romola*, 40.359.

52. See Elliot R. Wolfson, *Through a Speculum That Shines: Vision and Imagination in Medieval Jewish Mysticism*, Princeton, N.J.: Princeton University Press 1994.

53. *Romola*, 61.504.

54. *Romola*, 71.572.

55. Farley, *Divine Empathy*, pp. 64–5, 310–13.

56. On the dangers of theodicy, see Tilley, *The Evils of Theodicy*. Tilley discusses *Adam Bede* in chap. 8.

57. *Letters*, 2.403 (to Charles Bray, 15 Nov. 1857). In this respect she anticipated James Gustafson's stringent refusal of anthropomorphism in theology (see above, n. 47). It also marks her distance from Feuerbach's anthropomorphism.

58. *Daniel Deronda*, 60.725.

59. This argument is spelled out in 'The Modern Hep! Hep! Hep!' *The Impressions of Theophrastus Such*, pp. 135–55. See also *Daniel Deronda*, chap. 42.

60. Farley, *Divine Empathy*, pp. 258–62.

61. *Daniel Deronda*, 42.530, 537.

62. See the discussion of *Silas Marner* and *The Mill on the Floss* in chap. 4 and of *Romola* in chap. 5. The seasons of Christmas and Easter figure in several of the stories.

63. *Adam Bede*, 2.28. Compare this passage with the one quoted above (p. 166) from Farley, *Divine Empathy*, p. 295.

64. *Adam Bede*, 30.329–30.

65. Farley shows this; see *Divine Empathy*, chap. 18, where he interprets the figure of Jesus as universalizing the faith of Israel. See also p. 305, where he discusses the ideas of Martin Buber and Emmanuel Levinas.

Bibliography

Ally, Henry, *The Quest for Anonymity: The Novels of George Eliot*, Newark: University of Delaware Press 1997.

Arnold, Matthew, *Literature and Dogma: An Essay towards a Better Apprehension of the Bible*, London 1873.

Ashton, Rosemary, *George Eliot: A Life*, London: Hamish Hamilton 1996; London: Penguin Books 1997.

Atkins, Dorothy, *George Eliot and Spinoza*, Romantic Reassessment, No. 78, Salzburg: Salzburg Studies in English Literature 1978.

Baker, William, *George Eliot and Judaism*, Romantic Reassessment, No. 45, Salzburg: Salzburg Studies in English Literature 1975.

Barrett, Dorothea, *Vocation and Desire: George Eliot's Heroines*, London and New York: Routledge 1989.

Bonaparte, Felicia, *The Triptych and the Cross: The Central Myths of George Eliot's Poetic Imagination*, New York: New York University Press 1979.

Brown, Earl Kent, *Women of Mr. Wesley's Methodism*, New York: The Edwin Mellen Press 1983.

Carpenter, Mary Wilson, *George Eliot and the Landscape of Time: Narrative Form and Protestant Apocalyptic History*, Chapel Hill: University of North Carolina Press 1986.

Carroll, David, *George Eliot and the Conflict of Interpretations: A Reading of the Novels*, Cambridge: Cambridge University Press 1992.

—— 'George Eliot Martyrologist: The Case of Savonarola,' *From Author to Text: Re-reading George Eliot's Romola*, ed. Caroline Levine and Mark W. Turner, Aldershot: Ashgate 1998.

Chilcote, Paul Wesley, *John Wesley and the Women Preachers of Early Methodism*, Metuchen, N.J.: Scarecrow Press 1991.

Cobb, John B., Jr., 'Revisioning Ministry for a Revisioned Church,' unpublished paper, 1992.

Comte, Auguste, *Auguste Comte and Positivism: The Essential Writings*, ed.

Gertrude Lenzer, Chicago: The University of Chicago Press, 1975.

Cross, John Walter (ed.), *George Eliot's Life as Related in Her Letters and Journals,* 3 vols., New York: Harper & Brothers 1885.

Cunningham, Valentine, *Everywhere Spoken Against: Dissent in the Victorian Novel,* Oxford: Clarendon Press 1975.

Dodd, Valerie A., *George Eliot: An Intellectual Life,* London: Macmillan; New York: St. Martin's Press 1990.

Eliot, George, *Adam Bede* (1859), ed. Stephen Gill, London: Penguin Books 1985 (reprinted with new pagination).

—— *Daniel Deronda* (1876), ed. Terence Cave, London: Penguin Books 1995 (use has also been made of the previous edition, edited by Barbara Hardy, Penguin Books 1967).

—— *Felix Holt: The Radical* (1866), ed. Lynda Mugglestone, London: Penguin Books 1995.

—— *The Impressions of Theophrastus Such* (1879), ed. D. J. Enright, London: Everyman Library 1995.

—— *Middlemarch* (1871–2), ed. Rosemary Ashton, London: Penguin Books 1994.

—— *The Mill on the Floss* (1860), ed. A. S. Byatt, London: Penguin Books 1979.

—— *The Poems of George Eliot,* Cambridge: Cambridge University Press 1887.

—— *Romola* (1862–3), ed. Dorothea Barrett, London: Penguin Books 1996.

—— *Scenes of Clerical Life* (1857–58), ed. Jennifer Gribble, London: Penguin Books 1998.

—— *Selected Essays, Poems and Other Writings,* ed. A. S. Byatt and Nicholas Watten, London: Penguin Books 1990.

—— *Silas Marner, The Lifted Veil, Brother Jacob,* ed. with an introduction by Peter Mudford, London: Everyman Library 1996.

—— *Silas Marner: The Weaver of Raveloe* (1861), ed. David Carroll, London: Penguin Books 1996.

Ermarth, Elizabeth Deeds, 'George Eliot's Conception of Sympathy,' *Nineteenth Century Fiction* 40, June 1985, pp. 23–42.

Farley, Edward, *Divine Empathy: A Theology of God,* Minneapolis: Fortress Press 1996.

Feuerbach, Ludwig, *The Essence of Christianity* (1841), trans. George Eliot, New York: Harper & Brothers 1957.

—— *Principles of the Philosophy of the Future* (1843), trans. Manfred H. Vogel, Indianapolis: Bobbs-Merrill Co. 1966.

Glotzer, Leonard R., *The Fundamentals of Jewish Mysticism: The Book of*

Creation and Its Commentaries, Northvale, N.J.: Jason Aronson Inc. 1992.

Granlund, Helena, *The Paradox of Self-Love: Christian Elements in George Eliot's Treatment of Egoism*, Stockholm: Almqvist & Wiksell International 1994.

Gustafson, James M., *Ethics from a Theocentric Perspective*, vol. 1, Chicago: The University of Chicago Press 1981.

Haight, Gordon S., *George Eliot: A Biography*, London: Oxford University Press 1968; London: Penguin Books 1986.

—— (ed.), *The George Eliot Letters*, 9 vols., New Haven: Yale University Press 1954–6, 1978 (referred to in-text as *Letters*).

Harvey, Van A., *Feuerbach and the Interpretation of Religion*, Cambridge: Cambridge University Press 1995.

Hegel, George Wilhelm Friedrich, *Aesthetics: Lectures on Fine Arts*, trans. T. M. Knox, Oxford: Clarendon Press 1975.

—— *Early Theological Writings*, trans. T. M. Knox, Chicago: The University of Chicago Press 1948.

—— *G. W. F. Hegel: Theologian of the Spirit*, ed. Peter C. Hodgson, Minneapolis: Fortress Press; Edinburgh: T&T Clark 1997.

—— *Lectures on the Philosophy of Religion*, ed. Peter C. Hodgson, trans. R. F. Brown, P. C. Hodgson, and J. M. Stewart with the assistance of H. S. Harris, 3 vols., Berkeley, Los Angeles, and London: University of California Press, 1984–7.

—— *Lectures on the Philosophy of World History. Introduction: Reason in History*, trans. H. B. Nisbet with an introduction by Duncan Forbes, Cambridge: Cambridge University Press 1975.

Hick, John, *A Christian Theology of Religions: The Rainbow of Faith*, Louisville: Westminster John Knox Press 1995.

—— *An Interpretation of Religion: Human Responses to the Transcendent*, London: SCM Press; New Haven: Yale University Press 1989.

Hodgson, Peter C., *Winds of the Spirit: A Constructive Christian Theology*, Louisville: Westminster John Knox Press; London: SCM Press 1994.

Houlgate, Stephen, 'Hegel and the "End" of Art,' *The Owl of Minerva* 29, fall 1997, pp. 1–21.

Hughes, Kathryn, *George Eliot: The Last Victorian*, London: Fourth Estate 1998; New York: Farrar, Straus and Giroux 1999.

Irwin, Jane (ed.), *George Eliot's Daniel Deronda Notebooks*, Cambridge: Cambridge University Press 1996.

Johnson, Thomas H. (ed.), *The Letters of Emily Dickinson*, 3 vols., Cambridge, Mass.: Harvard University Press 1965.

Kaplan, Aryeh, *Sefer Yetzirah: The Book of Creation*, York Beach, Maine:

Samuel Weiser Inc. 1990.

Karl, Frederick R., *George Eliot: Voice of a Century*, New York: W. W. Norton & Co. 1995.

Kaufman, Gordon D., *In Face of Mystery: A Constructive Theology*, Cambridge, Mass.: Harvard University Press 1993.

Keller, Catherine, *Apocalypse Now and Then: A Feminist Guide to the End of the World*, Boston: Beacon Press 1996.

Knoepflmacher, U. C., *George Eliot's Early Novels: The Limits of Realism*, Berkeley and Los Angeles: University of California Press 1968.

—— *Religious Humanism and the Victorian Novel: George Eliot, Walter Pater, and Samuel Butler*, Princeton, N.J.: Princeton University Press 1965.

Lakeland, Paul, *Postmodernity: Christian Identity in a Fragmented Age*, Minneapolis: Fortress Press 1997.

Lawless, Elaine J., 'The Silencing of the Preacher Woman: The Muted Message of George Eliot's *Adam Bede*,' *Women's Studies* 18, 1990, pp. 249–69.

Lovesy, Oliver, *The Clerical Character in George Eliot's Fiction*, English Literary Studies, Victoria, B.C.: University of Victoria 1991.

McCobb, Anthony, *George Eliot's Knowledge of German Life and Letters*, Romantic Reassessment, No. 102.2, Salzburg: Salzburg Studies in English Literature 1982.

McGowan, John P., *Representation and Revelation: Victorian Realism from Carlyle to Yeats*, Columbia: University of Missouri Press 1968.

Mansell, Darrel, 'A Note on Hegel and George Eliot,' *The Victorian Newsletter* 7, Spring 1965, pp. 12–15.

Marshall, Ellen Ott, 'Dinah Morris: A Constructive Proposal for the Meaning of Christianity in the Nineteenth Century,' unpublished paper, 1997.

Mason, Richard, *The God of Spinoza: A Philosophical Study*, Cambridge: Cambridge University Press 1997.

Mebust, Kirsten A. S., 'The End of Suffering: An Eschatology of Word and Presence in *Adam Bede*,' unpublished paper, 2000.

Mintz, Alan, *George Eliot and the Novel of Vocation*, Cambridge, Mass.: Harvard University Press 1978.

Noble, Thomas A., *George Eliot's Scenes of Clerical Life*, New Haven: Yale University Press 1965.

Panikkar, Raimon, *The Cosmotheandric Experience*, Maryknoll, N.Y.: Orbis Books 1993.

Paris, Bernard J., *Experiments in Life: George Eliot's Quest for Values*, Detroit: Wayne State University Press 1965.

—— 'George Eliot's Religion of Humanity,' *English Literary History* 29, Dec. 1962, pp. 418–43.

Patrick, Anne E., 'George Eliot and Difference: Ambiguities of Genre, Gender, and Religion in *Daniel Deronda*,' *Papers of the Nineteenth Century Theology Working Group*, ed. Marcia Bunge and Gerda Schmidt, Berkeley: American Academy of Religion, 1990, pp. 1–16.

—— 'George Eliot's Final Experiment: Power and Responsibility in *Daniel Deronda*,' *Morphologies of Faith: Essays in Religion and Culture in Honor of Nathan A. Scott, Jr.*, ed. Mary Gerhart and Anthony C. Yu, Atlanta: Scholars Press 1990, pp. 321–42.

Paxton, Nancy, *George Eliot and Herbert Spencer: Feminism, Evolutionism, and the Reconstruction of Gender*, Princeton, N.J.: Princeton University Press 1991.

Ricoeur, Paul, *From Text to Action: Essays in Hermeneutics, II*, trans. Kathleen Blamey and John B. Thompson, Evanston, Ill.: Northwestern University Press 1991.

—— 'Religion, Atheism, and Faith,' in Alasdair MacIntyre and Paul Ricoeur, *The Religious Significance of Atheism*, New York: Columbia University Press 1969.

Rose, Phyllis, *Parallel Lives: Five Victorian Marriages*, New York: Alfred A. Knopf 1983.

Schleiermacher, Friedrich, *The Christian Faith*, ed. H. R. Mackintosh and J. S. Stewart, Edinburgh: T&T Clark 1928.

Shaffer, E. S., *Kubla Khan and the Fall of Jerusalem: The Mythological School in Biblical Criticism and Secular Literature, 1770–1880*, Cambridge: Cambridge University Press 1975.

Shalvi, Alice (ed.), *Daniel Deronda: A Centenary Symposium*, Jerusalem: Jerusalem Academic Press 1976.

Stockton, Kathryn Bond, *God between Their Lips: Desire between Women in Irigaray, Brontë, and Eliot*, Stanford: Stanford University Press 1994.

Strauss, David Friedrich, *The Life of Jesus Critically Examined*, translated from the 4th German edition (1840) by George Eliot, ed. Peter C. Hodgson, Philadelphia: Fortress Press 1972; London: SCM Press 1973.

Tilley, Terrence W., *The Evils of Theodicy*, Washington, D.C.: Georgetown University Press 1991.

Uglow, Jennifer, *George Eliot*, London and New York: Virago/Pantheon Pioneers 1987.

Valenze, Deborah M., *Prophetic Sons and Daughters: Female Preaching and Popular Religion in Industrial England*, Princeton, N.J.: Princeton

University Press 1985.

Vargish, Thomas, *The Providential Aesthetic in Victorian Fiction*, Charlottesville: University Press of Virginia 1985.

Whitehead, Alfred North, *Process and Reality*, New York: Macmillan 1929.

Willey, Basil, *Nineteenth Century Studies*, London: Chatto & Windus 1955.

Wolfson, Elliot R., *Through a Speculum That Shines: Vision and Imagination in Medieval Jewish Mysticism*, Princeton, N.J.: Princeton University Press 1994.

Wright, T. R., *The Religion of Humanity: The Impact of Comtean Positivism on Victorian Britain*, Cambridge: Cambridge University Press 1986.

Index

Fictional characters are indexed under the novel in which they appear.